PERCEPTIVE
LISTENING

PERCEPTIVE LISTENING

SECOND EDITION

FLORENCE I. WOLFF, PH.D.

PROFESSOR EMERITUS OF COMMUNICATION
UNIVERSITY OF DAYTON

NADINE C. MARSNIK, M.A.

INSTRUCTOR OF ENGLISH AND SPEECH
VERMILION COMMUNITY COLLEGE

HARCOURT BRACE JOVANOVICH COLLEGE PUBLISHERS

FORT WORTH   PHILADELPHIA   SAN DIEGO   NEW YORK   ORLANDO   AUSTIN   SAN ANTONIO
TORONTO   MONTREAL   LONDON   SYDNEY   TOKYO

EDITOR-IN-CHIEF: Ted Buchholz
ACQUISITIONS EDITOR: Janet Wilhite
PROJECT EDITOR: Margaret Allyson
PRODUCTION MANAGER: Jane Tyndall Ponceti
BOOK DESIGNER: Peggy Young

ISBN: 0-03-074549-7

Library of Congress Number: 92-72258

*This book is dedicated to our husbands, John M. Wolff and
George M. Marsnik, who listen.*

*We offer this book as a tribute to Dr. Ralph C. Nichols,
the Father of Listening. Dr. Nichols, researcher, teacher, mentor,
and friend, performed the pioneer work from which
the authors and others have developed today's research,
teaching, and training in the listening field.*

CONTENTS IN BRIEF

CONTENTS

PREFACE

Because listening skills are taught, not caught, we have designed a comprehensive book in listening to be used by college students, businesspersons, and other professionals.

For the student, we provide a highly readable text with pragmatic exercises; an incentive to retrain and to improve individual listening skills; and a workable tool to be used in the classroom, the workplace, and the social and personal environments.

For the instructor, we provide a truly "teachable" textbook, a series of effective classroom and seminar activities, and a pedagogical tool to motivate students to listen and learn.

Outstanding features of this newly revised second edition include an instructor's manual, listener log assignments, and retraining guidelines in each chapter. Within the text and instructor's manual are over 100 exercises to enhance the learning process. The easy-to-follow chapter format includes an opening consisting of a thesis, chapter objectives, and a chapter preview. A chapter summary, exercises, and notes close each of the eleven chapters. Further contributing to the strength of this text are clear explanations of comprehensive theory, relevant and contemporary examples, simplified models of major theories, and explicit illustrations. Major vocabulary words are italicized and defined.

The authors acknowledge the support of the editorial and production staff of Harcourt Brace Jovanovich, especially Janet Wilhite, Acquisitions Editor; Margaret Allyson, Project Editor; and Adele Krause, Editorial Assistant. We are grateful to Dr. James R. East of Indiana University — Purdue University at Indianapolis, Harvey L. Lamberson of Tulsa Junior College, and Warren Y. Gore of the University of Minnesota. Their comments and suggestions in reviewing both the previous edition and the revised manuscript were extremely valuable. We recognize and appreciate the staunch support of Dr. Don B. Morlan, Chair, Department of Communication, University of Dayton, as well as the technical support provided by Vermilion Community College. And finally we are grateful for the encouragement of our families.

A WORD ABOUT THE AUTHORS

Florence I. Wolff is Professor Emeritus of Communication at the University of Dayton. She is director of the Wolff Innovative Training Systems (WITS) and the recipient of the International Listening Association Research Award, the Ohio Professor of the Year Award, and five Outstanding Teacher Awards.

Nadine C. Marsnik is an instructor in the Departments of English and Speech at Vermilion Community College. She is President of Information Systems. She has served in several capacities on the Board of Directors of the International Listening Association and has received their Research Award, President's Award, and Special Recognition Award.

Both authors are founding members of the International Listening Association and teach courses in listening. They are well known as featured speakers and as corporate seminar trainers throughout the United States.

PART ONE

WHY
LISTEN?

CHAPTER 1

LISTENING TO SUCCEED

Make the most of your life; that is all there is of you.
— Ralph Waldo Emerson

THESIS   Every time we listen we learn, grow, and prosper.

CHAPTER OBJECTIVES

1. Realize the importance of perceptive listening for success in the classroom.
2. Understand how perceptive listening enhances learning in business, industry, and the professions in order to meet the global challenge of the twenty-first century.
3. Become motivated to replace unproductive listening habits with productive theories, techniques, and tools presented in this textbook.

CHAPTER PREVIEW

- Listen to succeed in the classroom.
- Listen to succeed in the corporate world.
- Listen to succeed as a professional.

LISTENING TO SUCCEED IN THE CLASSROOM

Which voluntary activity do you perform most frequently in a day, week, month, or year—in fact, throughout your whole life? Listening! Do you ever wonder if you are getting your money's worth from your classes, if you are learning enough to prepare you to pursue a successful career? Students who lack listening competency are at a disadvantage. They need to learn listening skills in order to perform adequately in their current careers as effective college students.

Most students have never received formal instruction in listening. They may enter college as "handicapped" listeners. Unfortunately, few students know how to listen and learn in class despite the fact that the majority of them will move into entry-level positions requiring constant on-the-job learning through listening. Some experts doubt that we as a nation are acquiring adequate knowledge to compete in the global market of the future.

A Tragedy in American Education

A tragedy in American education began sixty years ago when a climactic research conclusion was ignored. As early as 1928, the classic study by Paul Rankin at Ohio State University revealed that approximately 70 percent of an adult's waking hours is spent communicating. Approximately 9 percent of that time is spent in writing, 16 percent in reading, 30 percent in speaking, and 45 percent in listening. Rankin, a Detroit public–schools educator, also learned that reading (the second least-used communication skill) received 52 percent of the emphasis in classroom instruction and listening (the most-used communication skill) a mere 8 percent.[1] Today, more than sixty years later, thousands of students, mostly uninformed in the art of listening to learn, fill American classrooms.

We are a nation of poor listeners. Immediately after hearing a message, most people retain barely 50 percent of the content; eight to twelve hours later, they retain barely 25 percent. One reason for this problem is the failure of educators to include progressive units and course instruction in listening, from kindergarten through high school. Our school system has not prepared us to be proficient in the most frequently used human activity. We have not been taught how to listen.

The inability of students to listen and learn efficiently in class wastes valuable time, earnest effort, and hard-earned money. The real tragedy in American education, however, is that we have had little opportunity to acquire and develop "listen-to-learn power" while we are students. If you are reading this page to prepare a listening course assignment, you are fortunate. If you are reading this textbook to improve listening competency in personal and professional situations, you also are fortunate. The concepts and tools presented in this textbook, once learned, can be instrumental in greatly improving your listening competency. A perceptive listener becomes more confident and successful in social settings and job interviews. A good listener becomes a more "promotable" employee in the workforce and a more caring and involved family member.

Assessments written by University of Dayton students who have completed the listening courses offered during the past twenty years invariably include the following comments:

- I've become more motivated to listen and learn in class.
- My grade point average has improved.
- I feel more confident about job interviews and being successful on the job.

The International Listening Association

Educators have long been concerned about the lack of listening instruction in the schools. Finally, in 1979, the International Listening Association (ILA) was incorporated "to promote the study, development, and teaching of listening in all settings."[2] As a founding member of ILA, Lyman K. Steil, formerly at the University of Minnesota, served as the first ILA president. Today over 400 members receive information through annual conventions, summer conferences, and publications of the *Journal of the International Listening Association* and the *Listening Post*. ILA members include students, educators, business people, consultants, and professionals — including Dr. Ralph G. Nichols, whose invaluable research since 1928 has earned him the title of Father of Listening.

The Status of Listening Instruction

Since 1979 the ILA has promoted listening instruction in the United States and eight foreign countries. The number of listening course offerings is increasing — so the 60 percent of time students spend listening in and outside of classes during four years of college can be more productive.

Florence I. Wolff at the University of Dayton designed national surveys in 1979 and 1990 to assess the status of listening instruction offered in colleges and universities. The 1979 survey showed that only 14 percent of the 70 respondents offered courses in listening. The 1990 survey, however, revealed that 87 of 126 respondents (61 percent) offered listening instruction: 48 percent offered listening courses; 46 percent offered listening units in other courses.[3] Indeed, the future trend of listening instruction in colleges and universities appears promising.

The Need for Listening Courses in College

Consider the experiences of Tom and Lucy, typical of thousands of college students. Tom lost out; Lucy profited.

Tom's Problem

Tom studied intensely three days before the history mid-term exam; he needed an A. He was shocked to receive a test grade of D − after cramming for the test. After class Tom conferred with the professor:

Tom: "I expected a high grade on this test. I studied for hours three days before the exam."

Professor (scanning the test): "Hmmm, it appears that you failed to explain several rules. And here are six questions answered incorrectly about concepts I clarified in class. If you don't understand parts of the lectures, feel free to ask questions. Keep studying, and your grades should improve."

Feeling even more depressed, Tom walked away wondering if he should drop the course.

A logical solution of Tom's problem is to remain enrolled in the class. In addition to preparing assignments on time, he needs to maximize class learning time. Like many concerned students, Tom is unaware of the amount of time he wasted during twenty-one 50-minute classes before the mid-term exam. By applying the listen-to-learn power tools explained in Chapter 4, Five Power Tools of Listening, in every class, Tom could develop a progressive study routine for tests.

Although the brain is a remarkable computer-like organ, it cannot process, store, and retrieve large blocks of data that should be processed progressively. If Tom had used listening-learning tools during the 17 hours of class time prior to the test, he would have needed only a general review of the text and class notes to prepare for the test. Retiring at a reasonable hour to get more sleep would have enhanced his performance — resulting in a higher test score.

Lucy's Dilemma

Early in the listening course, students learn about powerful tools that really work (see Chapter 4, Five Power Tools of Listening). As soon as Lucy learned several new tools for listening to take notes, she began to use them in her psychology class. The night before a major test, she was unable to study. The next morning Lucy approached the professor.

Lucy: "Due to an emergency, I could not study for this test. May I take the test another time?"

Professor (looking directly at Lucy): "All your assignments have been well prepared. I've watched you sitting in the front seat and focusing on me as you listened intently to all lectures. You have learned in class. You know the material. I suggest you take the test."

Lucy took the test and earned a high test score. Now a firm believer in listen-to-learn power, Lucy explained to other students how the listening–learning tools can work to eliminate cramming before exams.

The "Aha" Learning Experience

Judith Hill, the 1990 National Student-Teacher of the Year, campaigns against students' greatest and yet worst ally — the ability to memorize quickly and to forget as soon as the last multiple-choice circle has been filled in. Hill reminds students:

> You can go through and just memorize things and regurgitate them on the test, but you don't have the ownership of your education. The ownership comes when you incorporate it and it becomes part of you. That's long-term memory.[4]

Rather than cram quickly and forget easily, we suggest that students seek ownership of their education by implementing listening–learning concepts and tools during each class session for greater success in college.

The Grade Hunter

Students can benefit from the work of Charles H. Swanson, professor of Speech Communication and Theatre, Fairmont State College. His Grade Hunter unit of listening instruction emphasizes these facts:

1. Students who get better grades are not smarter; they listen better.
2. Listen as though your grades depend on it — they do!
3. How can we expect our students to learn when we haven't even taught them to listen?
4. Listen to learn? Learn to listen![5]

Educators have become accustomed to "kicking listening around academically" while continuing to believe that this complex, transactional process of communication can be taught as sporadic units of instruction within other courses. To be taught and learned properly, listening must be incorporated in formal curricula: instructional units in kindergarten through eighth grade, and a separate listening course in high school, college, and university.

Listening to learn in class is hard work and requires self-discipline and great effort. Motivation and determination open the doors to success in achieving worthwhile goals in college.

Guidelines for Listening to Learn in Class

Students who challenge themselves to abide by the following guidelines have greater opportunity to succeed in college.

- **Attend all classes**. Borrowing and copying notes is a poor substitute for learning in class. Successful students use their own note-taking systems with symbols to jog memory when reviewing notes. Borrowed notes may be meaningless and incomplete. (See Note-taking Systems in Chapter 6, Three Basic Concepts to Enhance Listening Comprehension). In class, lecturers review assigned chapters and provide valuable insights and examples to help the *Primary Listener* (decoder of original messages) learn in class. Students often receive lower assessments on projects assigned in classes they did not attend. Receiving important information from another student can be risky for the *Secondary Listener* (decoder of a repeated message). Class experience may reinforce learning by triggering recall during a test, in another class, or later on the job.

- **Prepare for class**. Self-preparation to listen, as explained in Chapter 6, Three Basic Concepts to Improve Listening Comprehension, is mandatory for learning in class. What we don't prepare to do, we seldom do well—that applies to listening and learning in class. Arrive early to allow time for review of previous class notes to prepare for relevant cognitions (bits of knowledge) to be clarified in class. Reviewing and anticipating relevant cognitions creates a mind set (a readiness to learn and store cognitions in logical patterns).

- **Target class assignments**. The ability to complete class assignments correctly depends on a student's listening skills. Clearly understanding an instructor's intended meaning is crucial. For example, if an instructor says, "For the next class, read over Chapter 5," students might peruse the chapter to acquire general information. If an instructor says, "Study Chapter 5," students should know to read, learn, and store concepts and supportive data in long-term memory and be prepared to explain and apply concepts to resolve problems. (Most teachers give "study" assignments. Students learn quickly to be prepared for classes during which they may be selected to teach concepts in assigned chapters; soon they feel more confident facing the class.)

The Schuller Formula for Success

Robert L. Schuller, author and speaker, uses the word STRIVE as an acronym to explain his formula for success. Anyone striving to change listening behavior and achieve other goals may find the Schuller Formula helpful.[6]

S   START SMALL. Many large enterprises started in a small room with a small, used desk and chair. We can learn to apply perceptive listening techniques a little at a time.

T   THINK TALL. Use your fullest potential to set ceiling-level goals to achieve success. As we listen to learn, grow, and prosper, we are "thinking tall."

R   REACH OVER THE WALL. A banker asked a farmer requesting a loan to build a fence, "Are you going to fence-in to protect your property or fence-out to work more land?" The farmer answered, "Fence-out." He got the loan. Reaching over a wall of poor listening habits to perceptive listening habits is difficult and requires perseverance.

I   INVEST ALL. We grow and prosper by learning and investing in ourselves as we invest in others. By listening, we help others. We offer hope, human dignity, freedom, and the chance to pursue personal success.

V   VISUALIZE A BALL. Schuller suggests we picture what we hope to achieve. Visualization, a major component of the listening process, is explained in Chapter 6, Three Basic Concepts to Enhance Listening Comprehension.

E   EXPECT TO STALL. While learning to replace poor listening techniques with productive ones, we may stall occasionally by reverting back to former habits. The danger of falling is minimal if we strive constantly to use perceptive listening techniques.

LISTENING TO SUCCEED IN THE CORPORATE WORLD

No matter how hard one worked and played in college, striving for success in the corporate world revolves around learning, working, eating, and sleeping. While college calendars grant dozens of days off, plus summer vacation, employers usually offer new employees one week of vacation. A *U.S. News & World Report* poll of middle-level executives at twenty of America's best-known corporations (AT&T, Dow Chemical, NCR, General Motors, etc.) charts the hours managers work on the job:[7]

Under 30 hours	1%
40–49	21%
50–59	21%
60–69	20%
70 hours/over	6%

An ancient Chinese proverb says: Choose a job you love and you will never have to work a day in your life. Modern wisdom might add: But beware. If you took away the job, would there be any of you left?

What emerges from the survey is a new portrait of the organization woman and man — displaying strong feelings of corporate loyalty while balancing their careers with family and personal lives.[8] We also learn how much listening time is required in relation to the number of work hours consumed in management positions — 60 percent.

Learning on the Job

Robert Stempel and Roger Smith, General Motors chief executive officers (*CEOs*), claim that GM will hire and retain only those persons with the ability to learn in order for the corporation to operate in the highly competitive world market of the 1990s. Socrates claimed: "The way we speak is who we are." We may need to add, "The way we listen and learn is who we become."

The "and then some" Philosophy

Richard L. Weaver, professor of Interpersonal and Public Communication, Bowling Green State University, believes that three little words — "and then some" — make the difference between average people and top people. Top people do what's expected of them — and then some. They are considerate and kind toward others — and then some. They meet obligations and responsibilities fairly and squarely — and then some. They are good friends and can be counted on in any situation — and then some.[9] These three little words can revolutionize society and our academic, business, professional, and personal lives.

We can begin using the "and then some" philosophy in small ways: Leave a room cleaner than it was; close a door that needs closing; put debris in provided containers; place objects where they belong; selfishly grasp every opportunity to listen and learn; and take time to listen to and care about others — and then some.

Weaver offers two suggestions impacting on the degree of success one achieves throughout life:

- Become a sponge for knowledge.
- Don't allow floors to become ceilings to achieve goals. Go the distance — and then some.[10]

Listeners in business, industrial, and corporate environments can profit by integrating Weaver's "and then some" philosophy into their listening and training performance.

On-the-Job Learning and Training in Business

Entrepreneurs and corporations recognize the need for continuous learning and retraining on the job. Training programs for employees in entry-level to top-level management positions are therefore likely to receive more attention in the 1990s.

Responding to a questionnaire from Hendrick & Struggles, a management recruitment firm, 62 percent of the leaders of 264 large companies said, "Building and keeping a qualified work force is the most important business issue of the decade."[11]

Of the 55,000 members of the American Society for Training and Development, 85 percent are training managers and 11 percent are outside consultants or suppliers of training equipment. Training will cost about $15 billion more each year in the 1990s over the previous yearly cost of $30 billion.[12]

Listening Competency Needs in Organizations

Gary Hunt and Louis Cusella mailed 250 questionnaires to a random sample of Fortune 500 training managers to study listening needs in organizations. A relatively high return of 42 percent may indicate the level of interest among managers in listening. The training managers indicated that poor listening was "one of the most important problems facing them, and that ineffective listening leads to ineffective performance or low productivity."[13] Other conclusions evolving from the study are:

- Causes of listening problems appear to be lack of feedback about listening skills, lack of knowledge, lack of openness in organizations that discourage effective listening, and lack of employer motivation to practice effective listening.

- Poor listening performance is ranked as a serious problem during meetings, performance appraisals, and superior-subordinate communication.

- Trainers advocated emphasizing those skills associated with "active" listening above those associated with "informational" listening. (While all perceptive listening is active, we believe Hunt and Cusella referred to empathic listening, a specialized listening one does out of concern for another. Both interactional empathic listening and informational discriminative listening are fully discussed in Chapter 5, Five Kinds of Listening We Do.)

A study conducted by DiSalvo et al. revealed which communication skills recent college graduates use daily in entry-level positions to be successful on the job. The ranking included: listening, advising, routine information exchange, persuading, small–group problem solving, and instructing. The first three skills (listening, advising, and routine information exchange) were the most stable pattern in the study.[14] A study by Junge et al. identified the skill areas required for successful employment as speaking, listening, and writing.[15]

The Need for Listening Retraining in Management

Leland Brown, author of *Communicating Facts and Ideas in Business*, notes that corporate employees listen about 60 percent of the time on the job.[16] William F. Keefe, author of *Listen, Management*, states that listening consumes about 63 percent of an executive's workday;[17] Wolvin and Coakley conclude that 63 percent of an executive's salary is paid for time spent in listening.[18]

Judi Brownell, a professor at Cornell University, claims that effective management requires effective communication and that listening may be one of managers' least-developed skills. She administered questionnaires to 144 managers and their 827 subordinates at six hospitality organizations. After managers identified and rated their performance in 26 listening behaviors, subordinates revealed their perceptions of the managers' listening behaviors. Several conclusions of the in-depth study should be noted:

- Managers over 45 years of age are perceived as poorer listeners — possibly because they seem to be satisfied with current positions and not motivated to seek new information. Also, the younger subordinate population (mean age of 28) perceived older managers to be poorer listeners.

- Persons in current positions for less than a year are perceived to be more effective listeners — possibly because they are trying harder to succeed or because effective listening behavior helped them advance.

- Individuals who have had some listening training are more likely to be rated higher in listening behavior by subordinates. A high percentage of managers in the bottom quartile had no prior listening training.

- Nearly all managers rated themselves as "very good" or "good"; a few rated themselves as "fair." Yet managers in the bottom quartile received ratings as low as 3.6, with 3.0 indicating infrequent use of effective listening behavior.[19]

For the past ten years, your authors have noted a persistent pattern in thousands of trainees' written assessments completed at the conclusion of listening seminars.[20] The most frequent comments written by seminar trainees are:[20]

- "I realize how poor a listener I am. I'm eager to work on my weaknesses and improve my listening at home and on the job."

- "Everyone in our company needs this seminar — all levels of management and support staff."

- "I'm dealing with people all day, and what I learned about listening will help my job performance."

- "If I had had this seminar six months ago, I might have saved my marriage. Now I'm divorced and don't know what to do with my life. We stopped listening to each other."

- "Sales is more than just power-playing and manipulation. I know I'll be more successful when I listen more than I speak. This seminar was great."

Of the thousands seeking retraining in listening, many are sales representatives. They are eager to upgrade listening skills to meet customers' needs more exactly and to advance their careers in sales — the indisputable hub in the wheel of success in business and industry.

Listening to Sell

Listening to sell is rapidly replacing the old-fashioned loud, persistent-talking sales approach. Simply stated, the key to successful selling is: Find out what customers want — and give it to them. Sales and marketing expert Stephen Doyle uses a new term — customer-driven — to describe a company whose "entire business operation focuses on a new kind of responsiveness to customers' needs."[21] What better way to learn customers' needs, gain invaluable insights, and develop trust relationships than by using the listen-to-learn power tools in a lateral coordination effort.

Listening and Lateral Coordination in Organizations

Lateral coordination in organizations is a special type of teamwork in which groups of employees from truck drivers to CEOs share up-to-the-minute information about customers' desires. These companies consider customer responsiveness (meeting customers' needs and expectations) as a valuable resource on which to build lateral (across the company) coordination.

Doyle and Ben Shapiro, at Harvard Business School, suggest the following plan for operating customer-driven companies in which ultimate success may depend on employees' perceptive listening skills.

- **Dispatch a trained sales force**. A well-informed sales force must see customers regularly to listen and learn how customers feel and what they expect. Successful sales people know to listen more than they speak.

- **Dispense information**. Information gathered by the sales force (like pricing, purchasing, and advertising) is centralized by computer. To benefit from this challenging input system, all employees, from cleaning to administrative staffs, need training in listening to transmit correct information and to avoid delay and errors in serving customers.

- **Make an all-out effort**. Sales force promises made to customers can be kept only if thousands of people in all company divisions focus constantly on specific ways *their respective jobs* fulfill customers' needs. With employees trained as perceptive listeners, coordinated decisions based on customer information and insights can be made throughout the company.[22]

Listening to Win and Keep Customers

The greatest business secret in the world is knowing not only how to win customers, but more important, how to keep them. The following time-proven principles clarify this concept.[23]

- The average business spends six times more dollars to attract a new customer than it does to keep an existing customer. Yet customer loyalty, in most cases, is worth ten times the price of a single purchase! Thus employees with effective communication skills save employers "big bucks."

- Of customers who leave, 70 percent of them do so not because they're unhappy with the product or service, but because of an attitude of indifference. Somebody sent a message that read, "I don't care about you or your problems!" As employees apply Empathic Listening concepts (see Chapter 5, Five Kinds of

Listening We Do), they project caring rather than indifferent attitudes toward customers.

- Nice customers can ruin sales or even a business; they don't complain when they're not treated well. They simply walk away and don't come back — although they do tell friends about their dissatisfaction.

An important aspect of listening is interpreting customers' nonverbal messages discussed in Chapter 9, Listening to Nonverbal Messages. This listening skill enables salespeople and other employees to handle dissatisfied customers tactfully and continue selling to satisfied customers. However, when customers do not buy, sales persons need to use self-listening to offset feelings of rejection.

Positive intrapersonal communication (speaking and listening to one's self) improves sales performance by changing a negative self-image into a positive one.

Helpful Tips for Positive Self-Listening in Sales

The following tips can increase sales by overcoming negative, energy-wasting activities.[24]

- Listen to yourself list all activities you have achieved successfully.
- Listen to yourself recall the successful sales you have made.
- Listen to yourself point out that your value as a salesperson is at least equal to the importance of any client.
- Listen to yourself discuss how to update records and files and be better prepared for future sales encounters.
- Refuse to listen to yourself focus on any negative thoughts and emotions by using the "thought-zapping rubber band technique" (wear a rubber band around your wrist and pop it each time a negative reaction tries to take over).

Applying self-listening techniques (further clarified in Chapter 5, Five Kinds of Listening We Do) benefits salespersons, supervisors, mid- and high-level management, corporate leaders and front-line workers (those in direct contact with customers).

Professionals in other specialized areas need to apply listening retraining concepts and tools for successful on-the-job performance.

LISTENING TO SUCCEED AS A PROFESSIONAL

Today's professionals have an unprecedented number of major technological advances at their fingertips. Computerization and telecommunications have produced laser facsimiles, on-line databases, and magnetic imaging, all of which make it possible to gather, analyze and disperse enormous amounts of information at formerly undreamed–of speed.

Remember to listen as you tell yourself: "No one can make me feel inferior without my permission."

Despite using this technology to create more efficiency, many professionals are coming under fire for accomplishing less than their clients hope for. The public bemoans a rising tide of mediocrity in our schools. Lack of trust in medical experts has people turning to more litigation and malpractice suits against the very doctors to whom they turn for cures.

Why do receivers of professional expertise feel so unhappy? Why do people search out the knowledge and expertise of professionals and then respond with dissatisfaction and anger?

In *Megatrends*, John Naisbitt offered one explanation for this dissonance.

> What happens is that whenever new technology is introduced into society, there must be a counterbalancing human response—*high touch*—or the technology is rejected. The more high tech, the more high touch.[25]

Naisbitt has put into words something many of us have intuited: As we need and reach out for the results of high technology, we also need and reach out for a counterbalancing human response.

Listening: A High—Touch Response

We believe the counterbalancing human response for which we yearn is listening—the intellectual skill which requires no hardware, no software, no satellite, nothing to plug in, simply one person reaching out to another.

How can professionals—untrained in the skill of listening—incorporate it into their practices?

Educators Must Listen

In addition to students learning to listen, professors, teachers and administrators of educational programs also must listen to the needs of students.

One example of listening to student needs can be seen in the following example of adding a human response to educational technology.

New School Accepts Some Old Ways
Six months after President Bush's visit to St. Paul's Saturn School drew national attention to computers, technology and individualized curriculum, it resurrected some old—fashioned schoolhouse staples like homework, number two pencils and more interaction between students and teachers.[26]

The Saturn School did not abandon its efforts to find new ways to educate, but it did add a counterbalancing human touch—teachers and students spending more time speaking and listening in class. They believe this will help make the technology work. We agree.

In addition to making curriculum changes to meet student needs, thoughtful educators are making changes in teacher education so classroom interaction involves both speaking and listening by both teachers and students. Teachers in the field need to be encouraged to make a commitment to change their own listening habits.

Nussbaum and Scott report that a good teacher is an attentive communicator who likes to listen carefully and who deliberately reacts in such a way that students know the teacher is listening. They conclude that "these constructs can be incorporated into the training of teachers."[27] Wise educators suggest that schools of education focus on teaching the skill of listening and the art of teaching listening to all educators.

Physicians Must Listen

There is no doubt that physicians with the capabilities for magnetic resonance and ultrasound imaging, organ transplants, chemotherapy and nuclear medicine make use of state–of–the–art technology to find illness and treat it. People are alive today who, even twenty years ago, could not have lived. Yet 85 percent of those who responded to a University of California at Los Angeles survey of medical patients said they had changed or were thinking of changing doctors. The questionnaire revealed that these patients believed their doctors to be competent but were troubled by a lack of sensitivity and inability to communicate.[28]

Patients say the ideal physician is "one who listens, provides feedback and is an active participant in creating an environment where both physician and patient feel their needs have been met."[29]

The growing dissatisfaction by patients and a growing number of malpractice suits have caused medical schools to look seriously at some communication needs for all medical personnel. R. Sanson-Fisher and P. Maguire, reporting in the British medical journal *Lancet*, examined this need and reported that a doctor's skill—or lack of skill—in communication, primarily listening, was important in monitoring how patients and relatives adapt to illness and treatment . . . and how doctors interact with their patients.[30] They believe that a doctor's communication skills affect the adequacy of the clinical interview, patient compliance and patient satisfaction.

Almost a hundred years ago, William Osler told medical students it was more important to know what sort of patient has the disease than to know what disease the patient has.[31] When Newton Minow delivered the ninth annual James C. Hempill Lecture in 1990, he reminded medical professionals that they can—in fact, must—know both the disease and the patient because "knowledge of disease is useless if we do not understand the people who are afflicted by them."[32] Listening to the person who has the disease is the needed "high touch" in medicine.

Nurses Must Listen

Nurses must understand the technological tests and how to administer high–tech treatment such as chemotherapy (drug treatments for various kinds of cancer). Yet nurses' regular one–to–one interaction with patients gives them an opportunity to achieve a warm human response.

Nurses who receive training listening skills required for good interviewing not only recognize problems but also are able to make the necessary recommendations to reduce problems. A nurse who is trained to listen to patients achieves what

Kalisch calls "the ability to understand the current feelings of the patient."[33] When empathy is communicated, it can form the basis for a necessary helping relationship between nurse and patient. We believe the focal word in Kalisch's evaluation is "current." Nurses who *listen* to patients learn *today's* needs, fears and feelings and not those experienced yesterday or by another patient. This awareness of patients' current needs allows nurses to use high touch in responding to the real messages sent.

Dentists Must Listen

Although dentists' use of bonding, tooth replacement, caps, bridgework and ortho-dontia (tooth straightening) means none of us need suffer an unattractive smile, too many of us live in fear of the dentist. Studies show that this emotional state of mind actually can cause pain or exaggerate its presence.

A dentist who prepares to drill, extract or administer drugs to relieve pain, must talk to patients and listen to their responses. A dentist may say, "This shot is painful or uncomfortable for some people. Please let me know how you feel." The dentist who responds to these answers with empathic listening can develop deep trust. This trust helps dentists recognize emotional states and can be the basis for the best preventative and restorative dental care.

Pharmacists Must Listen

Pharmacists must listen to patients who ask questions. In fact, pharmacists encour-age clients to repeat all directions. Pharmacists often find themselves in the role of educator. Without relying on medical terminology or jargon they must explain special conditions and side effects of medication. An experienced pharmacist de-scribed a typical customer: "She is a tired, distracted mother carrying a baby and holding the hand of an older child. She is worrying about the one who is ill and attending to the one who is not. I must give her instructions and encourage her to question and give feedback." Equally important, the pharmacist must be very atten-tive to her questions, listening with great care to be sure she understands. With any customer, a pharmacist's listening skill is primary.

Lawyers Must Listen

Many attorneys plunge ahead armed with high–speed computers, laser facsimiles, portable telephones, legal databases, automated timekeeping systems and far too little regard for the input of their colleagues and their clients — and far too little listening to the other side.[34]

While we expect this technology from our attorneys, it can destroy the person-to-person skill most needed to succeed in the person-to-person activities of a legal practice. Practicing attorneys Lawrence Klun[35] and Schoenfield and Schoenfield[36] believe that the quality of listening in client counseling (sessions where the client defines needs and the attorney suggests procedures) and interviews (information gathering) are the greatest elements to be considered in determining the success or failure of a law practice.

Law professor Thomas Schaefer reiterates this by cautioning attorneys to develop tolerance for silences, to avoid interrupting, to create an accepting unevaluating climate and to "learn while he speaks."[37]

When listening in the courtroom, attorneys pay careful attention to qualifying words such as "in my opinion" or "theoretically" which must be clarified for a listening jury. Attorneys also must listen closely for gaps in the logical analysis of experts — that which is not said and those steps which are not explained. Attorneys also listen for the way witnesses recall stories — as they wish them to be. They listen carefully for verb tenses ("I would have," or "I might have") and to qualifiers ("I believe," or "I think") to ascertain bias or flaws in testimony.

Richard H. Millen, an attorney, puts his listening skills to work in mediation rather than in courtroom litigation. He believes courtroom confrontation involves "using the law against each other" whereas mediation "uses listening in a nonadversarial manner with empathic responses and 'I' messages in an effort to reach community."[38] Millen does not suggest that lawyers do away with litigation. He does, however, suggest ways that lawyers and clients together also can make use of the high–touch solution of mediation to control, manage, and participate in dispute resolution through listening.

Religious Professionals Must Listen

Even though computer technology adds several aids for religious professionals, they are not likely to abandon high touch. When people turn for help to pastors or rabbis, they expect them to ask thoughtful questions and show sensitivity to their need to talk. In short, they expect empathic listeners.

Lloyd Steffan explains this need by suggesting that people are in need of a "theology of listening, for a willingness to listen ultimately expresses an attitude of love."[39] We believe this love can be expressed in listening by religious professionals in the roles of teachers, preachers, and counselors.

Maurice Friedman eloquently sums up this "listening out of love" when he proclaims, "Only real listening — a listening witness — can plumb the abyss of the universal existential mistrust that stands in the way of genuine dialogue and peace."[40]

Not only religious professionals, but all professionals can seek to become this kind of listening witness. They may come closer to becoming listening witnesses through learning and practicing the skills discussed in this book.

WRAPPING IT UP: A SUMMARY

When we listen perceptively, we learn, grow, and prosper. Listening to learn leads to success in the classroom, the corporate world and as a professional.

The one voluntary activity humans perform most is listening, but our system of education has failed to include courses in listening instruction. We are a nation of poor listeners.

The ILA, incorporated in 1979 to promote research and instruction in listening, will continue to encourage listening research and instruction. Surveys show an increase both in listening course offerings and published textbooks in this field.

Certain concepts and tools can be applied to motivate students, businesspeople and other professionals in listening to succeed. Those include the "Aha" learning experience, the "and then some" philosophy, and tips for self-listening in sales.

Professionals, too, must learn to listen. Education professionals — both administrators and instructors — must personally learn to listen, as well as to teach the art of listening to other professionals and businesspeople.

Medical and legal professionals will prosper when they learn to view patients and clients as whole human beings rather than as cases. Listening skills ultimately can help avoid loss of life and lawsuits.

As perceptive listeners, religious professionals can reach out with greater spiritual comfort and direction.

DISCUSSION AND STUDY GUIDES

1. Explain whether you agree or disagree with the statement, "Few students know how to listen and learn in class, even though most students move into entry-level positions requiring on-the-job learning through listening."

2. Briefly explain the examples pertaining to Tom and Lucy. Have you had similar experiences in the classroom or on the job?

3. State the four concepts basic to the Grade Hunter. What are your reactions to these concepts?

4. As you begin studying this textbook, how would you rank your potential in listening to succeed in the classroom or in the work force? Circle the appropriate answer and defend your choice.

   Excellent   Very Good   Fair   Need to Retrain

5. Which professions noted in the section, Listening to Succeed as a Professional, would you rate as practicing the highest and lowest levels of listening skills? Clarify and support your selections with specific examples.

6. In your opinion, which type of professional would be most and least likely to seek help to retrain as a perceptive listener? What criteria (age, personality, etc.) are you using to formulate your judgments? Discuss this information with a colleague or friend.

LISTENING EXERCISES THAT WORK

EXERCISE 1. (Listening to Staff Workers) This is a self-inventory of your behavior while listening to staff workers on a part-time, entry-level, or career job. As you circle "yes" or "no" after each item, ask yourself how your associates would assess your behavior on the job now or in the future.

1. I plan time to listen on the job.   Yes   No

2. I listen to colleagues' problems even if their concerns have no relation to my job.   Yes   No

3. I treat those I work with as associates or peers rather than as subordinates.   Yes   No

4. I guard against pretending to listen to staff.   Yes   No

5. I courteously and infrequently interrupt when others are talking.   Yes   No

6. I clearly articulate responses after staff members stop speaking.   Yes   No

7. I make encouraging sounds and nonverbal signs while listening in the workplace.   Yes   No

8. I listen logically and separate facts from my peers' opinions.   Yes   No

9. I use the best place available when listening to staff.   Yes   No

10. I recall an associate's prior work and ideas right before listening.   Yes   No

11. I conceal any disapproval I might feel when listening to a staff member.   Yes   No

12. I try to create a comfortable and congenial setting when listening to peers.   Yes   No

Please Total Each Column   _____   _____

EXERCISE 2. (Your Staff Worker Self-Inventory) Using the total number of "yes" responses, note your degree of successful listening on the job as indicated on the chart below.

"Yes" Responses	Degree of Success
11–12	Excellent
9–10	Very Good
6–8	Fair
5 and below	Need to Retrain

Form into small groups. Share with others your specific plans to change listening behavior in relation to those items marked "no." From this exercise, what have you learned about yourself in the role of listener on the job?

EXERCISE 3. (Achieving Success) Select two of your friends or acquaintances who are successful in the work force. In small groups, discuss which of the concepts and tools described in this chapter appear to be the basis of their success.

EXERCISE 4. (Listening and Medicine) Interview a friend or acquaintance who has had a negative or a positive experience with a medical professional. Through discussion, determine the kind of listening role played by the professional and by the patient. In small- or large-group interaction, share your findings and clarify which concepts presented in this chapter were revealed during the interviews.

EXERCISE 5. (Listening and the Professions) Arrange to interview a professional person (an educator or a medical, legal or religious professional). Ask the person to evaluate the role listening plays in the field, explain how success or failure in the professions relies on listening competency, and assess the actual listening behavior being used to fulfill job responsibilities. Share the interview report with your peers.

NOTES

1. Paul T. Rankin, "The Importance of Listening Ability," *English Journal* (College Edition) 17 (October 1928), 623–30.
2. Lyman K. Steil, President, Communication Consultants Association, remains active in the ILA.
3. Florence I. Wolff, "A 1977 Survey: General Insights into the Status of Listening Course Offerings in Selected Colleges and Universities," *North Carolina Journal of Speech Communication*, 12 (Winter 79), 44–52; "A Pragmatic 'Sharing' Workshop in Listening Pedagogy: Who's Teaching Listening and How?" presented at the first annual *ILA* convention, Atlanta, GA, February 19, 1980; and "1979 and 1990 Studies: Listening Instruction Trends in Randomly Selected Colleges and Universities," at the 12th annual *ILA* convention, Jacksonville, FL (Nadine C. Marsnik, co-speaker), March 7, 1991.
4. Sally Ann Flecker, "The 'Aha!' Experience," *Pitt*, (published by the University of Pittsburgh), Vol. 5, No. 2 (April 1990), 14.
5. Charles H. Swanson, "Teaching Students How to Listen as Students: A Flexible Unit," (from *Grade Hunter*, by Charles H. Swanson), presented at the 11th *ILA* convention, Indianapolis, March 9, 1990, and the 12th *ILA* convention, Jacksonville, FL, March 8, 1991.
6. Robert L. Schuller, ABC Network Hour of Power telecast, January 6, 1991.
7. Jerry Buckley, "The New Organization Man," U.S. News & World Report, January 16, 1989, 41–43.
8. Buckley, 40.
9. Robert L. Weaver II, "And Then Some: Give More, Get More, Want More From Life!" *Concept*, 1990–1991, 38–40. (Speech delivered at Golden Key National Honor Society's 1990 Fall Reception and Initiation, Bowling Green State University.)
10. Weaver, 40.
11. Elizabeth M. Fowler, *New York Times* News Service, "Chairmen put new emphasis on worker training," *Dayton* (OH) *Daily News*, January 6, 1991, 2-F.
12. Fowler, 2-F.
13. Gary T. Hunt and Louis P. Cusella, "A Field Study of Listening Needs in Organizations," *Communication Education*, 32 (October 1983), 393–401.
14. Vincent DiSalvo, David C. Larsen and William J. Seiler, "Communication Skills Needed by Persons in Business Organizations," *Communication Education*, 25, 4 (November 1976), 275.
15. Denis A. Junge, M. Harry Daniels and Joseph S. Karmos, "Personnel Managers' Perceptions of Requisite Basic Skills," *Vocational Guidance Quarterly* (December 1984), 138–46.
16. Leland Brown, *Communicating Facts and Ideas in Business*, Englewood Cliffs, NJ, 1982), 380.
17. Wiliam F. Keefe, *Listen, Management* (New York: McGraw Hill, 1971), 10.
18. Andrew Wolvin and Carolyn Gwynn Coakley, *Listening* (Dubuque, IA: Wm. C. Brown, Publishers, 1988), 14.
19. Judi Brownell, "Perceptions of Effective Listeners: A Management Study," *Journal of Business Communication* 27, 4 (Fall 1990), 401–15.
20. Florence I. Wolff, Director of WITS (Wolff Innovative Training Systems), and Nadine C. Marsnik, President of Information Systems, travel extensively, conducting corporate and military communication seminars.
21. Anne R. Field, "Your Service Underground: What the Truck Driver Can Teach the CEO," *Success*, February 1990, 38.
22. Field, 39.

23. Michael LeBoeuf, "How to Win Customers and Keep Them for Life," six audiocassettes, Nightingale-Conant Corp. 7300 N. Lehigh Ave., Chicago, IL 60648-9951 (800-323-5552).
24. Terri L. Darrow, "Conquering Call Reluctance," *Sky* (Delta Air Lines magazine), May 1988, 119–22.
25. John Naisbitt, *Megatrends: Ten New Directions Transforming Our Lives* (New York: Warner Books, 1982), 35.
26. James Walsh, "New School Adopts Some Old Ways to Bolster Scores," *Minneapolis Star and Tribune* (November 4, 1991), 1B.
27. Jon F. Nussbaum and Michael D. Scott, "Instructor Communication Behaviors and Their Relationship to Classroom Learning," *Communication Yearbook* 3 (1979), 566.
28. Edward Krupat, "A Delicate Imbalance," *Psychology Today* 19 (November 1986), 22.
29. Ronna Zimmerman and William E. Arnold, "Physicians' and Patients' Perception of Actual Versus Ideal Physician Communication and Listening Behaviors," *Journal of the International Listening Association* 4 (1990), 147.
30. R. Sanson-Fisher and P. Maguire, "Should Skills in Communicating With Patients Be Taught in Medical Schools?" *Lancet* 2 (September 6, 1980), 523.
31. William Osler, *Albany Medical Annals* (1899).
32. Newton Minow, "Communication in Medicine: Do Doctors and Lawyers Know How to Listen?" *Vital Speeches* 521 (December 1990), 122.
33. Beatrice J. Kalisch, "What is Empathy?" *American Journal of Nursing* 73 (September 1973), 548.
34. Minow, 122.
35. Lawrence J. Klun, Attorney at Law, Ely, MN 55731 (personal interview), May 1991.
36. Mark K. Schoenfield and Barbara Pearlman Schoenfield, *Interviewing and Counseling* (Philadelphia: American Law Institute-American Bar Association Committee on Continuing Professional Education, 1981), 2.
37. Thomas L. Schaeffer, *Legal Interviewing and Counseling in a Nutshell* (St. Paul: West Publishing, 1976), 117–18.
38. Richard H. Millen, Early Dispute Resolution Consultant, 15235 Valley Vista Blvd., Sherman Oaks, CA 91403 (personal interview) March, 1991.
39. Lloyd Steffen, "The Listening Point," *The Christian Century* 107 (March 1990), 1087.
40. Maurice Friedman, "The Community of Otherness and the Covenant of Peace," in paper presented by Richard H. Millen at the International Listening Association Convention, Jacksonville, FL (March 1991).

CHAPTER 2

LISTENING POWER GENERATES KNOWLEDGE

There is only one good, knowledge, and only one evil, ignorance.
— *Socrates*

THESIS Understanding the intricate process of listening enables one to accelerate learning and generate knowledge.

CHAPTER OBJECTIVES

1. Know that the roles of speaker and listener are equally important for successful communication.
2. Understand the functions of the six integrated components in the Wolff-Marsnik model of the listening process.
3. Realize the urgent need to conserve and protect the delicate mechanism of hearing in our noisy world.

CHAPTER PREVIEW

- Terms of the circular process of oral-aural communication.
- Verbal and nonverbal messages.

As Sally rushes across campus to take a chemistry test, Sidney enters a corporate meeting called to clarify new procedures for hiring staff. Both are concerned. Do they have adequate knowledge to perform their respective tasks successfully? Most likely they do if they have been applying the listening concepts exposed in this textbook, beginning with the process of oral-aural communication.

THE PROCESS OF ORAL-AURAL COMMUNICATION

Oral-aural communication is a two-way (speaking-listening) process. Therefore we are wise to learn and practice specialized speaking *and* listening theories, techniques, and skills. Even though all communication situations differ, we need to understand certain terms and major components necessary to initiate, carry on, and complete the ongoing process of oral-aural communication.

DEFINITION BOX 1: Terms Relating to Oral-Aural Communication

Oral: mouth; via the mouth

Aural: ear; via the ear

Verbal message: words spoken or written to express a thought

Nonverbal message: body language used to express a thought

Receptive: readiness to accept and respond to a message

Transmit: send from one place or person to another

Channel: sound wave transmission via air or other devices

Encoding: selecting verbal and nonverbal symbols to express and transmit messages

Speaker or Source: encoder and transmitter of verbal and nonverbal messages

Decoding: interpreting the speaker's verbal and nonverbal symbols to understand messages

Listener or Receiver: decoder and responder to verbal and nonverbal messages

Transactional: response from the speaker to listener to speaker to listener; circular pattern of communication.

Feedback: verbal and nonverbal responses from the listener and speaker that are received, interpreted and transmitted

Internal stimuli: hidden sensory activity from within; (feelings of hunger, anger, joy, discomfort, etc.)

External stimuli: persons, objects and events in the immediate surroundings perceived via the sensory system (hearing, seeing, touching, smelling, and tasting)

Covert responses: hidden messages from within

Overt responses: exposed verbal and nonverbal messages

The Popcorn Episode

Imagine you are attending a movie with a friend and the aroma of buttered popcorn triggers an idea: Why not buy some hot popcorn? You have become a *source* or *generator* of a message about to be spoken.

As you sensed a desire for popcorn, you were *encoding* or using a set of words or language symbols to express a thought—to buy popcorn. You assume the role of *speaker* as you whisper to your friend, "Carl, would you like some popcorn?" You are transmitting an oral (via the mouth) message carried by sound waves through a *channel* (air) to your friend's ears. Also, you are sending nonverbal messages or clues to enhance your message (emphatic whispering, gestures, or facial expression).

If Carl is attentive to your message, he assumes the role of *listener* or *aural receiver* (via the ear). Carl **interprets** or *decodes* the meaning of your words and

---

The beginning of wisdom is the definition of terms. — Socrates

immediately **re-creates** or *encodes* your message reflecting his interpretation and understanding of your verbal-nonverbal message, "Why not buy some popcorn?" While encoding this message in preparation for his response, Carl may experience a *covert* or *internal stimulus* (hunger pangs) and an *overt* or *external stimulus* (smell of hot butter). When Carl whispers, "That's a good idea; get a large box," this oral response or *feedback* indicates that your verbal and nonverbal messages have been received, processed and correctly interpreted in spite of competing stimuli.

While conversing about the popcorn and trying to watch the screen, you and Carl may have experienced a sudden muscle contraction in the arm or leg or a digestive pain. If so, both the speaker and the listener have processed internal stimuli (generated within) and external stimuli (from outside) i.e., viewing the movie. To make the decision to purchase popcorn you and Carl briefly interacted, causing a reversal of roles.

The circular process of communication occurred as you and Carl reversed listener-speaker roles for the encoding and decoding of responses. Carl, the former listener, assumed the role of speaker, saying, "That's a good idea; get a large box." You assumed the role of an interpreting and re-creating listener. You correctly decoded and encoded or re-created Carl's *intended* message — to buy popcorn.

A MODEL OF THE CIRCULAR PROCESS OF ORAL-AURAL COMMUNICATION

At the top left corner of Figure 2–1, note the internal and external stimuli involving the speaker who is encoding a message with verbal and nonverbal symbols via the sound–wave channel.

The listener or aural receiver responds to the message, speaker and internal and external stimuli while decoding the speaker's message. After interpreting the listener's nonverbal and verbal messages, the speaker encodes an adapted or new message. As soon as the listener makes an oral response, the speaker-listener roles are reversed. The listener has assumed the role of speaker; the speaker has assumed the role of listener. And the circular, transactional process of oral-aural communication may or may not continue.

With the oral-aural circular process of communication in mind, how can we define the complex process of listening?

LISTENING DEFINED

Dictionary definitions of listening, "to apply oneself to hearing something; to pay attention; give heed," do not adequately address the complex process of listening. We need to understand how communication experts define listening.

Scholars in the discipline identify a variety of concepts which they believe are operational in the process of listening. Ethel Glenn, at the University of North Carolina in Greensboro, examined the commonalities and differences in fifty definitions of listening. Seven concepts with synonyms stating the same thought were

FIGURE 2–1   A Model of the Circular Process of Oral-Aural Communication

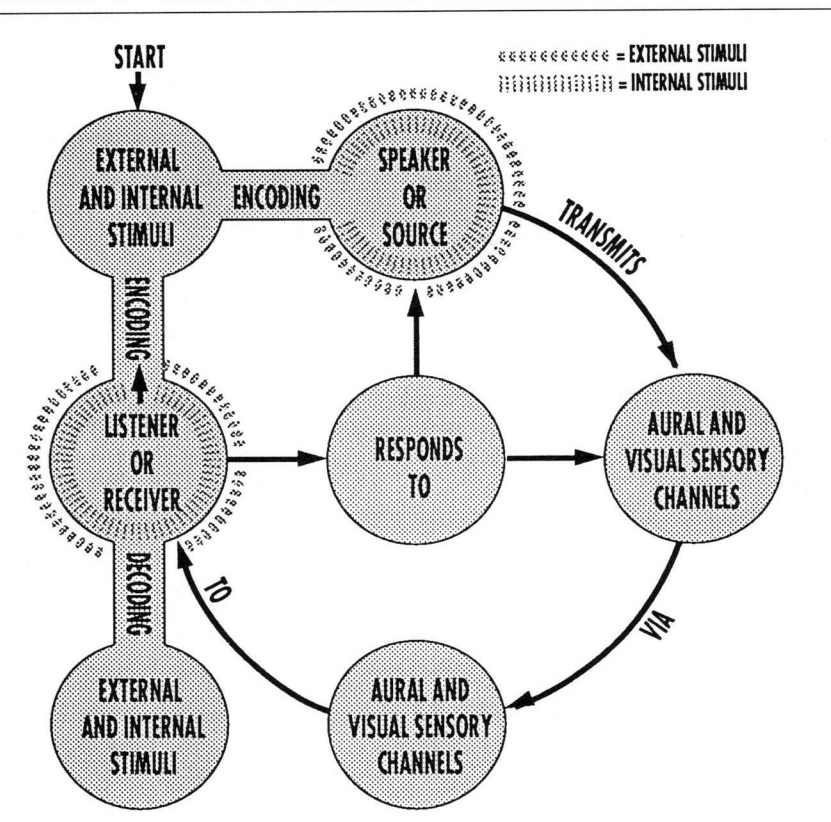

noted: perception, attention, interpretation, remembering, response, spoken sounds, and visual cues.[1]

Judi Brownell, State University of New York, clusters the major listening skills into six major components: hearing, understanding, remembering, interpreting, evaluating, and responding to messages. Brownell emphasizes the overlapping functions of understanding, interpreting and evaluating messages.[2]

Wolvin and Coakley define listening as "the process of receiving, attending to and assigning meaning to aural stimuli."[3]

As we develop the concepts and theories in this textbook, we base the learning on the Wolff-Marsnik sequential definition and model of listening that follows.

The model depicts the receptive-transactional process of incorporating six (one physical; five mental) sequential activities of listening. Without hearing we could not perceive and attend the message. Without interpreting or attaching meaning to the message, there could be no re–creating and retaining the message in short-term memory. Nor could we covertly and overtly respond to the speaker and message without storing the data in short-term memory long enough to do so. From begin-

> **Wolff-Marsnik Definition and Model of Listening**
>
> Listening is a receptive-transactional process of oral-aural communication involving hearing and attending, interpreting and re-creating, retaining and responding to verbal and nonverbal messages. (Model Formula: ha-ir-rr:v/n-m or ha-ir³v/n-m)

ning to end of this intricate, sequential process, the listener needs to maintain attention and concentration — listening is hard work.

Let's examine the six sequential, interdependent activities involved in the complex process of listening. Hearing and attending initiate the listening process.

Hearing and Attending

Hearing is a physical activity that occurs automatically as we mentally select to perceive and attend aural messages. Although the complete sensory and perceptual

FIGURE 2–2   Wolff-Marsnik Model of Receptive-Transactional Process of Listening

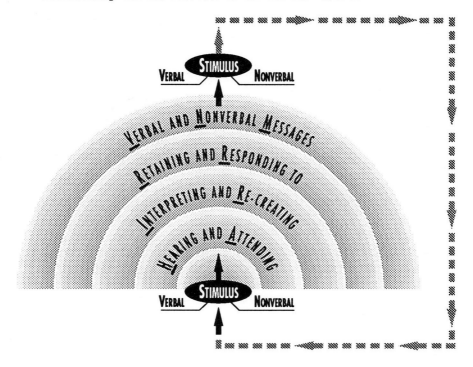

Easy-To-Remember Formula of the Process of Listening HA-IR-RR:V/N-M or HA-IR³-V/N-M

system (hearing, seeing, smelling, tasting, touching) is embodied in the listening process, hearing is the primary sensory receptor initiating listening.

How Do We Hear?

The almost magical operation of the sensory channel of hearing enables us to perceive sound. Sound waves are the physical stimuli for everything we hear. The air is not a vacuum but a collection of *molecules* constantly moving, colliding, and exerting pressure on one another. When there is no sound or wind, the molecules are evenly distributed in the air around us and exert uniform pressure. When there is a sound, changes in pressure move through the air as waves do on the surface of water. Sound–pressure waves are usually generated by the vibration of a physical object in the air causing the molecules close by to be pushed together. Thus, a *positive pressure* is created which, in turn, directs the sound-pressure waves through the air at about 760 miles per hour.

Because most objects do not move in just one direction when they are struck, a partial vacuum or *negative pressure* is created behind the wave of positive pressure. The alternations in air pressure moving in all directions from the source are called sound waves. Different vibrations produce different sound waves. This is the physical energy that impinges upon our ears.[4]

We perceive sound through the ear. It consists of three major parts: the outer ear, which collects the energy; the middle ear, which transmits the energy; and the inner ear, which transforms the energy into nerve impulses directed to the brain.

The Process of Hearing

Referring to Figure 2–3 may help us to understand better the miraculous process of hearing.

The *pinna*, the oval, wrinkled flap attached to the head, is an important part of the *outer ear*. It catches sound waves and reflects them into the circular, inch-long tube (the little hole in your head), called the *auditory canal*. The pressure waves are funneled through this partially wax-filled canal toward the *eardrum*, causing the drum membrane to vibrate.

Beyond the eardrum is the *middle ear*. In this air-filled space are three little bones named after objects they resemble: the hammer, anvil, and stirrup. As the vibrations of the eardrum are transmitted through the inner ear, the three small bones amplify the vibrations. The hammer transmits the pressure waves of sound energy to the anvil, causing it to move back and forth. In the same way the anvil moves the stirrup. The stirrup is connected to another membrane, the *oval window*, which transmits the vibrations to the inner ear. By the time sound reaches the oval window the vibrations are many times stronger than when they first struck the eardrum.

The oval window is at the entrance to the inner ear. The inner ear consists mostly of the *cochlea*. This bony, snail-shaped structure is filled with thin liquid. Inside the cochlea is the *basilar membrane* that runs the length of the spirals in the cochlea. The basilar membrane is adjacent to hairlike nerve cells called *receptor neurons*. These cells change the *pressure vibrations* to *nerve impulses*, which are transmitted to the *auditory nerve* and then to the brain. And then we hear the infinite sound of life.[5]

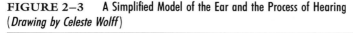

FIGURE 2–3   A Simplified Model of the Ear and the Process of Hearing (*Drawing by Celeste Wolff*)

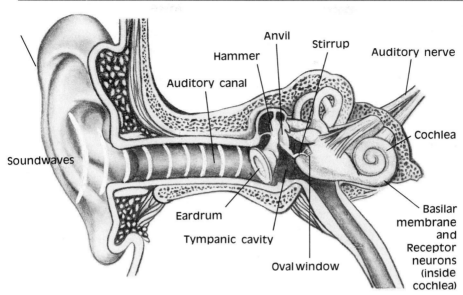

Levels of Hearing

There are three levels of hearing: primary, secondary, and tertiary. On the *primary level* of hearing, sound waves are transformed into auditory nerve impulses via the *voluntary* or central nervous system. These are the types of messages we plan to listen and react to, whether in a philosophy class or at a community meeting. On the *secondary level*, both the central nervous system and the *involuntary* or autonomic nervous system are at work as we concentrate on reading an assigned article or the morning paper. While reading, we might also half-consciously hear the sound of a jackhammer down the street or a lawn mower in an adjacent yard. Finally, on the *tertiary level*, the autonomic nervous system processes the aural stimuli exclusively. For instance, a heavy chandelier crashes to the floor immediately behind us. There is no time to think about what happened. We hear and shudder with fear. Therefore our *hearing acuity* (sharpness in perceiving aural stimuli on the three levels of hearing) influences our ability to communicate and adjust to the world around us. (We are assuming that the listener has normal or unimpaired hearing. Someone with hearing disabilities should consult an audiologist.)

Since hearing initiates the overall integrated process of listening, it behooves us to safeguard the sensitive mechanism that enables us to hear.

Guarding Against Loss of Hearing

Noise (unwanted or harmful sound) is the most pervasive pollution in our society. We need to be alert and guard against the loss of hearing.

Many believe that hearing loss is an inevitable part of aging. But research indicates that those living in low-noise environments experience very little hearing loss in old age. David Lipscomb, former professor of audiology, University of Tennessee at Knoxville, tested more than 1,000 incoming freshmen. He learned that six of every ten students had hearing loss typical of the elderly. Rock music and high-tech gadgets, such as powerful portable stereos, are among the apparent causes of hearing loss in our deafening culture.[6]

Decibels (db) are used to measure sound intensity; each doubling of energy adds ten decibels. We just read how the delicate hairlike receptor neurons in the cochlea of the inner ear convert sound vibrations into nerve impulses for transmission to the brain. When exposed to loud noises, the receptor neurons shrivel and die. Hearing is permanently impaired. Every noise we're exposed to chips away at our hearing. Thus, we need to be informed about the decibel intensity of sound in our environment. Let's check the decibel noise levels established by a federal agency, the Occupational Safety and Health Administration (OSHA).

Hearing Loss and Damaging Noise Levels

OSHA claims that continued exposure to any noise above 85 db (a car horn or electric typewriter) will in time damage hearing. The louder the noise above 85 db, the less time required for damage to occur. Other decibel levels of noise or cacophony (harsh, discordant sound) that we may encounter are noted below.[7]

SOURCE OF NOISE	DECIBEL LEVEL
rocket launch	180
rock concerts	140
boom cars	140
gunshot	140
gasoline-powered lawn mower	130
jet plane	120
inboard motor boat	110
cacophonous night club (near speakers)	110

110 db or more of sound for one-half hour or less = hearing loss

chain saw, jackhammer, subway train	100
screaming child	90
shrill alarm clock	80
heavy traffic	75
hair dryer	70
conversation, air conditioner	60
refrigerator	50

Frequent exposure to noise over 85 db = hearing loss

Sources: Better Hearing Institute, 2nd American Academy of Otolaryngology

In addition to loss of hearing, noise can damage our physical and mental health.

Other Damaging Effects of Noise

We need to be informed about the damaging effects of noise on our health. Here are five points to consider.

1. Noise can cause higher levels of cholesterol and blood pressure; stomach and intestinal ulcers; heart disease; fatigue; impaired sleep; stress; labored breathing; tinnitis (constant ringing, hissing, or buzzing in the ear); babies born with below-average weight, harelip, cleft palate, slower verbal development; and stressful conflict at home and on the job.

2. Recently, medical experts report seeing an increasing number of patients in their 20s, 30s and 40s complaining of hearing loss. Many 20-year-old employees are entering the work force with 60-year-old ears; the premature hearing loss will only increase.

3. The ear-splitting volume at a rock concert causes hearing loss to musicians, sound engineers, and the audience. The Who's guitarist, Pete Townshend, has severe hearing loss. He advises, "Don't listen to music loud at all — ever." Sound experts claim that going to one rock concert (calculated at 140 db) is the equivalent of two and one–half years of aging in hearing.[8]

4. Recognize the signs of hearing loss: difficulty understanding the higher frequencies of speech (words containing the letters s, f, t, sh, ch or h); misunderstanding the spoken word; not hearing the phone ring or your watch tick; and being unable to hear conversation in the midst of background noise.

5. Be prepared to protect your hearing at noisy events. We carry proper equipment to special events. Carry ear-protection equipment to rock concerts and safeguard your hearing.

Ways to Counteract Noise

We can try to observe the following suggestions to make our world quieter.[9]

1. Soundproof your home. Cover tile floors and bare walls that amplify noise with carpets, drapes, and bulky furniture to soak up sound. Place rubber mats under washing machines and other appliances. Seal cracks around windows and doors; plant window-height leafy trees and bushes to absorb outside sounds.

2. Press your hands against your ears when exposed to sudden loud noise. When using noisy tools (lawn mower, power saw, etc.) use foam-plastic-cylinder ear plugs that expand to fill the ear canal rendering 20 db of protection. Plugging the ears with cotton offers little protection (7 db). Take advantage of the new anti-noise devices used in headsets, hearing aids, automobile mufflers, factory machines, etc. that nullify repetitive, cacophonous sounds.

3. Speak up for silence. A Pittsburgh suburb ticketed an ice-cream truck driver

for loud chimes, and noisy street musicians received the same treatment in San Francisco. Freedom from excessive noise is a civic right. We need to create our own oasis of a regular time and place for quiet without intrusion from others. Then the sounds of silence truly become golden, and we are better equipped to retrain and become perceptive listeners.

As we hear (which is not listening), the brain speeds through the next integrated activity called *attending*. Since hearing is a physical activity, attending is the first of five mental activities in the listening process.

Attending the Message

Attending the speaker's *intended* message is a crucial part of the listening process because we are constantly bombarded with a barrage of information stimuli. *Selective perception*, referred to as selecting or "discriminating among stimuli," is a defensive mechanism for the human nervous system. As shown in Figure 2–1, both *external stimuli* and *internal stimuli* compete for our attention. But we can *attend* or be primarily attentive to only *one* stimulus at a time, even as we are aware of other competing stimuli.[10]

The amount of aural stimuli we process in a normal 14–18-hour day is almost infinite. We often find it impossible to recall the countless number of aural stimuli we selected to attend on the previous day. It is also impossible to estimate the even greater number of aural stimuli that never got through to us. Without a selection process, the endless array of external and internal stimuli engulfing us could cause a neural overload. This could result in an eventual breakdown in the voluntary and involuntary nervous systems transmitting data to the brain. For example, in what order would you select to attend or direct your attention to the external and internal stimuli vying for attention in the following situation? On a sunny Sunday morning, as you awaken and reach to turn off the radio alarm (external stimulus), you are seized with violent choking (internal stimulus). Simultaneously, you hear the ringing of the telephone and the doorbell (additional external stimuli). How would you react to such an array of aural stimuli? Let us consider what each of us would probably do.

Determining Factors

Three factors determine which stimulus we select to perceive and attend: (1) the immediate importance of the stimulus, (2) our related experiences, and (3) our emotional state.

The importance we attach to specific stimuli determines whether we attend or filter them out. In the situation noted above, the basic human need to survive takes precedence. Controlling the choking seizure either by self-treatment or by seeking assistance from others is of primary importance. Once we clear the trachea (windpipe) and the choking ceases, the other competing stimuli can be selected for processing according to their importance.

Second, our cumulative *experiences* also influence which stimuli we select for processing. Actually, regarding aural stimuli, we hear what we expect to hear. The reluctant student may have squandered most of the high school and college years by napping rather than listening to the astronomical number of aural messages generated in the classroom. This *nonlistener* (one who arranges not to hear and perceive aural stimuli) would not be able to respond to an unexpected question directed to the class.

Unfortunately many times we tend to ignore information not consonant with our feelings, attitudes, and beliefs. For example, years ago the ecumenical movement would have been condemned as heresy. Roman Catholics were forbidden to participate in services held in a Protestant church. Protestants were reluctant to attend any ceremony in a Catholic church. This effort to block out information contrary to one's beliefs and ideologies curtails learning and personal growth.

And finally, *emotional state* can adversely affect selective perception of stimuli. In reference to aural stimuli, "when our emotions overstimulate our brain it tends to put cotton in our ears. This is particularly true when the more negative emotions are aroused."[11] Heightened emotions (anger, fear, grief, hostility, and jealousy) create psychological roadblocks. Upon receiving that unforgettable phone call reporting the death of a parent or close friend, one feels numb with grief.

On August 1, 1990, most Americans were shocked by the news detailing Iraq's invasion of Kuwait. Subsequently, we listened to threatening reports from Saddam Hussein, the Iraqi dictator, to use Iraqi-backed terrorist organizations to perpetuate violent crime in the United States. During times of great emotional upheaval, our ability to attend and process aural and other sensory stimuli becomes restricted and disoriented. We tend to function abnormally. We may have difficulty interpreting and recreating to decode the speaker's message.

Interpreting and Re-creating

Our model of the listening process (see Figure 2–2) designates the two integrated processes of interpreting and re-creating as occurring after hearing and attending to aural stimuli. Interpreting and re-creating is searching and encoding in the listener's mind, a re-creation of the speaker's intended message.

Interpreting and Re-creating Meaning

We rely on language when we interpret and re-create the meaning of messages from sensory stimuli. *Language* is a universal system of word symbols representing objects and events in the world. Through the use of language we are able to link current stimuli and responses with our experiences. For example, we examine a pair of expensive boots and listen to the salesperson expound on the stylish design, quality leather, and the comfortable, durable inner lining which are the prominent selling features. We link the current stimuli (the sales pitch) with previous knowledge of the pertinent words in the message (boots, leather, stylish, comfortable, and lining).

Uses of language range from the sublime (scriptural and Shakespearean messages) to the ridiculous (the typical American cocktail party prattle). However, the essential function of language, according to Joseph DeVito, is "taking an idea . . .

that exists inside the head of the speaker, shaping it so that it can be transmitted as a message, then actually transmitting the message — and hoping that approximately the same idea will somehow miraculously reappear inside the head of the listener."[12] That we are capable of manipulating language symbols in the processing of thought is humanity's unique achievement.

Language and Thought

Engaging the mind to mold ideas into language symbols is *thinking* or *thought*. Listeners apply four kinds of thinking when assimilating aural messages: concept formation, problem solving, creative thinking, and reasoning.

When the symbols of language and thought pertain to more than one object or event, we are engaged in *concept thinking*, as in learning the six activities integrated in the listening process discussed in this chapter. When we manipulate the symbols of language and thought in an effort to reach a particular goal, we are involved in *problem-solving thinking*, as in listening during a seminar on preparing federal income tax returns. When we unconsciously rearrange language and thought symbols and use imagery to achieve loosely defined goals, we are engaged in *creative thinking*, as in synthesizing several unique ways to improve our listening competency while we study this text. The fourth kind of thought is *reasoning*, or directing thought according to a set of well-defined rules of logic — for example, replacing careless listening habits with productive techniques will probably lead us to reason and conclude that the level of listening competency can be improved. Also, detecting the speaker's use of exclusive and inclusive language can improve listening competency.

Listening to Exclusive and Inclusive Language

As perceptive listeners of the English language, we need to recognize a speaker's use of exclusive language with restrictive, traditional, and sexist word symbols and inclusive language with broad, contemporary, nonsexist word symbols. Listeners can decode messages more accurately when speakers use gender-inclusive language as noted below.

GENDER-EXCLUSIVE LANGUAGE	GENDER-INCLUSIVE LANGUAGE
mankind	humankind
chairman	chairperson
policeman	police
mailman	mail carrier
workmen	workers
businessmen	business people
horsemen	horse riders
salesmen	salespersons
flight stewardesses	flight attendants
poetess	poet
cleaning ladies	cleaning staff

Adapting to and practicing gender-inclusive language has created several awkward language structures.

The "He-She/His-Her" Construction

The awkward "he-she/his-her" word syndrome clutters messages, adds confused meaning to messages and is no longer used by most publishers. These terms can be eliminated by restructuring language. For example:

A student who cuts classes tends to limit his or her opportunity to be the best he or she can be.

Restructured: Students who cut classes tend to limit the opportunity to be the best they can be.

Any manager needs to review his or her 1991 sales quotas.

Restructured: Sales managers need to review their 1991 quotas. Awkward structures weaken and distort the beauty of language, creating an additional burden as listeners decode messages.

"The beauty of the American English language is that it is a flexible language, one that changes to meet the needs of society."[13] A crop of new words surfaced during the Persian Gulf War. Listening to and reading the daily progress reports, we learned a series of terms used by the military: jeep (hummer); 16 mm rifle (pea shooter); tent (hootch); air dog fight (fur ball); anti-aircraft attack (triple A). Such creative, accepted, and widely used terms by military personnel may have expedited communication, contributing to the victory for United Nations forces.

After hearing and attending, interpreting and re–creating the aural stimuli via language and thought, we organize the speaker's message into appropriate categories in the apperceptive portion of the brain.

Organizing into Categories

In order to attach meaning to aural stimuli, the complicated network of the brain sorts and assigns input data into categories or groupings. We have thousands of categories of stored information in the apperceptive mass of the brain. Categories are created as the result of one's formal learning and everyday experiences. The mind sorts and assigns *every word* in our language into categories. Upon hearing the words *chair, boy,* and *sat,* we evoke meaning from the *criterial attributes*. These are the universal characteristics of meaning we have assigned to these words — *seat* for *chair*, *child* for *boy*, and *reclined* for *sat*. Constantly, we must quickly decide to which category an aural stimulus belongs as the brain makes a search for only one category assignment at a time.

Meaning from Subcategories

Modifiers, or words that add to the meaning of other words, evoke meaning from *subcategories*. Note the following two sentences and the additional, pertinent meaning the listener can evoke from subcategories specified by the modifiers in the second sentence: "The boy sat in the chair"; "The *little* boy *happily* sat in the *dentist's* chair." Hearing and perceiving the italicized modifiers, the listener can assimilate and organize additional meaning evoked from the subcategories. Obviously we understand much more about the boy in the chair. The more we listen the more we expand and refine the apperceptive mass of the brain. But an exchange student with meager knowledge of American English may not have created a subcategory for the word *dentist*. Consequently the listener either conjectures some sort of meaning for the word or bypasses it. Either way, the speaker's intended meaning is distorted.

In addition to criterial attributes or commonly known meanings, a category that includes the objects and events we assign to it has many *noncriterial attributes*. These attributes or characteristics are not universal but are individually assigned as the result of each person's unique experience. For example, the words *students, management,* and *motorcycles* are names of categories with criterial attributes. However, the noncriterial attributes arbitrarily assigned from one's personal experience could evoke such meanings as: students are irresponsible; corporate vice presidents are secure and happy; and motorcycles are deathtraps. Much to his chagrin, Mark Twain could not give a serious speech. Regardless of what he said, listeners were looking for concealed humor in his words—and they found it. Many used noncriterial attributes to categorize and interpret Twain's messages. Speakers' messages are distorted when listeners fail to organize words into the correct universal categories the speaker intended.[14]

Retaining and Responding to Verbal and Nonverbal Messages

The third interrelated activity of listening, retaining and responding to verbal and nonverbal messages involves the storage of information or *memory*. Learning and memory take place in large areas of the brain rather than in small networks of brain cells. *Memory* is stored data duplicated over and over again.

Short- and Long-Term Memory
Short-term memory is the storage of data for a few seconds. *Long-term memory* stores data for hours, days, years, or even a lifetime. After we hear, attend, and perceive an aural stimulus (the phone rings), and interpret and recreate the meaning of the message (the manager states that all vacations scheduled during the next month must be canceled), we momentarily retain the message in short-term memory while preparing a covert response ("What a tough break!"). The process of listening is constant and rapid. It exercises short-term memory or retention during the actual listening process. Later we ponder our employer's need to revise vacation schedules. Subsequently we relay the disappointing news to sympathetic friends. Thus we have stored the information in long-term memory channels of the brain. In spite of keen disappointment, we probably will be back to work as usual during the previously scheduled vacation week. Retaining aural messages in long-term memory is not a *part* of the listening process. It is the *result* of perceptive listening.

Occasionally we may become impatient and even discouraged at the scanty amount of information that we are able to retain in immediate or short-term memory. We forget. Basically there are two reasons why we can't seem to remember certain data for even short periods of time. First, the storage capacity of short-term memory is limited. Second, short-term memory is easily disrupted.

The results of short-term memory research by psychologists are interesting. Our memory span for a single repetition is about seven items long, the equivalent of a seven-digit telephone number. Most of us cannot retain more than seven items or numbers unless we have learned to organize the information into chunks. The trick is to group the data as we interpret or assign meaning to it.

Chunking Aural Data

We can better retain data in memory by noting the logical, similar, and different patterns in letters, words, and numbers. For example, we can "chunk" the logical sequence and the *ing* endings of three sets of activities performed by the listener: hear*ing* and attend*ing*, interpret*ing* and recreat*ing*, and retain*ing* and respond*ing* to aural and nonverbal stimuli. The telephone number 293-5234 can be remembered by storing *293* as the first chunk, separated by the *5* and followed by the sequential numbers *234* as the second chunk.

The U.S. postal system's use of nine-digit zip codes in mailing addresses requires more storage than the seven-item capacity of short-term memory. In a paper entitled, "The Magical Number Seven, Plus or Minus Two," G. A. Miller claims that the average person can retain seven items or letters or numbers in short-term memory.[15] Under certain circumstances, we can easily retain ten bits of chunked information by remembering a concept as demonstrated in these numbers: 2 4 6 8 0 1 3 5 7 9 (the odd-even number concept). Actually the limit of short-term memory is **seven chunks**.

How would you chunk the following zip codes to store in short- and eventually long-term memory? (Dayton, OH 45419-3805; New York, NY 10008-3734; Mission, KS 66201-2768; and Somerset, NJ 08875-6742) The Dayton and New York codes already are chunked into easy memory patterns. But the Mission and Somerset codes require greater effort to retain the chunked data. (Chapter 4, Five Power Tools of Listening, explains how listeners can retrain to store more information in short- and long-term memory.)

Not only is short-term memory limited in capacity, it is also highly susceptible to disruption by other sensory stimuli competing for our attention. However, we can sustain a reasonable amount of interference. We may be able to retain data in short-term memory while making a brief comment or noting an unfavorable grimace on a clerk's face. We can do so if only a small amount of information is being stored for a short period of time, such as a person's height and weight. If the stored information includes a friend's height, weight, and four items to buy for a fishing trip, memory may be disrupted. An efficient listener who understands information overload in relation to short-term memory capacity would revert to note-taking to record and retain the data. (Chapter 6, Three Basic Concepts to Enhance Listening Comprehension, describes ways in which the listener can aid understanding by using appropriate note–taking systems.)

Responding: The Last Act of the Listening Process

The final act of the listening process is responding to the speaker's verbal and nonverbal messages. This means that the listener is processing two kinds of responses: covert and overt responses to the speaker's words and body language or nonverbal messages.

Covert Response. After hearing and attending, interpreting and recreating, and retaining the speaker's message in short-term memory, the listener inwardly responds to the message. Remember the example in which all employees' vacation schedules had to be changed. The covert response of those who had planned to visit Hawaii probably was "What a tough break!" with mixed feelings of disappointment and frustration. During the phone call, they responded to the manager's words (vacations changed) and *paralinguistic cues* (the volume, pitch, rate and quality of the manager's voice).

Overt Response. The listener's overt response is a reflection of the listener's covert response to the message and occurs almost simultaneously with the covert response. Overt responses are the listener's observable nonverbal reactions to the speaker and message. Remember the time you apologized for arriving late at an important meeting. You listened as the administrator commented, "Here's a copy of the new inventory policy discussed before you arrived at the meeting." Yet nonverbally the message transmitted was, "Why couldn't you be on time for the meeting? — we needed you here." The listener's covert and overt response to the speaker and message is called *feedback*.

Kinds of Listener Feedback

The receptive-transactional process of oral-aural communication requires a listener response — or feedback — to the speaker. As noted earlier in Definition Box 1, our definition of feedback highlights verbal and nonverbal responses — between listener and speaker — for reception, interpretation, and transmission of messages. Feedback helps the speaker assess how messages are being processed and understood by the listener. Little or no feedback may be the beginning of a breakdown in communication.

Lyman Steil, a communication consultant, lists four classes of feedback response:[16]

1. **Verbal Feedback:** Listeners utter encouraging, noncommittal sounds (uhuh, yes, or repeating a speaker's word). This type of indirect verbal feedback occurs during the listening process. Answering a speaker's question is direct verbal feedback that occurs after the listening process.

2. **Nonverbal Feedback:** The perceptive listener continuously transmits nonverbal messages via body language and vocal sounds. These signs help inform the speaker that listeners, indeed, are receiving and reacting to the message.

3. **Combined Verbal and Nonverbal Feedback:** Using both the verbal and nonverbal feedback is the clearest signal of listener response to the speaker's message. Again referring to the vacation-schedule example, the covert response ("tough break") may be reinforced by a series of overt, nonverbal messages (grim facial expression, clenched hands and stiffened body stance). We complete the last act of the listening process as the mouth opens to make a relevant,

direct verbal response. At this point, the listener-speaker roles are reversed: The listener assumes the speaker role; the former speaker assumes the listener role.

4. **Silence** (the absence of intended verbal and nonverbal feedback): Silence can be interpreted as angry, sympathetic or indifferent feedback. We sense the anger of "the silent treatment" in an unresolved conflict. We feel the deep sympathy conveyed by one unable "to find the right words." We are confused by those whose indifference provides no clue of listener response to the speaker.

(Further discussion of silence as a listener response is noted in Chapter 10, Ten Listening Retraining Techniques.)

Since listeners are responsible for decoding verbal AND nonverbal messages, we will discuss nonverbal communication in greater detail (see Chapter 9, Listening to Nonverbal Messages).

The listener's desire and ability to decode messages and provide meaningful feedback to the speaker depends on the competent use of countless listening-related subskills.

Listening-Related Subskills

Because we listen to different speakers with different purposes stating different messages in different situations, we need to develop an array of different subskills. In *Human Listening: Processes and Behavior*, Carl Weaver identifies what he calls "a long but not complete" list of 41 listener-related subskills, ten of which are noted below.[17]

Listener-Related Subskills

To get the central idea	To listen under bad conditions
To get main ideas	To adjust to the speaker
To retain pertinent content	To understand oral instructions
To take notes	To listen to difficult material
To use contextual clues to determine "word meaning"	To resist the influence of emotion-laden words/arguments

Perceptive listening is a complex and difficult communication process requiring hard work and self-discipline. Other important perceptive listening concepts and related subskills presented in this textbook can upgrade our level of listening competency to learn, grow, and prosper in the classroom, on the job and in family and social environments.

WRAPPING IT UP: A SUMMARY

The popcorn incident at the movie exemplifies the oral-aural process of communication involving the encoding speaker, verbal and nonverbal messages, the channel, and the decoding and encoding listener. Speakers and listeners are affected by internal and external stimuli.

The six sequential, integrated activities of the receptive process of listening are: hearing and attending, interpreting and re–creating, retaining and responding to verbal and nonverbal messages.

Young people are suffering hearing loss. They are exposed to loud music and noise at concerts and by turning up volume controls on radios, television, stereos, and head sets. We need to protect the sensitive hearing mechanism from damage caused by noisy environments.

The listener's interpretation and re–creation of messages involve covert and overt responses. There are four classes of listener feedback: verbal, nonverbal, combined verbal and nonverbal, and silence.

The awkward "he-she/his-her" syndrome of exclusive language should be re-placed with inclusive language.

The Listener Log

Your instructor may suggest keeping a Listener Log to record special assignments and unique listening experiences, particularly the exercises that follow. An inch-thick spiral notebook can be used. Reserve the front pages for taking class notes. A paper clip placed at the top of a page for the Listener Log section serves as a convenient divider. Follow the format and writing style required by the instructor. By the end of the course, the Listener Log can be a valuable tool for continued improvement in your listening behavior and a major factor in your grade.

DISCUSSION AND STUDY GUIDES

1. List and briefly describe six interrelated activities in the process of listening. Explain the interdependent relationship of each and the impact on the listening process.

2. How would you explain the miracle of hearing? Which practical suggestions would you share with a friend regarding ways to safeguard and protect hearing?

3. Distinguish between oral and aural. Visualize and explain the oral-aural process of communication, using and giving major definitions of ten related terms. When and by whom would short- and long-term memory be used?

4. Make a list of five exclusive– and five inclusive–language words you or others have used. Write two paragraphs explaining your feelings and plans to use exclusive and inclusive language.

LISTENING EXERCISES THAT WORK

EXERCISE 1. (Getting Acquainted in a Classroom or Seminar) (Use appropriate data) Gather into small groups, four to six persons. Without taking notes and within the next 15 minutes, learn the pronunciation and spelling of each other's first and last names. Listen attentively to the exchange of the following personal data: home city and state, size of family and parents' occupations, reasons for selecting this college or company, academic year, major, professional aspiration or current position, idea of an exciting social date. After the allotted time, two persons from each group, randomly selected by the instructor, introduce each other to the whole group. Any error resulting from careless listening during small–group discussion may be corrected by the person being introduced after the introduction. Continue the 30-second introductions until all have been introduced. General discussion may follow: Was it difficult to listen attentively and retain the personal data for the introductions? If so, why? In addition to meeting new acquaintances, what have you learned about the receptive-transactional process of listening?

EXERCISE 2. (Power Listening Generates Knowledge) In the Listener Log, list ten concepts clarified in this chapter. Form into small groups. Discuss how and why the application of the listed concepts can accelerate learning and generate knowledge. Write a summary paragraph of the discussion in the Log.

EXERCISE 3. (Activating the Definition of Listening) In the local newspaper, check the weekly radio or television programs. Plan to listen to a program about a topic relatively unfamiliar to you. As the program is aired, take no notes but be conscious of your behavior in respect to the six components of the listening process: hearing and attending, interpreting and re–creating, retaining and responding to verbal and nonverbal messages. Later, write a short paragraph in the Listener Log describing what and how you learned during each of the six activities in the listening process.

EXERCISE 4. (Selective Perception) Go to a crowded shopping mall or other busy area with two members of your listening class. Stand or sit together for 20 minutes and listen to the conversations of people passing by. Each student will write in a small notebook the major-word themes of as many conversations as possible. Subsequently, compare your recorded data with that of the other two students. Which of you selectively perceived and listened to the most conversations or aural stimuli? How many different major-word themes were recorded in the three notebooks? What have you learned about people by listening to conversations?

EXERCISE 5. (Short-Term Memory) An excellent way to become acquainted at a social gathering is to play the short-term memory game. The first person makes an introductory comment, such as "I am Jack Medcalfe; I love to play tennis." Each person attempts to repeat the names and bits of information before adding to the series of introductions. Those participating in the game will be somewhat surprised to note how difficult it is to listen and retain data in short-term memory. Later briefly record this experience in the Listener Log. Then answer the following questions: How many persons' introductory data could most listeners retain? How can you account for this pattern of retention in relation to the discussion in this chapter? Specifically, how could you improve your performance in a similar situation in the future? What suggestions could you give others who wish to improve short-term and long-term memory?

EXERCISE 6. (Exclusive and Inclusive Language) Write five short sentences containing exclusive language (he, she, his, her). Rewrite the sentences using inclusive language. Form into small groups and share your writing. Why is inclusive language more appropriate than exclusive language? What impact do these language structures have on the listener? Was it difficult to convert from exclusive to inclusive language? Explain.

NOTES

1. Ethel C. Glenn, "A Content Analysis of Fifty Definitions of Listening," *Journal of the International Listening Association* 3 (1989), 21–31.
2. Judi Brownell, *Building Active Listening Skills* (Englewood Cliffs, NJ: Prentice-Hall, 1986), 13.
3. Andrew D. Wolvin and Carolyn Gwynn Coakley, *Listening*, 3rd ed. (Dubuque, IA: Wm. C. Brown, Publishers, 1988), 92.
4. Clifford T. Morgan and Richard A. King, *Introduction to Psychology*, 4th ed. (New York: McGraw Hill, 1971), 630, 633–38.
5. Neil and Mary Carlson, *Psychology, the Science of Behavior*, 3rd ed. (Boston: Allyn and Bacon, 1990), 198–200.
6. Lowell Ponte, "How Noise Can Harm You," *Reader's Digest*, March 1989, 121–25.
7. Better Hearing Institute and American Academy of Otolaryngology, "How noise can harm your hearing," *Good Housekeeping*, June 1987, 215.
8. Sue Chastain, Knight-Ridder News Service, "Every noise we're exposed to chips away at our hearing," *Dayton [Ohio] Daily News*, November 23, 1989, 3-A.
9. Ponte, 124.
10. Guy R. Lefrancois, *Psychology* (Belmont, CA: Wadsworth, 1980), 115.
11. J. Dan Rothwell and James I. Costigan, *Interpersonal Communication: Influences and Alternatives* (Columbus, OH: Charles E. Merrill, 1975), 169.
12. Joseph A. DeVito, *Language: Concepts and Processes* (Englewood Cliffs, NJ: Prentice-Hall, 1973), 13.
13. Barb Fedders, "The search for inclusive language," *Dimensions*, University of Dayton Publication, August 1986, 4–5.
14. For further information of cognitive structuring into categories and subcategories, see Carl H. Weaver, *Human Listening: Processes and Behavior* (Indianapolis: Bobbs-Merrill, 1972), 42–59.
15. G. A. Miller, "The magical number seven plus or minus two: Some limits on our capacity for processing information," *Psychological Review* 63 (1956), 81–97; cited in Neil R. Carlson, *Psychology: The Science of Behavior* (Boston: Allyn and Bacon, 1990), 259.
16. Lyman K. Steil, *Effective Listening: Key to Your Success* (New York: Random House, 1983), 125.
17. Weaver, 10–11.

CHAPTER 3

TEN AXIOMS ABOUT LISTENING

We should not be able to talk without listening, yet there are many who do.
— Gerald Nierenberg and Henry Calero

THESIS Humans listen before they speak, speak before they read, and read before they write. Thus learning and refining listening skills provides a foundation for the entire process of human communication.

CHAPTER OBJECTIVES

1. Recognize that awareness of the ten axioms about listening can improve our ability to learn how to listen perceptively.
2. Know that the axioms about listening underlie everything we learn about listening.

CHAPTER PREVIEW

- Listening is a mental operation.
- Listening is active.
- Listening is learned.
- Listening is complex.
- Perceptive listeners must be trained.
- Listeners share responsibility for communication success.
- Listening is as vital a communication skill as reading.
- Teaching listening differs from teaching reading.
- Listening and agreeing are separate acts.
- Listening is crucial to all communication.

Before Mike Wilson began his first listening training session, he told a co-worker, "This listening training is really important for our people. Personally, I get most of my information from reading, but I know the value of listening. I'm a pretty good listener myself, and I can listen when I want to."

Mike meant to show his positive endorsement of listening training. However, what he did show was a pervasive lack of understanding about listening which had skewed his thinking and had kept him from making progress toward truly efficient listening.

When we, like Mike, agree that listening training is important but catch ourselves saying, "I've been listening all my life so I'm pretty good at it," or "I can listen if there's a good speaker," we signal that we really don't know what listening is.

It is imperative that we understand some of the established and accepted principles that form a foundation for our study of listening. The early work of such listening pioneers as Dr. Ralph G. Nichols uncovered several facts about listening ability and performance which are so fundamental to learning to listen that we consider them to be axiomatic—underlying everything we say about listening.[1]

Because not knowing or understanding these axioms can sabotage our entire study of listening, we present some of them here. Let's look at our own understanding of listening. If it is spotty and vague, we can attempt to learn these axioms and retrain ourselves to become perceptive listeners.

AXIOM 1. LISTENING IS A MENTAL OPERATION

We realize listening is a mental operation when we consider the steps in listening: hearing and attending, interpreting and re–creating, and retaining and responding. With the exception of hearing, all are mental operations. Listening begins as soon as the physical act of hearing—together with other sensory receptors like seeing and touching—occurs. Once we hear, we may or may not move into the next five steps of the listening process.

Hearing Is Physical, Listening Is Mental

Equating the physical act of hearing with the primarily mental act of listening has been a serious and persistent mistake made by prospective listeners in the past.

It is not unusual for a supervisor to recommend a hearing test for a trainee who has listening difficulties. Many of us assume that when we test a person's hearing, we have concluded our search for listening problems. Naturally, it is important to find hearing difficulties and to deal with them, but eradicating them cannot eradicate all listening difficulties. Statistically only about 6 percent of schoolchildren exhibit hearing problems. However, any teacher will agree that more than 6 percent of schoolchildren demonstrate listening problems.

Listening does not happen physically in the ears but mentally between the ears. Sara Lundsteen, in an effort to teach this difference, devised a checklist for roadblocks to listening. She suggests identifying both specific difficulties with hearing and specific difficulties with listening. We can check our *hearing* roadblocks by responding to such statements as: (1) "I often have trouble hearing what people say," (2) "The room was too noisy," (3) "The speaker talked loudly enough, but not clearly." We can then identify our *listening* roadblocks, which are all mental activities, by responding to statements such as: (1) "I wasn't interested," (2) "I was thinking of what I was going to say," (3) "I was thinking about other things."[2]

Although Lundsteen designed this tool for children, anyone who wishes to identify specific roadblocks to the physical act of hearing and the mental act of listening will find it useful.

Aural Understanding

Aural understanding begins with hearing ability. When we move from hearing and attending to interpreting, we *understand* the aural message. We may *hear* a ticking sound and select it, but we *listen* to a clock because we understand it is a clock. We may hear discordant sound coming from a room, but our friend listens to a favorite rock group. We may hear the sounds of someone speaking German, but only someone who understands German can listen to it.

It is possible to experience aural understanding without the physical ability to sense by hearing. Several years ago, a young deaf woman surprised people when they met her because they presumed she heard. She became an efficient listener by substituting lip reading and nonverbal signals for her loss of hearing. She worked her way through school as a salesperson and most of her customers never imagined that she did not hear what they said. She listened without hearing ability (sense of hearing) because she was forced to substitute other senses for hearing.

We make a mistake when we assume that efficient hearing produces efficient listening. We can agree that hearing is the initial step in the complex process of listening, but several additional steps must follow. We conclude that listening is a complex mental operation that demands active participation.

Retraining Guidelines: Listening Is a Mental Operation

- Remember, good hearing and good listening are not the same. Even though you have heard a message, you may not have listened to it.
- Recognize physical hearing roadblocks (noises, poor hearing acuity) and remove or correct them.
- Recognize mental listening roadblocks (daydreaming, worrying, poor habits of concentration) and resolve to set them aside.

AXIOM 2. LISTENING IS ACTIVE

Listening involves several intellectual operations — a process listeners *do* rather than one done to them. Many approach the average classroom, problem-solving session or meeting as a place to lean back, glance through papers, or chat with neighbors while waiting to be "fired up." Many have long assumed that listening is easy and passive. Those who believe this enter into communication presuming a masterful speaker will successfully conquer their apathy. It takes two to communicate. Even if speakers talk forever, if listeners refuse to take an active part there will be no communication.

Speakers experience an accelerated pulse, fluctuating skin temperature, and blood pressure when sending messages. Speakers also show evidence of mental activity in their gestures, facial expressions, body movement, eye contact, and choice and expression of words. We know the speaker expends energy because we can see, hear, and sense it. Listeners, too, need to expend energy.

The Act of Listening

Listening is mostly internal. Because we cannot see people perform the mental process of listening, we presume that it is passive. We become expert in ways to pretend we are listening: staring, nodding, writing, or doodling. After completing one listening course in college, Joanne, a freshman, remarked, "I really needed this course in high school. There I trained myself to be a proficient nonlistener. If I thought speakers were boring, I simply leaned back and tuned out the minute they started talking. I had dozens of techniques for faking attention, but I was asleep with my eyes open. It never occurred to me that I should be giving energy to the actual mental process of listening!"

Such proficient nonlisteners as Joanne enter colleges, vocational schools, and jobs every year. There they spend more time using listening than any other communication skill.

Carl Rogers defined active listening as a situation in which we do not passively absorb words spoken to us but actively attempt to grasp the facts and feelings in what we hear.[3]

The Need for Active Listeners

The need for active listeners is evident if we think of a listener coming into an important listening situation as like an athlete entering a contest—keyed up, set, ready. When Ivan Lendl walks onto the court at Wimbledon, he is physically and mentally ready, and he expects to expend enormous amounts of **physical and mental energy** both when serving and receiving the ball. As listeners, we should likewise be ready to expend energy to receive messages. But how many of us walk into classrooms, business meetings, or personal relationships with little or no expectation of actively expending energy receiving those messages?

Listening is active. Listeners who believe it is passive or who believe that faking physical activity will convince others that they are listening will waste valuable energy and cheat themselves in the process. Oral communication is an ongoing, ever-changing process demanding conscious mental and physical action by listeners.

Retraining Guidelines: Listening Is Active

- Assume an active role. Refuse to believe that listening is passive.
- Plan to be a message receiver ready to do whatever is necessary to interpret, re—create, respond to, and retain messages.

- Remind yourself that a speaker is only one part of the communication team and that you, as listener, are the other.

AXIOM 3. LISTENING IS LEARNED

When considering how listening is learned and in discussing the way we learn, James I. Brown said:

> At birth we know nothing about language—not even what it is. Amazingly enough, however—usually in our first five years—we will complete the greater part of the basic acquisition process with no formal instruction—depending solely on listening . . . the learning through listening during those early formative years seems almost miraculous.[4]

Brown used these lines to explain how listening is used to learn language. However, many of us, perhaps because we must listen before we can speak and because we learn so much through listening, assume that listening is a "miraculous" innate power that is not learned. Unfortunately, this presumption can keep us from recognizing that listening is a learned skill which can be improved or allowed to deteriorate. In his book, *How to Speak, How to Listen*, Mortimer Adler quotes Gertrude Stein: "Everyone, when they are young, has a little bit of genius; that is, they really do listen . . . then they grow a little older and many of them get tired and listen less and less. But some, very few, continue to listen."[5] He uses Stein's words to show that while children do learn the almost miraculous act of listening, as they get older they learn careless habits. Without training we simply become less and less proficient listeners. Listening is a learned skill, just as reading is a learned skill. We hear with the ear just as we see with the eye. But we listen with the brain, just as we read with the brain. We do not have to be taught to see, but we do have to be taught to read by interpreting words through mental processing. Similarly, we do not need training to hear, but do need it to listen.

Although listening is not automatic, the manner in which we listen can be automatic. That is, we may have developed a collection of listening habits that we use automatically. The beliefs, values, and motives that govern our behavior in other roles also influence this process. Sometimes we hear a message but do not attend to it; sometimes we hear and attend to messages that come from friends, sometimes from enemies. Sometimes we listen eagerly; at other times we can't wait to get away. Sometimes we bring pressing personal problems to listening; at other times we are free from worry. We bring these conditions, values, and beliefs to listening, and these experiences are some reasons why we cannot listen automatically.

So many variables govern every step of listening that the ability to do so is not only not automatic, it is remarkable. The axiom that we must learn to listen truly describes a growing and, perhaps even miraculous process.

Retraining Guidelines: Listening Is Learned

- Remember that listening is not an automatic response.

- Remember, efficient listening habits create perceptive listening skills, and careless listening habits create poor listening skills.

AXIOM 4. LISTENING IS COMPLEX

Listening is a complex act consisting of one physical and five mental activities. When someone says, "He's so stupid, you can't tell him anything; he doesn't listen," that is not only being unfair, but is also demonstrating a lack of knowledge about the complexity of the listening process.

No doubt a relationship between listening and intelligence exists. Intelligence does limit or control everything we do, but we often exaggerate its importance in relation to listening. If we have not learned specific listening skills through experience or training, then our ability to listen will be limited no matter what the degree of intelligence.

As a result of a 1988 study of listening in organizational environments, Marilyn Lewis and N. L. Reinsch, Jr. concluded that listening in the work environment is, indeed, complex. They identified 38 categories of listening activities needed in the workplace. This large number of activities also took place in the milieu of time pressures, interruptions, and ongoing relationships.[6] We can underscore the complexity of listening by pointing out that workers often attempt listening with no formal training.

Imperfect practice creates imperfect listeners. One of our favorite basketball coaches says, "Practice doesn't make perfect. Practice makes permanent." He believes that if we practice daily doing something the wrong way, we will simply make the wrong way permanent. With no training at all, we may be practicing slovenly listening habits until they become permanent.

Evidence of this can be seen in the results of an informal survey of listening ability conducted among schoolchildren. Each teacher interrupted what she was saying in her class and announced, "Time out." The teacher then asked: "What were you thinking of?" and "What was I saying just before I called time out?" In lower grades, pupils responded privately to teachers who wrote down the results. In higher grades, students wrote out the answers without revealing their names. Results from the first–graders showed that 90 percent were listening to their teachers when "time out" was called, and over 80 percent of second–graders were listening.

The percentages tapered off in higher grades. In junior high school, only 43.7 percent of students were listening, and in high school, the average dipped to a low of 28 percent.[7] Perhaps college professors and business executives who saw these results cringed as they imagined the percentages among older listeners with deeply ingrained, careless listening habits. This informal survey seems to emphasize that, without training, the 90 percent listening efficiency of first–graders deteriorates. Inefficient habits practiced over and over create even less efficient listeners.

Nonlistening training actually exists in many homes and schoolrooms. Therapist Franklin Ernst believes that not only do we allow repeated practice to make inefficient listening permanent and allow ourselves to believe that daily practice eliminates the need for listening training, but also that many of us actually receive training in nonlistening. He believes that, from earliest years, children receive a steady diet of edicts such as, "Don't pay any attention to him," "He didn't mean what he said," or "We don't listen to that in this family." He asserts that typical parents not only make these statements but reinforce them by their own inattention and frequent interruptions. Often parents provide, by word and deed, training in nonlistening.[8]

When children leave the nonlistening environment of their homes and enter school, this behavior is often further reinforced. Most teachers are themselves untrained so that they, too, demonstrate and put up with inattentiveness and interruptions that create roadblocks to listening. In addition, many classrooms are organized with large blocks of time for listening without opportunities for responding. Students who cannot listen for long periods without doing any responding learn to turn off their minds. If we recognize these habits in ourselves, we can take steps to remove them by training.

Those who have not been trained to listen or who have presumed good listening to be a matter of intelligence are similar to novices in any field. When theatergoers admire skilled actors, they recognize that actors have worked hard for many years and have trained with the best available directors in a variety of theater companies. Thoughtful theater audiences don't expect the star of an elementary school production to exhibit the same skills. They know that style, skill, and consistency come from learning fundamental skills of acting and from practicing them. Most people are amateurs in listening, yet we often dismiss them as too stupid to listen because they stumble along with few skills. Hearing and attending, interpreting and re–creating, and retaining and responding demand as much skill as actors making entrances, picking up cues, and remembering lines.

Retraining Guidelines: Listening Is Complex

- Realize that the one physical and five mental activities in perceptive listening are part of a complex operation.
- Recall that perfecting the complex skill of perceptive listening takes time. Anticipate improving gradually.

AXIOM 5. PERCEPTIVE LISTENERS MUST BE TRAINED

Many of us nurture the false assumption that daily practice in listening eliminates any need for training. We often hear people say, "Well, after all, we do it all the time. Who needs training?" Or, "I can listen when I want to." Such reasoning suggests that because we daily take part in many listening situations we will daily become more efficient listeners. Unfortunately, we may very well be practicing and reinforcing faults rather than skills. Listening training must be accepted and put to work day by day. Most of us walk and many of us run every day, and most of us have been doing so since we were about a year old. Yet none of us expects to become a track star or marathon runner simply because we have been using our legs for 20 or more years. We wouldn't dream of entering a marathon without specialized training. We would do warm-up exercises and run a little more each day until we were in perfect condition to use those same legs on which we had been walking for all but a year of our lives. Let us consider this same idea in relation to listening. We can train ourselves, a little more each day, until we are as aware of our level of listening efficiency as athletes are of their level of physical efficiency.

Now and then we hear a potential listener say, "I know I'm not a good listener, but I can listen when I want to." We can only imagine the same person saying, "I know I'm not a good swimmer, but I can swim when I want to." We know that when a canoe capsizes and the only hope to survive is to swim to shore, all occupants *want* to swim. However, the nonswimmers and the poorly trained swimmers will be the ones likely to drown, not because they didn't want to swim but because they hadn't been trained to swim. No matter how much we want to listen, we can only do so to the level at which we have been trained.

Retraining Guidelines: Perceptive Listeners Must Be Trained

• Resolve not to accept the false assumption that because we listen daily we do not need training.

• Agree to put as much effort into listening training as into training to learn any other skill.

• Realize that we can only listen to the level to which we have been trained.

AXIOM 6. LISTENERS SHARE RESPONSIBILITY FOR COMMUNICATION SUCCESS

The fact that listeners share responsibility for communication success is a totally new concept to some communicators. Many believe that when they master the technique of speaking well their communication will be completely effective. They believe that a good speaker carries 100 percent of the burden for communication. Hundreds and thousands of dollars have been and continue to be spent on programs to make message transmissions clear, concise, and correct so that anyone could understand them. However, speech communication is a two-way transaction between a speaker and a listener. We listeners are the "anyone" who should be trained to receive these costly messages. Listeners complete efficient communication.

We can compare communicating to a baseball game. The pitcher throws a ball but the catcher must be trained to catch it. We do not expect him to be hit by the ball; we expect him to move his arms and body and follow the ball with his eyes in order to catch it. Even with the most skillful pitcher, the catcher will have to move fairly often, sometimes even throw off the catcher's mask and run backward to catch the ball.

Similarly, even with the most skillful speakers, listeners will have to exercise their minds and sometimes do some fast mental maneuvering to catch the message. Good listeners will call upon all their skill, energy and training no matter how poorly they believe the message has been sent.

Speaker and listener share equal importance. Unless we listeners recognize our equal responsibility, speakers might as well bounce their messages off a blank wall the way a tennis player does when practicing a stroke. When it is time for a game, tennis players want a live partner who receives and responds. So do speakers.

Efficient Listeners Expend Effort

When efficient listeners expend effort, they no longer put the entire responsibility for success on the speaker. They no longer excuse lazy listening with, "He's so dull, who can listen to him?" Or, "I guess she really knows what she's talking about, but I just can't listen to such a boring speaker." When we believe this, we accept the misconception that if we cannot function as listeners, it is somehow the fault of the speaker.

Communication consultant Lyman K. Steil suggests a strategy for counteracting this attitude. He proposes that if we agreed to put 51 percent of the effort needed for communication into the act of listening, almost all communication would improve dramatically.[9] We listeners would accept literally the admonition to go more than halfway in communication. When we do this we keep communication alive by receiving a message and doing something with it. If we put all responsibility for communication on the speaker, we can make the mistake of writing off even a good idea or drifting off into daydreams because of a fumbling delivery. When we put forth 51 percent or more of the effort, we will feel an obligation to listen to a message, and do a better job of listening.

Results of Listener Effort

Results of listener effort can be dramatic. For example, a few years ago two students decided that trying to deal with an instructor whom they judged to be dull and disorganized was too frustrating. They decided to write off a whole class as a failure by dropping out. After counseling with their listening instructor, they agreed to go more than halfway in the communication process by giving effort to listening for just one week. They tried several additional listening strategies, which will be discussed fully in following chapters, with this result: On the very first day of their effort, the speaker became so inspired by these two people who actually seemed to care what was happening that he responded directly to them. He became far more animated and his delivery improved; he made a more dynamic presentation. The entire class, recognizing the speaker's new enthusiasm for the subject, began to respond. The class became so exciting that members continued discussing the subject during the break. The speaker improved because he discovered that someone was listening.

The students who listened completed the communication circuit begun by the speaker. They set up an alternating current that passed from speaker to listener and from listener to speaker and recharged them both. When these students worked at listening they prospered. So did the speaker.

What these people discovered illustrates a very important truth: Speakers crave people who listen, not bored "attendees." They respond to listeners who accept the responsibility for communication. Trained listeners who put effort into their role in communication go far toward creating a speaker's success. Believing that the speaker is totally responsible for success in communication creates much of the apathy in classrooms, boardrooms, and business offices. When teachers, business executives, and other speakers believe they carry the entire responsibility for communication, they struggle to court listeners. They know that without a responsive audience they are licked from the start.

One high school teacher exclaimed, "They expect me to be Walt Disney, and I'm just the guy who teaches them algebra." Efficient listeners in his classroom would not create in him the entertaining ability of Walt Disney, but they would make him a far more enthusiastic speaker. Without doubt, they also would learn more about algebra.

Energetic listeners can unlock any other area related to language — science, history, mathematics, government, the whole of life. They also can unlock speakers' realizations that they are making contact and that the communication process is complete and dynamic.

Retraining Guidelines: Listeners Share Responsibility for Communication Success

- Never blame a speaker for your own lazy listening habits.
- Resolve to expend at least half of the effort needed to reach communication success.
- Remember that both listener and speaker share equal importance in communication.
- Look forward to dramatic communication improvement whenever you take responsibility for listening.

AXIOM 7. LISTENING IS AS VITAL A COMMUNICATION SKILL AS READING

We cannot deny the importance of reading as a communication skill. We are writing this book to be read, and much of what we present here we learned by reading. Reading profoundly influences human behavior. However, because we listen at least three times more than we read, listening exerts a more profound influence on human behavior, and learning this skill is crucially important. In discussing children's learning to organize and create meaning, Sally Jackson said, "Because the task of the listener is so complex and integrative, we should not be surprised to find that children must develop listening skills just as they must develop speaking skills."[10]

Listening and Speaking

Listening and speaking precede other communication skills. We learn to analyze and comprehend through what we hear even before we can speak and long before we can read. Reading may depend so closely upon listening as to be built upon it. We learn to speak because we are able to listen. As children we imitated as we listened to our parents who taught by modeling and by reinforcing approximations of correct speech. They patiently spoke words and trained us to listen and imitate.

Influence of Listening

The influence of listening is far reaching. The Survey Research Center of the University of Michigan sought to determine why people voted as they did in a presidential election. They learned that 58 percent of voters got their information from listening to radio and television, and only 27 percent from reading magazines and newspapers. A 1989 survey conducted by the Roper Organization for the Television Information Office revealed that nearly 65 percent of those polled rely on television as a primary source of news. The study concedes that print news tends to be more "factual and complete, but information retrieval from print works only when the individual is motivated to do the retrieving."[11] Most people surveyed had not been so motivated.

Adolf Hitler mesmerized a nation and led it to its downfall, not so much because Germans read what he wrote, but because they listened to what he said. What we eat, the headache remedies we take, the style of car we drive, and the moral codes we believe in are all affected by the way we listen. The most persuasive salespersons do not rely on writing; they listen and talk because they realize the profound influence of listening in our lives.

Listening has a profound effect among nonreaders. Millions of people in the world are unable to read and must gather all they learn through listening. In many developing nations, people send few printed messages compared to those transmitted in person and by radio. Listening exerts a powerful influence in such countries, but it also plays a mighty role in literate societies. Many people do not read, even though they can. Many do not find pleasure in reading and therefore are not motivated to turn to it for information, opinion or relaxation.

Listening in industry, as pointed out in Chapter 1, Listening to Succeed, is vital. A study conducted by the U.S. Department of Health, Education and Welfare reports that the single most consistent complaint voiced by American workers is that supervisors fail to listen when they make suggestions for improving work processes.[12] In modern industry, managers who refuse to listen are being replaced rapidly by managers who feel they have a lot to learn from workers and who are eager to demonstrate their willingness to listen.[13]

Listening and Learning

Listening is the backbone of learning. Many who have spent six years studying reading grew up assuming that everything of importance in a classroom, on a job, or in life could be learned from printed matter. Much is, of course, but if we daydream away our listening-to-learn time expecting always to be able to read it later or when we need it, we cheat ourselves of potential for power. Both reading and listening are necessary skills. When we make use of both receiving skills — each at the appropriate time — we can witness startling results.

Retraining Guidelines: Listening Is as Vital a Communication Skill as Reading

- Remember that it is a mistake to presume you can get all the information you need by reading.
- Recall that we spend an average of 45 to 80 percent of our communication time listening and an average of 16 percent of that time in reading. Resolve to spend that listening time actively listening.
- Plan to use all listening-to-learn opportunities.

AXIOM 8. TEACHING LISTENING DIFFERS FROM TEACHING READING

Teaching listening differs from teaching reading. The idea that learning to read will teach us how to listen appears to have taken root in our educational system. Reading gives us the necessary skill for receiving the written word. Listening gives us the necessary skill for receiving the spoken word. Abundant research shows that the best way to develop any skill is to provide direct training designed to improve that skill, not another. Assuring one that teaching reading will improve listening is a little like telling a parent to feed Joe in order to make Ernie grow. All parents know they had better feed them both. In training, too, we work on both because reading and listening are separate processes. True, some of the ingredient skills are common to both, but other ingredient skills are markedly different.

Differences Between Listening and Reading

Differences between listening and reading deserve serious attention. The essentially social activity of listening differs in many ways from the solitary activity of reading. In fact, many circumstances make listening far more difficult than reading.

Readers Can Go Back and Reread. Readers can go back and reread when they become distracted or find the material difficult to comprehend. Listeners do not have the permanence of a printed message. If we don't understand or are distracted, the message is gone and we have missed it.

Readers who do not understand a word can look it up or ask another about it. Listeners who do not understand a word simply lose that meaning as the word goes by. John Bonee cautioned public relations students about this when he reminded them that "the spoken word is ephemeral. The words I'm speaking now pass through the air. You can't bring them back unless *I* bring them back. When I do, that's *not* repetition. That's amplification."[14]

Because listening is a social activity, we often listen among our fellow communicators. They can impede our attentiveness with whispered comments, tapping pens or feet, sniffles, or general shuffling. These distractions can make us lose our focus or misunderstand the message. Bonee reminds us that even if we ask to have something repeated, we probably will not receive the same message sent in precisely the same way. Speakers do not replay a message word for word as if they were tape recorders. Readers can simply go back and reread. Listeners cannot.

Readers control the rate at which they read. We read at the rate comfortable for us. If the material is difficult or if we are inexperienced, we can take it slowly. If we read for pleasure or to skim, we move as rapidly as our reading skill allows. As listeners, however, we must accept the rate set by the speaker. If we receive material that is too difficult or is beyond the level of our experience and understanding, we can become permanently lost. Conversely, if a speaker talks too slowly, we can become bored, distracted, and, once again, lost. However difficult, we must accept the rate of the speaker.

Readers can choose the place where they read. Readers have always been able to choose the most productive place to read. If a room is hot, noisy or filled with people who distract us, we can go off to a private place to continue reading. We furnish our libraries with study carrels, our schoolrooms with reading corners, and our homes with comfortable chairs and good reading lamps for just this purpose. Listeners very often have no choice of the place in which they listen.

Jean Kerr, author and playwright, often explained that she locked herself in the family car to find the privacy she needed to read and write — solitary activities. She could not escape to a quiet place to listen; that takes place wherever the message comes. Therefore, listeners either learn to handle the distractions that naturally occur when other people are around, or lose listening concentration altogether.

Readers are trained; listeners are not. Most readers have been trained through at least six years of elementary school. Research shows that listening skills do not improve at the same rate when only reading is taught. In general, in first grade we were better listeners than readers. As our schooling progressed, we received a great deal of formal reading instruction and no formal listening instruction. Our ability to read continued on an upward curve while our listening ability declined. By the time we reached age 9 or 10, our skill in reading probably was so much better than our skill in listening that most of us could understand our lessons better by using our eyes than by using our ears.[15]

It was probably at this point that we began to believe we could afford not to listen in class because we could read it later. From this point on, listening drops further and further behind. Most of us graduate from high school as fair readers and poor listeners into a world so structured that we may spend up to 80 percent of our time listening.[16]

Similarities Between Listening and Reading

Listening and reading are both receiving skills and, because we begin to listen before we begin to read, we can say that reading is superimposed upon a foundation of listening. Listening vocabulary and reading improvement are related. We enrich our vocabulary, learn to pronounce words correctly, and use our language precisely by listening to others who use the language well. We can continue to enlarge our listening vocabulary, command of language, and reading ability throughout a lifetime by careful listening.

Several years ago a young Peruvian student spent a year with a North American family. When she began attending classes in the local public schools, she was greatly frustrated both in understanding the spoken language and in reading assigned lessons. As she listened to the spoken vocabulary around her and gradually enlarged her listening vocabulary, her reading ability improved. She learned to make a connection between the symbols she read and the more familiar symbols she had come to understand better through listening.

Common listening and reading skills do exist. When we begin to read we may translate a symbol from the printed page to a symbol we have first understood through listening. We may sound out or listen intrapersonally to difficult or unfamiliar words. When we understand a component, such as a drop in pitch or a definite pause in spoken language, we can transfer this understanding to a similar component, such as punctuation in written language.

Listening and reading make use of the common skills of thinking and understanding. Listening and reading call upon many of the same feelings, background, experiences, and thought strategies. A written language that we find difficult to understand when we read it may present similar difficulties when we listen to it as a spoken language.

The assumption that learning to read will teach us automatically how to listen is false. The reverse actually may be true. Learning to listen more efficiently might help us learn to read more efficiently.

Retraining Guidelines: Teaching Listening Differs from Teaching Reading

- Remember that listening is generally more difficult than reading and demands careful attention to each step.
- Realize that teaching reading does not teach listening.
- Work toward incorporating specific listening classes into all levels of education — kindergarten through college.

AXIOM 9. LISTENING AND AGREEING ARE SEPARATE ACTS

Many believe that if we listen to another point of view we will appear to agree. Carl Weaver, a pioneer listening researcher, believes that assuming that listening means agreement creates a serious impediment to interpreting verbal messages.[17] Perhaps all of us have said, "He won't listen to anything I say," when in fact we mean, "He won't agree with my point of view." Many conversations die and discussions end because we think listening suggests agreement.

Immaturity and Fear

The immaturity and fear of the child within us is what Sigmund Freud referred to when he suggested that we harbor a childish part of our personalities which demands immediate gratification for all wishes. Whenever we frustrate the child in our personality, we feel tempted to throw temper tantrums or display some other form of immature behavior. When we hear a point of view with which we disagree, we can experience such real frustration that we allow the child in us to refuse to listen. We do this often because we mistakenly imagine that by listening we will show agreement.

Sometimes we exhibit such immaturity in responses like: "I don't want to listen, I want people to listen to me." This reveals fear that listening weakens our position of authority or that it might be a kind of surrender. Listening shows not a failure to lead but a willingness to communicate.

Perhaps the false assumption that listening means agreement stems from our seeing authority as the single means to control. Our social environment affects us all, and misconceptions are part of that social environment. All cultures foster prejudices about human conduct. Dozens of folk sayings suggest that people cannot change no matter how hard they try: "Like mother, like daughter," "You can't fight city hall," or "You can't change human nature." If we believe we cannot listen because that indicates agreement, we have fallen victim to still another stereotype. Change is always possible if we are diligent enough to find the input that will cause the change we desire.

Listening provides one way to find the input that could change a family, a group or a society. By doing so, we might discover the response that could change the thinking or action of the person or group that we disagree with. By ignoring the message — by refusing even to hear, which is the first step in listening — no one is likely to change.

Listener Responsibility

Listener responsibility suggests that, once we have learned the importance of listening before we agree or disagree, we must remember that others to whom we listen also may believe that because we listened, we agreed. If it is an important issue and if we do not agree, we must, after listening carefully, let the speaker know this. "I admire the strength of your belief and support your right to feel this way; however, I do not agree," is one way to handle this without shutting off communication.

Listening Demands an Open Mind, not Agreement

Our attitude or frame of reference largely determines the way we receive a message. Refusing to change agreement creates a defensive attitude. Teen–agers who view any question that parents ask as snooping, insecure breadwinners who explode whenever their spouses mention money, or touchy parents who consider children's questions to be threats to their wisdom are all victims of the attitude that listening means surrendering authority. Listening demands neither surrender nor agreement, but an open mind.

After we listen to aural stimuli, we may or may not agree. This is another intellectual operation — an operation that will be impossible if we do not listen to the message. We must attempt to set our defensive attitude aside. Doing so will increase our listening efficiency immeasurably.

Retraining Guidelines: Listening and Agreeing Are Separate Acts

- Take the time to listen to opposing viewpoints
- Keep an open mind while listening to another's point of view, and practice all steps in the process of perceptive listening.
- Realize that your agreement or disagreement with another point of view should be based on a clear understanding of the other's position, which should come after careful listening.

AXIOM 10. LISTENING IS CRUCIAL TO ALL COMMUNICATION

The cost of careless listening can be extremely high. Many of us admit to being careless listeners and do so with a good-natured shrug that indicates we consider it to be no more than a charming idiosyncrasy. People who recognize this quality admit, "I can sit and look at a person and never hear a word he says," or "My husband is always complaining that I don't pay attention to a thing he says." They assume that what they missed was of little importance.

When we have difficulty listening efficiently, we have difficulty understanding our families, our co-workers or our friends. We have difficulty making sense to one another, and we find one marriage in two in the divorce courts. Listening is a major part of communication, and lack of skill in this area creates many of the communication problems we experience with others.

Abraham Kaplan, a professor of philosophy at the University of Michigan and a follower of Martin Buber, whose "I–Thou" philosophy states that we define ourselves by engaging others, believes that most of us engage in duologue, not dialogue. Kaplan said a "duologue" describes when everybody talks and nobody listens. Duologues take place in churches, homes, schools, and parties. They are little more than monologues presented to glazed and indifferent audiences. Kaplan says there is nothing lonelier than two humans involved in a duologue, and nothing more marvelous than two people genuinely engaged in listening. Kaplan believes we pay the price of not listening with the loss of dialogue, loss of contact, and loss of knowledge that comes through listening. Careless listening can cost friendship, time, and positive feelings. Caring listening can help people change their attitudes about themselves, become less defensive and more open to new experiences.[18]

The importance of perceptive listening is crucial in areas from the boardroom to the war room. Business and industry calculate the costs of careless listening in dollars and cents. At a large midwestern manufacturing plant, engineers ordered a large roller made of magnesium, a fairly light metal. The shop workers, who listened carelessly, made it from manganese, a metal so much heavier that the roller could never be used. Time, effort, and money were wasted to create a tool impossible to use. Results such as these and the possibility of financial catastrophe have forced many business people to insist on written memos. Although writing and sending messages is more expensive and time consuming than speaking, careless listening is even more expensive. Business executives believe that expense is too great to hazard. Because we don't trust people to listen, it can cost money.

When the president of the United States wishes to send a message, he speaks because he is aware of the powerful impact of a spoken message. But he speaks from a written text which later will be sent to the news media. The carefully prepared, written text is vital because untrained listeners could misinterpret his remarks which could affect global incidents. Careless listening to official messages can create enormous consequences.

In January 1991 President George Bush made the official declaration of war in the Persian Gulf, speaking directly to millions of people in a carefully prepared televised message.[19] A few days earlier, when U.S. Secretary of State James Baker met with Iraqi Foreign Minister Tariq Aziz, their willingness to listen to each other was of vital importance to a large part of the world. News stories written shortly after the talks suggested that very little listening took place.[20] John Bierman reported, "The President had already declared that Baker would offer 'no negotiations, no face-saving, and no rewards for aggression.' At the same time Iraqi officials claimed they would not surrender Kuwait."[21] Throughout the crisis, world leaders did a great deal of speaking, but apparently were unable to listen as often as they spoke. What many believed to be a show of power might well have been a show of the high cost of not listening.

Minor consequences of careless listening can range from a salesperson's loss of a commission to a student's embarrassment at handing in a report late. Major consequences can be the loss of dollars for industry, the breakup of a marriage, or the threat of international crisis. Listening is crucial to all communication, and the consequences of careless listening can be monumental.

Retraining Guidelines: Listening Is Crucial to All Communication

- When careless listening occurs, calculate the cost of it in your own life.
- When world leaders attempt to solve political issues through conferences, note the listening practices on each side and calculate the possible cost to each country and to world peace.

We believe these axioms prepare the way for learning to be a perceptive listener. We suggest that the axioms be considered also as underlying rules for more specific study of the listening process, listening behavior, and listening retraining.

WRAPPING IT UP: A SUMMARY

Years of research and experience have shown that several basic truths underlie most of what we teach about listening. The ten axioms discussed in this chapter provide a foundation upon which to build perceptive listening.

DISCUSSION AND STUDY GUIDES

1. Consider the best listener you know. What does this person do that others do not do? What qualities does this person possess that you would like to develop?

2. Consult with two or three persons who know you well. Ask them to identify your listening habits. Which of them may be a result of lack of knowledge about listening axioms? Name the axiom.

3. Can you identify times in your life when careless listening cost you time, embarrassment, money, or a relationship?

4. What do you think is the most important reason to study and apply the listening axioms? Can you identify some times in which attention to axioms would help you, your family, or friends listen more perceptively?

LISTENING EXERCISES THAT WORK

EXERCISE 1. (Active or Passive Listening) Identify the most difficult listening situations you encounter during one week. Choose two or three of these and analyze your listening behavior during each by answering these questions:

1. Did you expect the speaker to break through your apathy?
2. Did you refuse to listen because you thought the speaker dull?
3. Did you refuse to listen because you disagreed with the information?
4. Did you actively put effort into understanding the message?
5. Did you set aside your prejudices?
6. Summarize your overall performance by determining whether you are: very active, moderately active, barely active, very relaxed, passive.
7. Which axioms about listening were at work in this exercise? Explain.

EXERCISE 2. (Personal Analysis Questionnaire) Mark each statement below *true* or *false*. Attempt to discover the extent to which you are aware or unaware of the importance of the axioms about listening.

_____ 1. I feel that the people who don't listen to me are too stupid to appreciate my ideas and that intelligent people are able to listen.

_____ 2. I think that training people to listen is about as foolish as attempting to train people to breathe.

_____ 3. I believe that, since I have listened all my life, I have already developed good listening skills.

_____ 4. I believe it is more important to concentrate on becoming a good speaker than a good listener, since the speaker determines the quality of communication.

_____ 5. I believe that it is more important to learn to read than to learn to listen. After all, we can always go back to check material when we read.

_____ 6. I believe I was adequately trained to listen at home, in school, and on the job.

_____ 7. I believe I should be able to just sit back and enjoy a speaker. I dislike the idea of making listening work.

_____ 8. I really can't listen to people who are bigoted or put forth preposterous ideas; I disagree too strongly.

_____ 9. I believe I miss very little by not listening, and I dislike scare tactics which suggest that I should work at listening.

_____ 10. I know I can listen very well if I want to; when I want to, I do.

Each *true* answer reveals a lack of understanding about listening axioms. Count the number of *true* answers and assess your personal attitude toward listening retraining.

0–1 = You are remarkably aware of axioms about listening training.
2–4 = You have a positive attitude toward listening training.
5–7 = You are aware of listening retraining, but are allowing lack of understanding to warp your thinking.
8–10 = You have built a brick wall of listening misinformation that keeps listening axioms from being useful to you.

EXERCISE 3. (Listening and Agreement)

1. Write down five specific subjects you hate to discuss.

2. What is your pattern of listening when these subjects come up?

3. Why do you listen or not listen in this manner?

4. Have you been assuming that listening to these subjects would show agreement with the speaker?

5. What can you do to improve your listening performance in the future?

EXERCISE 4. (Communication and the Responsibility of the Listener and the Speaker)

1. List three speakers whom you consider to be boring or poorly organized. (To designate speakers, use numbers rather than names.)

2. What is your pattern of listening when communicating with these speakers?

3. Do you blame the speaker for poor communication?

4. Do you give 51 percent of the effort to these communication situations? Do you accept 51 percent of the blame for poor communication?

NOTES

1. Ralph G. Nichols identified several "false assumptions" about listening which helped subsequent scholars to perform future research in listening (see *Perceptive Listening*, 1983), Chapter 2.
2. Sara Lundsteen, *Listening: Its Impact on Reading and Other Language Arts* (Urbana, IL: ERIC Clearinghouse, 1979), xv.

3. Carl H. Rogers, "Active Listening," in Richard C. Huseman et al, *Readings in Interpersonal and Organizational Communication* (Boston: Holbrook Press, 1973).

4. James I. Brown, "Listening—Ubiquitous, Yet Obscure," *Journal of the International Listening Association* 1 (Spring 1987), 5.

5. Mortimer Adler, *How to Speak, How to Listen* (New York: Macmillan, 1983), 85.

6. Marilyn H. Lewis and N. L. Reinsch, Jr. "Listening in Organizational Environments," *Journal of Business Communication* 25 (Summer 1988), 63–64.

7. Ralph Nichols and Thomas Lewis, *Listening and Speaking* (Dubuque, IA: Wm. C. Brown, Publishers, 1954), 8.

8. Franklin H. Ernst, Jr. *Who's Listening: A Handbook of the Transactional Analysis of the Listening Activity* (Vallejo, CA: Addressó Set, 1973), 32–34.

9. Lyman K. Steil, "Effective Listening," (lecture) Bemidji State University, Bemidji, MN, July 1978.

10. Sally Jackson, "Conversational Implications in Children's Comprehension References," *Communication Monographs* 48 (September 1981), 238.

11. "TV vs Print: Which is Best?" *USA Today* (August 1989), 6.

12. Zane K. Quibble, "Quality Circles: A Well-Rounded Approach to Employee Involvement," *Management World* 10 (September 1981), 238.

13. John DeGaetani, "The Business of Listening," *Business Horizons* (October 1980), 41.

14. John R. Bonee, "The Care and Feeding of the Executive Speaker," *Vital Speeches* 158 (January 15, 1982), 201.

15. Nichols and Lewis, 37.

16. Lyman K. Steil, Larry Barker and Kittie W. Watson, *Effective Listening: Key to Your Success* (Reading, MA: Addison Wesley, 1983), 11.

17. Carl H. Weaver, *Human Listening: Processes and Behavior* (Indianapolis: Bobbs-Merrill, 1972), 4.

18. Abraham Kaplan, "The Art of Not Listening," in William W. Wilmot and John R. Wenburg, *Communication Involvement: Personal Perspective* (Huntington, NY: Robert E. Krieger, 1979).

19. Brian Duffy, et al, "Desert Storm," *U.S. News & World Report* 110 (January 28, 1991), 20–28.

20. Lisa Beyer, "Last Gasps on the Negotiation Trail," *Time* 137 (January 21, 1991), 30–31.

21. John Bierman, "At the Brink," *Macleans* 104 (January 14, 1991), 20–21.

CHAPTER 4

FIVE POWER TOOLS OF LISTENING

*The human brain is reputedly the single most complex structure
in the entire universe.*[1]
— *Guy R. Lefrancois*

THESIS The brain is the power center of listening; the ability to listen perceptively relies primarily on the ability to use the power tools of listening.

CHAPTER OBJECTIVES

1. Clearly understand the basic concepts applied in the power tools of listening discussed in this chapter.
2. Use the power tools of listening to improve competency as a perceptive listener.
3. Realize that not using the power tools of listening may limit one's learning and career-development potential.
4. Determine to correct and retrain listening behavior to act in accordance with the power tools required for holistic listening.

CHAPTER PREVIEW

- One-process brain concept.
- STTD (speech-thought-time differential).
- Self-concept influence.
- Motivation and listening goals.
- Listener behavior ("D" formula).

"I didn't understand the new marketing strategy explained at the last meeting; I was thinking about my scheduled eye surgery."
"Why can't I remember her name?"
"We planned to meet here for lunch at noon; why isn't he here?"
Many of us have had experiences similar to these. Had we known how to use several power tools of listening, each of the incidents might have been resolved differently.

This chapter introduces five power tools of listening. To understand how and why the power tools can work for us as perceptive listeners, we need to understand the basic operations of the central nervous system and the brain. Keep in mind the definition of listening, explained in Chapter 2, Listening Power Generates Knowledge, as we discuss Listening Power Tool 1.

LISTENING POWER TOOL 1: THE ONE–PROCESS BRAIN CONCEPT

Understanding the One–Process Brain Concept

How many times have we failed to listen because we haven't understood the one–process brain concept?

The central nervous system directs those tasks requiring focus of attention and concentration. Once we focus attention on another task, the brain relinquishes control of the listening process — and we stop listening.

Once we understand the importance and application of the concept we can use it in countless situations. For example, a friend comes by to share exciting news as we are engrossed with an important telephone call. We now make one of two decisions: to end the call and concentrate on our friend's news or to ask our friend to wait until the call has ended. We cannot listen simultaneously to our friend and the phone message — because of our one–process brain.

The Power-Center Brain and Listening

Observing the one–process brain concept is vital in view of the intricate operation of the brain in directing the process of listening. The brain converts countless bits of information into intelligent thought by evaluating, sorting, deciding and redeciding on sequences and relationships, filling in the blanks with bits of information from its files and filing the new images for later use.[2]

Neurologists and psychologists describe the human brain as the most complex structure in the universe, but it functions as a one–process brain when directing tasks processed by the central nervous system. (Figure 4–1 shows various parts of the brain listed in Definition Box 2.)

DEFINITION BOX 2:   Terms Relating to the Central Nervous System

NOTE: Although the central nervous system directs the operation of all human activity involving the complete system, we have selected several structures to explain the operation of the central nervous system in the process of listening.[3]

mental: pertaining to the mind

The one–process brain concept means that we can concentrate on only one activity at a time.

neural: pertaining to the nerves

neurons: nerve cells that communicate with each other and receive information from the body and environment

central nervous system (CNS): human nervous system that includes the brain and spinal cord (listener's ability to concentrate)

peripheral nervous system (PNS): neural networks from the CNS; linked to all sensory organs and their muscles and glands; directs physiological activities — respiration, heart action, digestion, sweating and crying (listener's ability to respond with feeling)

autonomic nervous system (ANS): the other part of the PNS; directs action of muscles and glands not under conscious control (listener's uncontrolled reaction reflecting careless habits)

sympathetic nervous system (SNS): division of the ANS; prepares the body for emergency: fast heartbeat, increased adrenalin, dilated pupils, etc. (listener's response to shocking messages)

parasympathetic nervous system (PaNS): opposes bodily functions accelerated by the SNS; readjusts bodily functions back to normal (listener's recovery from shocking messages)

spinal cord: major neural pathway connecting brain centers with the muscular, glandular, and sensory systems

brain: a convoluted and wrinkled, three-pound grayish mass; functions as the body's power computer by processing bodily and environmental information; has billions of electro–chemical parts; makes decisions for behavioral strategies (see Figure 4–1)

brain stem: handle of brain; controls physiological functions and automatic behavior; joined with top of spinal cord

cerebrum: Outer covering of the brain, also called cerebral cortex; involved in thinking, remembering, creative problem solving, decision making, sensation, and perception; divided into halves: the left and right hemispheres with dominant functions (directs the process of holistic listening)

corpus callosum: cluster of thick nerve fibers; connects the flow of data between the left and right hemispheres

cerebrum lobes: both cerebral hemispheres have four lobes: a. temporal lobes: under temples on both sides of brain; control language and hearing (primary modality of listening); b. frontal lobes: in upper, front half of cerebrum; control involuntary muscles and higher thought processes; c. parietal lobes: above temporal lobes, behind frontal lobes; regulate body sensations; d. occipital lobes: rear part of cerebral hemispheres; control vision (secondary modality of listening)

cerebellum: hindbrain; attached to the brain stem; looks like a miniature version of the cerebral hemispheres; controls/coordinates movement (listener's nonverbal reactions)

The brain and the spinal cord are primary parts of the central nervous system. The spinal cord is a massive tract of nerve fibers inside the spine. It relays upward and downward messages between the brain and the body, directing voluntary and involuntary actions.

The beginning of wisdom is to call things by their right names. — Chinese proverb

FIGURE 4–1   Some Major Structures of the Human Brain

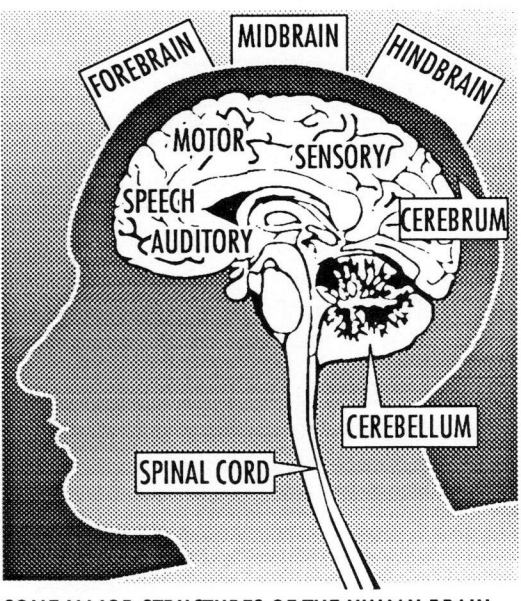

SOME MAJOR STRUCTURES OF THE HUMAN BRAIN

Voluntary and Involuntary Actions

In Definition Box 2, we include four subsidiary systems of the central nervous system: peripheral, autonomic, sympathetic, and parasympathetic nervous systems. It is the linkage of electro-chemical switches in the brain that operates these systems. This intricate network enables us to perform two kinds of behavior: voluntary acts (willful action under one's control) and involuntary acts (spontaneous action, not subject to control).

Many people enjoy relaxing with the sound of background music before working on a complex report or studying for an exam. Remember, the state of concentration required for listening is a voluntary act. Also, remember that involuntary behavior, when not consciously monitored, may lead to minor or fatal accidents. For example, a veteran jogger thinking of possible solutions to a family problem crosses over the jogging path and is struck by a car. A bicyclist timing for top performance hits rough terrain and loses control of the bike. Such events verify that, while our brains are remarkable organs, they operate as a one–process brain each time concentration is required to process a task — including listening.

Neurologists claim that a typical adult's brain contains 15 billion to 100 billion neurons or nerve cells. Using the lower 15 billion figure means we can remember two-to-the-ten-billionth-power bits of information. Just to write out this number that represents the items the mind is capable of holding, we would have to write one zero per second for ninety years. The brain is a very big place in a very small space.[4] It is often referred to as the split brain.

The Split Brain and Holistic Listening

A deep groove, the central fissure, splits the brain down the center from front to back creating two halves: the left and right hemispheres. We have been educated primarily to use the left hemisphere, which responds to structured input, and seldom to use the right hemisphere, which responds to creative processing.

Professor Paul J. Kaufmann at Iowa State University defines holistic listening as "assigning meaning with both right and left brain to all sense input."[5] Thus the holistic listener uses both hemispheres of the brain and all sensory systems, including hearing, seeing, smelling, tasting, and touching.

Your authors believe that the process of holistic listening is "creative" and "re–creative." Perceptive or holistic listeners focus on receiving the intended meaning of the speaker's "created message" for "re–creation" in the listener's left and right hemispheres — the whole brain. **Perceptive listening** is holistic listening, requiring self-discipline, hard work, and training.

Kaufmann claims that the creative and nonverbal aspects of the brain's right hemisphere are vital to holistic listening. He compares the split–brain functions as follows:[6]

Split-Brain Functions in Holistic Listening

LEFT HEMISPHERE	RIGHT HEMISPHERE
Verbal: use words to clarify meaning	Nonverbal: use body signs to clarify meaning
Analytic: reasoning from parts	Synthetic: reasoning from the whole
Abstract: a small bit of data to represent the whole	Analogic: seeing likenesses between things
Temporal: keeping track of time	Nontemporal: no sense of time
Rational: conclusions based on reason and fact	Nonrational: judgment suspended; playful
Digital: use numbers as in counting	Spatial: see relations to where things are
Logical: Conclusions based on reasoning	Intuitive: insight based on hunches, feelings
Linear: convergent conclusion from linked ideas	Holistic: divergent conclusions from the whole

The left side of the brain processes structured data in an analytical and logical way using numbers, words, and other symbols; the right side is creative and processes nonverbal messages in images and pictures. The perceptive or holistic listener needs **to use both hemispheres of the split brain**. We use left–brain thinking to decode and respond to the intended meaning of the speaker's words. We use right–brain thinking to decode and respond to the speaker's nonverbal messages, comprising 80–90 percent of the listening act.[7] This "zigzag" thinking processed by the split brain enables us, as listeners, to search for hidden meanings as we decode and re–create the speaker's intended message.

Retraining: Guidelines for Productive Use of the One–Process Brain Listening Power Tool

1. Respect the unique trait of the one–process brain: the ability to concentrate on one activity at a time.
2. Monitor your listening behavior to avoid misusing the one–process brain.
3. Immediately recognize a conflict situation in which you are tempted to stop listening. Decide which message or activity to attend and quickly adjust your listening behavior.
4. Stop talking as soon as you realize that others have stopped listening and are occupied with other tasks.
5. Establish a goal to use Listening Power Tool 1 by integrating the one–process brain concept into all listening events.

Another tool which we can use to capitalize on the unique operation of the brain is Listening Power Tool 2, the speech-thought-time differential (STTD) concept.

LISTENING POWER TOOL 2: SPEECH-THOUGHT-TIME DIFFERENTIAL (STTD) CONCEPT

Understanding the concept enables listeners to capitalize on "spare brain time." Unfortunately this valuable resource is often ignored or misused.

Speakers talk at a rate of about 120 to 180 words a minute, but our brains process messages at a speed of 400-800 or more words a minute. This means that we can think three or more times faster than we can speak. We handicap ourselves by not capitalizing on thought speed, which, according to Dr. Ralph G. Nichols, "breeds false feelings of security and mental tangents."[8] If we perceive the message coming to us and select to attend to it, we make use of the STTD. If we do not, the brain goes looking for something to think about. That means we are wasting, not using, the built-in advantage of the valuable STTD power tool. When we permit the brain to process any digression of the mind from the speaker's message, we have stopped listening.

Our minds are designed to soar, yet we present and receive words — the tools of thought — at a plodding rate. Our minds flit from idea to idea while we periodically return to keep tabs on the entering words. Difficulty arises when we occasionally flit to an idea so fascinating that we stay with it and forget to go back to the message arriving in words.

This is what we mean when we say the rapid speed of thought creates the disadvantage of distraction. When we begin to read, we handle words slowly. As we gain proficiency, we handle them more and more quickly until we can read quite rapidly. We can add speed because we control the rate at which we receive the printed matter. With listening, no matter how rapidly we might be able to operate with practice, we have been limited by the rate at which people send messages. The slower rate at which people speak provides us with extra thinking time — to be used wisely as time for listening.

It would be a bonus if we could receive words as rapidly as we can process them. For this reason scholars and researchers began to investigate the effect of speeded speech on listening and comprehension of information.

Speeded Speech Research and Technology

Speeded speech technology enables us to make a lucrative investment in listening time. What we do with that extra time determines whether we will be efficient listeners or remain trapped by reinforcing mind-wandering, nonlistening habits.

Conclusions of speeded speech research have been conducted by Harry Goldstein (1940), W. D. Garvey (1949), G. A. Miller and J. C. R. Licklider (1950).

Goldstein found that as we listen to speech at more than two and a half times the rate at which we regularly hear it, we have a great capacity for comprehending information. However, we are limited by the rate at which it is fed to us.[9]

Garvey determined that by cutting and splicing taped material, the time to present a message can be shortened by two and a half times with the message still understandable.[10]

By deleting portions of phonetically balanced words, listeners can comprehend with almost half the word deleted, according to Miller and Licklider.[11]

Modern technology has produced machines whereby messages can be played far beyond 300 or so words per minute or slowed to a rate to accommodate a beginning reader, a student of a foreign language or a learning-disabled person.

The results of using speed-controlled tapes are dramatic. The blind, who read braille at an average of 90 words per minute, can listen at rates approaching the 300 to 400 words per minute of speed reading. A blind college freshman, who knew her severe visual impairment would make heavy university reading requirements a difficult barrier, found that an electronic tape recorder gave her equality. She could speed up messages recorded at about 150 words per minute by her family to 300 or even 400-plus words per minute. She not only managed to handle a full load of university work, but also her increased concentration from listening at a rapid rate helped her get top grades.[12]

Students with limited study time, professionals reviewing new material, and managers evaluating material find they can save time and increase understanding with fewer distractions when they increase the rate at which they listen. Students can review taped notes from lectures in a short time and suffer fewer distractions when they speed the playback. Busy professionals who must keep abreast of new information and technology in their fields have long used the tape recorder to review. The possibility of speeded review could save countless hours and more than double the amount learned and retained. Medical and police teams can use speeded tapes to review records of medical procedures, emergency room activity, or arrest reports. Listening to compressed speech via speeded tapes offers a real time stretcher since busy executives spend up to 80 percent of their time listening.

Unfortunately we can use speeded speech only for information-sending messages. Perceptive listeners, however, can learn to use speeded speech when possible and thus take advantage of the speech-thought-time differential.

Advantages of Using STTD Productively

Some of the advantages evolving from proper use of the STTD power tool are:

- We realize the positive impact of speed thinking on our ability to listen. We strive to take advantage of the STTD resource knowing that our brains can process at a rate of about 400–800 words a minute a person's message spoken at about 120–180 words a minute.

- We learn to adapt the processing of messages from slow- and fast-speaking persons. Research indicates that many listeners prefer rapid speakers. They believe that a person talking at a rate of 180 words or more a minute helps them sustain attention longer and comprehend the message better.

- Both time and money can be saved. Due to the high cost of TV commercials, we are exposed to more rapid-fire, 15-second commercials. During the speed–thinking time provided by the STTD power tool, viewers are aware of two aspects of the commercial: the 15-second-time lapse and a rather mundane message. However, the intent of the commercial to grab a listener's attention is fulfilled.

- The overall level of listening competency is improved. But we constantly need to retrain to use the STTD power tool during both formal and informal listening events.

Disadvantages of Using STTD Nonproductively

Those who use the STTD power tool nonproductively have serious obstacles to overcome. Three harmful results of using the STTD resource improperly and hindering our ability to listen are:

- Productive listening techniques are replaced with nonproductive techniques. One of many nonproductive techniques is pretending to listen while directing the brain to perform other mental tasks: inwardly arguing with the speaker, making plans, trying to resolve problems, etc. Speakers easily detect unresponsive behavior despite the fact that nonlisteners often are pleased about their deceitful coverup. Actually, the lack of relevant feedback to the speaker confirms the nonattentive status of the receiver.

- The habit of ignoring the extra thinking time to listen and learn is reinforced. People often resist acquiring knowledge for fear of disrupting their deep-rooted beliefs and value systems. Such inflexible minds are closed rather than open to process new bits of information.

- The STTD spare brain time is wasted by useless worry. Rather than capitalizing on proper use of the STTD power tool, we waste the spare listening time worrying about personal or work-related problems, which everyone faces.

Regardless of the nature of a problem, we need constantly to remind ourselves: The most useless human activity is worry—particularly during listening time, which consumes so much of each day. To prove this concept, let's take a "worry test."

- Stop reading. Think of the most serious problem bothering you, one which you need to resolve.
- Locate an uncluttered wall. Place your crossed arms against the wall. Close your eyes. Position your head within the circle of your arms.
- Now start worrying about the problem—worry without interruption for ten minutes.
- At the end of ten minutes, lift your head, open your eyes and ask yourself: Does the problem still exist? (Yes.) Has it changed or been resolved? (Of course not.)

This test emphasizes the uselessness of worry. As listeners attempting to retrain and upgrade the level of competency, we need to answer this question: Should we trade the valuable spare listening time for useless worry time? If your answer to this question is a firm "no," you have passed the worry test.

We need to eliminate the "worry distraction" as we listen in order to properly use the STTD power tool. Dale Carnegie quotes Mark Twain: "I've had a lot of problems in my day—most of which never happened."[13] He believed that worry is interest paid in advance on a debt you may never owe.

A logical plan to resolve problems without useless worry interfering with listening-learning time consists of four parts:

1. Select a quiet place. Write a brief statement of a troublesome problem; write three possible solutions.
2. Select one solution for immediate action. After a reasonable time, try another solution if the problem remains unchanged.
3. Keep working on the problem, not worrying about it. If possible, share your concerns with a spouse or trusted friend.
4. Monitor your listening behavior throughout each day to ensure that useless worry does not restrict your ability to attend speakers' messages.

Retraining: Guidelines for Using STTD

1. Keep in mind that we listeners have a valuable resource of additional listening time. We can either waste it or use it to help us upgrade listening competency to learn, grow and prosper.
2. Keep the one—process brain listening power tool handy to use with the STTD listening power tool. Exercise your power of self-discipline to use the tools jointly to enhance listening to interpersonal and public messages.

3. Carefully monitor your listening behavior. Review the productive and non-productive use of the STTD tool. Realize it is your choice whether or not you benefit from the STTD resource.

4. Reinforce what you have learned from being exposed to this tool. Make it a part of your daily listening encounters.

5. Reflect on the ways you may have lost out in past listening experiences by not using the one–process brain and STTD listening power tools. With these at your disposal, be determined to retrain as a perceptive listener — now and in the future.

We have explained the one–process brain and STTD concepts, and shared suggested guidelines for successful use of two listening power tools. However, changing the pattern of listening behavior depends, to a great extent, on that unique person residing in each of us — the "listener self."

Our self-concept influences the way we fulfill the role of listener. The listener's physical, mental, and emotional responses to the speaker and message are directly related to the listener's positive or negative concept of self. Listener self-concept is the focus of Listening Power Tool 3.

LISTENING POWER TOOL 3: LISTENER SELF-CONCEPT

Listener Self-Concept Defined

Listener self-concept means understanding who we are and how we feel when listening.

Authors Teri and Michael Gamble believe it is important to ask: "How do your employer and friends picture you?" If people who are important to you have sent messages making you feel accepted, valued, worthwhile, lovable, and significant, you probably have developed a positive self-concept. If those important to you have made you feel left out, small, worthless, unloved, or insignificant, you probably have developed a negative self-concept.[14] Our ability to listen is dependent on both the physiological (hearing) and psychological facets (self-concept) while receiving, decoding, and responding to the speaker's messages.

Professor Judy Pearson, of Ohio University at Athens, notes specific self-concept terms which can be useful in clarifying who we are.[15] The listener's perception of self determines the way one relates to oneself and to others. To the terms used to identify one's self-concept, we note the perception and behavior of the listener self in Definition Box 3.

DEFINITION BOX 3   Terms Relating to Listener Self-Concept

self-image: the sort of person we think we are (make a concerted effort to be a willing and capable listener — try to imitate friends and colleagues who appear to really listen)

self-esteem: how well we like ourselves (visualize a positive self-image as a competent listener — build up the listener self)

self-awareness: distinguishing between self-image and self-esteem (want and plan to use new listening power tools — be prepared to reverse the roles of "aggressive speaker" and "thoughtful listener" at social and professional events)

self-disclosure: making verbal and nonverbal statements to inform others (willingly give open nonverbal feedback to speakers while listening and logical verbal responses after listening — keep an open mind and respond with sincere relevant feedback)

self-control: strategic and analytical response to others' demands and expectations (suppress the desire to talk rather than listen — control the urge to angrily interrupt a sales clerk)

self-focus: perceiving an improved view of oneself (visualize a "new me" in the role of listener — set aside the newspaper, turn off the TV, and listen to a friend expound on events of the day)

self-improvement: developing clear goals for ourselves (convert the specific power tools presented in this chapter into listening goals as directives for personal growth — use the power tools at the next listening event)

self-fulfilling prophecy: becoming what others expect us to become (speakers expect listeners to respond — be attentive to the minister's homily at a religious service or to the actors performing on stage)

Through language, relationships, and interaction, we sense others' acceptance or rejection of the perceived vision we have of ourselves. In the listener role, we may find it difficult to attend the messages of those rejecting our self-concept. Regardless, we use Listener Self-Concept Power Tool 3 by exercising self-discipline to attend and respond to the speakers.

Self-Discipline

One dictionary definition of self-discipline is "the training and control of oneself and conduct, usually for personal improvement."[16] We increase self-discipline as listeners knowing that we can control a spontaneous decision to stop listening. In doing so, we honor others' expectations and feelings of self-worth while accomplishing our personal goals to strengthen the power of self-discipline and, possibly, gain valuable knowledge.

Our desire and ability to exercise self-discipline as a perceptive listener is an integral part of the listener's concept of self and self-confidence. Many listening events occur unexpectedly at inconvenient times.

You probably remember forcing yourself to listen to a droning baccalaureate speaker, a "pushy" salesperson, or a talkative passenger on a plane. Under such circumstances, one has two choices: Remove oneself from the listening event, or discipline oneself to direct a change of attitude and participate as a willing perceptive listener. Exercising self-discipline or directing ourselves to listen under certain circumstances requires strenuous effort. Remember, the decision not to listen carries with it the burden of not having that knowledge or relationship with another human which, in the future, might be crucial to our well-being.

Retraining: Guidelines for Exercising Self-Discipline While Listening

1. Create a listener self-discipline goal and practice it initially during selected listening events. Gradually extend the self-discipline goal and behavior to all listening events.
2. Remind yourself of the need to exercise self-discipline before and during those listening events in which you might be tempted to "turn off" the speaker.
3. Be aware of the ongoing change in your listener self. Retrain to place a greater demand on yourself as a perceptive listener motivated to learn, grow, and prosper.

One way of seeking confirmation of one's self-concept is to apply the principles of self-disclosure. Authors Lawrence B. Rosenfeld and Roy M. Berko claim that "self-disclosure is intentionally letting the other person know who you are by self-revealing information."[17]

Let's examine how knowledge shared through self-disclosure can maintain, develop, and enhance the speaker-listener relationship and interaction.

Self-Disclosing as a Listener

Authors Ronald Adler and Neil Towne use a progressive Johari Window design to explain the importance of self-disclosure in interpersonal communication.[18] Listeners on the receiving end of the interaction need to be aware of the importance of self-disclosure. The following four steps indicate this.

1. Imagine a frame containing everything there is to know about you: your dreams, goals, likes, dislikes, needs. (See Figure 4–2.) Actually, this is impossible. We can't be aware of everything about ourselves. Each day we change and discover new things about ourselves.
2. Let's divide the frame containing everything about you vertically into two sections: On the left is the part you're aware of (known to self), and on the right is the part you're not aware of (not known to self), as in Figure 4–3.
3. Now we divide the frame containing everything about you horizontally into two sections: The top part represents things about you that others know (known to others); the bottom part contains things about you that you keep to yourself (not known to others), as in Figure 4–4.

The willingness and ability to exercise self-discipline can be one of the most powerful tools of perceptive listening.

FIGURE 4–2   Johari Window, Step 1

FIGURE 4–3   Johari Window, Step 2

FIGURE 4–4   Johari Window, Step 3

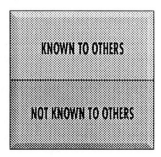

4. Finally, we overlay the last two frames onto the first frame. We have the design of the Johari Window, as in Figure 4–5.[19]

How can the Johari Window help listeners assess the traits of self-awareness?

FIGURE 4–5   Johari Window, Step 4

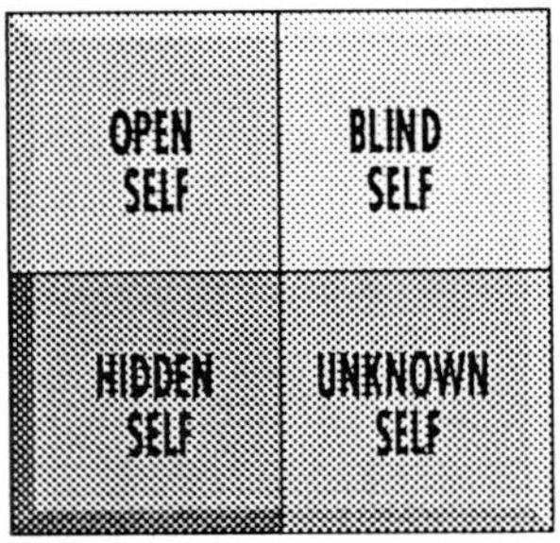

Listener Self-Awareness and the Johari Window

Using the Johari Window is one way to assess listener self-awareness. The window is named to reflect the first names of its creators, Joseph Luft and Harry Ingham.[20]

The meaning of listener self-awareness evolves from a logical premise. To understand ourselves as listeners we need to understand our way of looking at the world. To understand others, we must understand how they look at the world. Becoming more aware of ourselves and our potentials as communicators is vital to all communication, including listening.

The quadrants of the Johari Window represent the levels of awareness of the whole person in relation to others. The window can help us realize how we, as listeners interacting with others, view ourselves and how others view us. Knowledge of self derives from interactions with others. We learn to know others based only on how well we know ourselves. However, knowing our own likes and dislikes does not guarantee that we automatically know the likes and dislikes of others.

In the process of communication we attempt to enter the private world of the person to whom we're listening. We need to realize that every person has individual preferences, priorities, experiences, and backgrounds. It is that world of differences that determines the extent of the response which listeners make to others as they attempt to communicate—and "see" into the private world of others.

Our ability to see into the private worlds of those with whom we communicate is determined by the levels of self-awareness of the listener and speaker and their awareness of each other. A student who goes to the library ostensibly to study or a supervisor engrossed in checking a computer printout pays little attention to a passer–by interested in superficial conversation, because the private worlds and personalities of the parties are different **at that time**.[21] Listeners and speakers need to develop greater awareness of these differences. The Johari Window concept helps us do that.

The Johari Window and the Personality Quadrants

Let's examine each quadrant of the Johari Window for assessing personality.[22]

Quadrant 1, Open Area: This area represents the feelings and behavior known to others and to oneself. The larger this area, the greater contact the listener has with the real world. The needs and abilities of the listener are more apparent and understood by the listener self and others.

Attentive listeners show genuine interest in the speaker and the message and willingly transmit relevant feedback to the speaker via the open area quadrant. This means that, at this particular time, we are in touch with our feelings. We feel the need to communicate with others and have them communicate with us.

Quadrant 2, Blind Area: This area represents feelings, behavior, and motivation not known to self but apparent to others. You are in the blind quadrant area when others have a great amount of information about you which you do not know about yourself.

The blind quadrant includes the impatient listener whose involuntary and annoying mannerisms distort the overall process of communication by restricting the flow of valuable feedback.

Quadrant 3, Hidden Area: This area represents those feelings and behaviors known to oneself but unknown to others. The hidden area includes listeners who attempt to conceal feelings by a coverup response to the speaker. For example, a seemingly confident CEO of a customer-driven company encourages the staff to be frank. Yet inwardly the CEO feels threatened listening to any opposition to company policy and is operating in the hidden quadrant.

Quadrant 4, Unknown: This area represents the inner realm of feelings and behavior unknown to oneself and others. This quadrant includes information about ourselves that we don't know we don't know. Some experts reason that, by increasing the open quadrant, we can decrease the unknown quadrant. Others believe that, since we can't identify the unknown, we can't ever decrease the unknown quadrant.

This area is presumed to exist because we discover from time to time new attitudes, behaviors, and motives which probably were within us all the time. Such listeners, because of information emerging from the unknown area, set aside an opposing view of a controversial issue held over a long period of time.

Now that we understand the four areas or "selves" of the Johari Window, it would be an easy task for listeners to use it and other tools described in this chapter to assess self-concept. Actually, self-concept assessment is an important aspect of retraining to listen.

Retraining: Guidelines for Productive Use of the Listener Self-Concept

1. Review the content of Definition Box 2. Quietly reflect on how you feel about yourself in relation to each of the eight self-concept terms. On paper write the goals you need to pursue to develop and maintain a positive self-concept.

2. As much as possible, be prepared for listening encounters that, from past experiences, have required self-discipline to fulfill the listener role. Act upon the retraining guidelines for the self-disciplined listener (see page 72).

3. Remember that one's self-concept is subject to ongoing as well as drastic change. We need to be aware of such changes because the way we attend others' messages can affect their self-image, self-esteem, and ability to interact. Regularly

use **intrapersonal communication** (speaking and listening to self) to help sustain a positive self-concept. (Self-listening is discussed in Chapter 5, Five Kinds of Listening We Do.)

4. Store an image of the Johari Window in your long-term memory. Close your eyes and visualize the quadrants: open, blind, hidden, and unknown. Do the Johari Window check often to assess your listener self. Try to expand the open quadrant for increased and meaningful contact with speakers.

5. Above all, we need to love ourselves and realize that a positive self-concept and genuine happiness are within us.

Knowing and feeling confident about our inner selves nurtures a force from within called motivation. This is Listening Power Tool 4.

LISTENING POWER TOOL 4: MOTIVATION

Motivation refers to a driving force that moves us to a particular action. Certain behaviors are likely to help us gain success (earning an academic degree), recognition (competing in sports), and financial well-being (investing in real estate) to fulfill our needs.[23] We can understand why self-discipline (directing oneself to listen) and motivation (wanting to listen in order to learn, grow, and prosper) are crucial elements in achieving success, recognition, and financial well-being. In addition to applying the concepts in Chapter 1, Listening to Succeed, we listeners can gain valuable advice by listening to others. Furthermore, we develop our potential by focusing on motivation factors requiring us to listen, learn, and react to new *cognitions* or bits of knowledge. As we develop our potential, we learn more about the listener self.

Motivation and Knowing the Listener Self

Motivation power is generated by the desire to answer human needs. We listen to and learn from messages to the degree the message answers our needs. As we interact with others we need to understand their needs and how they look at the world. Also, we need to identify our needs and the way we look at the world. These observations enhance our sense of self-awareness, vital to all functions and forms of communication.

A leader-manager, conducting an assessment interview with an associate manager, expects an attentive listener, eager to receive the performance assessment report. However, if the employee recently decided to change positions, regardless of the outcome of the assessment interview, there is little or no security-need motivation. Conversely, if the employee desperately wants to remain in the position, there is a high degree of security-need motivation. The better we know ourselves and our ever-changing need levels, the better we interact.

Maslow's Hierarchy of Needs

We select to attend those messages directly related to satisfying human needs. The listener's motivation pattern of processing messages generally follows five hierarchical levels of human needs; basic, security, belonging, love or esteem, and self–actualization, formulated by the psychologist Abraham Maslow.[24] In the Pyramid of Needs (see Figure 4–6), note that the lower levels include the stronger needs and the higher levels, the weaker needs. Also note that the higher-level needs are not superior to the lower ones. They are merely different and, in all likelihood, are tied in with prepotency (weaker needs emerge only after stronger needs are met).[25]

As listeners, our motivation patterns of response change accordingly with the prepotency status of our personal needs. We listen eagerly to a TV report explaining the repair of a water main and restoration of service in our area (basic-need prepotency). An hour later we listen anxiously as a special friend accepts our dinner invitation (emotional-security prepotency).

Maslow's five-level hierarchy of needs would include such examples as these: basic — air, water, food, shelter, sex, sleep; security — steady job, home; belonging — club, church; love or esteem — closeness to spouse, family, friends, peers; self-actualization — employee award, weight loss. The route to self-actualization leads up from the four lower levels in the pyramid. Psychologist James V. McConnell states that not all of us have a chance to become self-actualized persons, primarily because we have simpler needs that must be satisfied first. He claims: "Unless you have confidence in yourself, you will not dare to express yourself in your own unique way, make your own contributions to society, and thus achieve your own inborn potential."[26]

FIGURE 4–6   Maslow's Pyramid of Needs

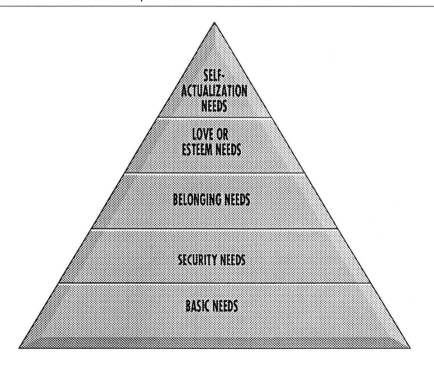

Your authors stress the fact that listening perceptively to learn can enable us to satisfy simpler needs more expeditiously. Thus we can become a self-actualized nation—better equipped to meet the challenges of the twenty-first century and to hold our rightful place in global competition with world powers.

Retraining: Guidelines for Exercising Motivation as a Listener Power Tool

1. With perceptive listening as a goal, we can direct feelings of motivation during interactions. The speaker benefits by having a more responsive listener. The listener benefits by learning and responding to the speaker's intended message.
2. Be motivated to listen during each interaction—even when a concerted effort is required to generate the feeling. Realize that different messages may require stronger or weaker feelings of motivation. Form the habit of listening as a motivated responder.
3. Memorize Maslow's Pyramid of Needs. Each time you listen, identify the corresponding need level to which the speaker and message relate.
4. The external environment can affect feelings of motivation, but remember that motivation comes from within. It is within our power to direct the level of motivation during listening encounters.
5. Retrain yourself to become a highly motivated, perceptive listener.

The last listening power tool is a formula of receptive and perceptive listener behavior. The listener's receptive behavior involves attending the speaker's verbal and nonverbal messages for decoding and responding. Perceptive behavior involves gaining additional insight into the speaker's intended message from the overall speaking-listening event. This includes the setting; physical, mental and emotional distractions; speaker presentational skills; topic of conversation or speech; speaker-listener relationship; speaker-listener attitudes toward selves and each other; and the listener's behavior skills.

Learning to use the listener behavior formula can improve the level of listening competency. It can readily be adapted for use by students, managers, supervisors, professionals, spouses, children, relatives, friends, and acquaintances. The formula for responsive and productive listener behavior is Listening Power Tool 5.

LISTENING POWER TOOL 5: LISTENER BEHAVIOR "D" FORMULA

We present this formula early to enable you to start listening retraining immediately. It is vitally important to begin applying the three "D" elements of the formula now rather than waiting until Chapter 10, Ten Listening Retraining Techniques in which the complete formula will be presented. Here is the formula:

- DDOT—Don't Do Other Tasks.
- DMP—Don't Make Plans.
- DD—Don't Daydream.

We suggest you memorize the formula. Exercise self-discipline to apply it each time you listen, during planned listening events (meetings, classes) and during unplanned listening events (unexpected encounters with colleagues, friends, and clients).

Let's examine Listening Power Tool 5 and learn how to apply "the three D's" of the listener behavior formula. The first "D" element, DDOT, directly relates to the quality of **listener feedback** (any response sent to and received by the speaker).

Don't Do Other Tasks

When we advise listeners not to perform other tasks, we refer to any physical or mental activity unrelated to the listening event. To heed this advice, we need to practice self-discipline to use the one–process brain and the STTD power tools properly. Also, we need to be aware of our listener self and have the self-confidence to change behavior immediately when we realize we are attending to other tasks unrelated to the message during listening time.

We abuse the extra listening time provided by the STTD resource by directing the brain to process counter-productive or improper tasks unrelated to the listening event. Improper tasks include: criticizing the speaker and message, taking a mental "stroll," glancing around, inspecting or repairing fingernails, doodling, talking, whispering, rearranging books and supplies, removing lint from a garment, repositioning a contact lens, cleaning eyeglasses, shuffling papers. There are hundreds of nonlistening tasks we direct the brain to process — and we stop listening. Why? We have a one–process brain; we can concentrate on only one activity at a time.

However, there are certain tasks, listed below, that need to be performed during listening time.

The more knowledgeable we become about those tasks which we should perform during listening time, the less listening time we have available to waste doing improper tasks.

Here are six major tasks conducive to perceptive listening, particularly if we are committed to begin listening retraining:

1. Review the main ideas of the speaker's message. As the speaker talks, focus on the major words of ideas presented. Do not review the message too long for fear of losing the speaker.
2. Preview the message. Try to anticipate what the speaker might be saying next. Again, do not preview the message too far ahead for fear of losing the speaker.
3. Assess the value of the message to fulfill your needs. Selfishly ask: What's in it for me? And grab the information — it's free.
4. Observe the speaker's nonverbal behavior throughout the message. Carefully monitor the speaker's eyes, face, voice, and movement.
5. Use PIM (Pictures In Mind). Use your imagination to visualize the meaning of major words as they are spoken. (The PIM concept is fully discussed in Chapter 8, Attention, Concentration, and Memory Can Be Improved.)

6. Jot down questions **in major words**. Whenever it is obvious that a speaker cannot be interrupted, use the listening time to write only the major words of questions to be asked later and data to be recorded.

These are some of the worthwhile tasks that can enhance the listening process. To retrain and successfully change listening behavior, practice using, not just reading about, the new concepts and techniques.

Conversely, it is important to be aware of another behavior that wastes listening time. We refer to indifferent listeners who become engrossed in making plans, the second element of the formula, DMP.

Don't Make Plans

The luxury of having spare time eludes most of us. Erroneously, many believe the extra listening time can be used to make plans instead of attending the message. We direct the brain to stop listening while we formulate plans unrelated to the speaker's topic.

Here is an example of poor planning: While attending a meeting to learn about group insurance coverage, David wonders about lunch after the meeting. Then he tries to decide which format to follow in developing a project report due within the week. David was planning and processing information totally unrelated to group insurance. The group health insurance message contained information David needs to know. Yet he had neither the self-discipline nor motivation to listen and learn. Nor did he perform the proper tasks during the listening time.

Indeed, we do have the luxury of using the extra listening time but only for message-related tasks. To upgrade listening competency, David needs to retrain by learning to use the listening power tools, including the listening behavior formula element, DMP.

Let us briefly look at the third element of the formula, DD.

Don't Daydream

The temptation to use listening time to make plans is as powerful as the desire to use listening time to daydream. In each instance, as soon as the brain directs the processing of planning or daydreaming—again, we have stopped listening.

We daydream or fantasize to relax and define personal and career goals. Everyone needs to daydream, but not while listening to others or working on the job.

As we daydream to project and visualize goals, we are involved in self-communication (speaking and listening from within). At different times in the past, we listened to ourselves daydream—the daydreams evolved into who we are, what we are achieving, and where we are going.

We can enjoy and benefit from daydreaming at proper times: during a lunch break, right before falling asleep, immediately upon awakening. We must be cautious, however, not to confuse daydreaming with creative thinking about resolving problems.

Retraining: Guidelines for Using the Listener Behavior Formula

1. Memorize the listener behavior formula. During each listening event, use part of the STTD listening time to apply the formula to monitor your listener behavior. Adjust your behavior accordingly.

2. Note the many nonproductive tasks performed during listening time noted in this chapter. Make a list of the tasks you persistently perform instead of listening. Review the list frequently for recall during listening encounters.

3. Learn to identify when you perform listener receptive behavior (verbal message processing by the left brain) and listener perceptive behavior (nonverbal message processing by the right brain). Become aware of when you use both brains to decode messages. Retrain to become a holistic perceptive listener.

4. Keep in mind the one–process brain concept and the (STTD) additional listening time as you apply the listener behavior formula.

5. Be prepared and motivated during future listening encounters to incorporate the concepts, guidelines, and suggestions presented in this chapter while using the five listening power tools.

Final Suggestions for Applying the Five Power Tools of Listening

While retraining to use the power tools of listening, keep in mind these suggestions:

1. Focus on your goal: to retrain to become a motivated perceptive listener reaching for the highest level of listening competency.

2. Don't criticize yourself when you have not fulfilled the goal of perceptive listening behavior. Instead, analyze the careless behavior preventing you from achieving your goal.

3. Be dedicated and persevere. Do not abandon the power tools of listening and resume careless listening behavior.

4. Prepare to enjoy listener retraining. Relish the thought that more than ever you are listening, learning, growing, and prospering in your personal and professional life.

5. End each listening event on an upbeat note. This generates a positive upward push for your self-concept.

6. Ask yourself: Who or what is the greatest obstacle preventing me from persistently using the power tools of listening? Who or what prevents me from developing into an open-minded, willing, and intelligent listener? Who or what is the enemy preventing me from improving my level of listening competency to learn, grow, and prosper?

Perhaps the author of the following poem has the answer.[27]

The power to become perceptive listeners lies within each one of us.

The Unknown Foe

An enemy I had, whose face I stoutly
    strove to know.
For hard he dogged my steps unseen,
    wherever I did go.
My plans he balked, my aims he foiled,
    he blocked my onward way.
When for some lofty goal I toiled, he
    grimly told me, 'Nay.'
One night I seized and held him fast,
    from him the veil did draw,
I looked upon his face at last, and lo —
    myself I saw.

WRAPPING IT UP: A SUMMARY

This chapter covers basic concepts and techniques relevant to using the five power tools of listening: the one–process brain concept, speech-thought-time-differential concept, the listener self, motivation, and the listener behavior "D" formula.

DISCUSSION AND STUDY GUIDES

1. Identify the quadrants of the Johari Window. How can applying the concept influence the ability to listen? Which of the quadrants do you need to adjust to upgrade listening competency?

2. Explain Maslow's Hierarchy of Needs and the "prepotency of needs." Currently, which need levels are affecting your listening behavior? Why?

3. Why is worry described as the most useless activity of humans? What did you learn after taking the worry test? If you are a "worrier," what are your plans to eliminate worry as an obstacle to listening?

4. Explain how awareness of the split brain can enlighten our understanding of the intricate process of perceptive or holistic listening. Review the split–brain operations. Are you a left–brain or a right–brain listener? Explain.

5. What lesson can you extract from the poem, "The Unknown Foe"? Ask yourself: "Is the 'unknown foe' impeding my progress in retraining to use the listening power tools?" If so, how can you remedy the situation?

LISTENING EXERCISES THAT WORK

EXERCISE 1. (Perceiving Myself as a Listener) On a sheet of paper, write this statement, "I am a————listener." Repeating the statement over and over, make a long list of words appropriate for filling in the blank. After you believe you have exhausted your supply of words, continue saying the statement and writing additional words. After completing the list, place a "P" after the positive adjectives, an "N" after the negative ones. Total the number of P's and N's. Ask your friends or staff to react to your self-perceptions. Do they agree or disagree with the P's and N's? Summarize these data in the Log.

EXERCISE 2. (Projected Use of the Power Tools of Listening) Check your next-week calendar; select five events you plan to attend. Under each, list the power tools of listening that would help you respond as a perceptive listener. Which tools might be difficult to use and easy to use? Specifically, what could you do to make the difficult tools easier to use? Discuss the results with your friends and record a summary report in the Listener Log.

EXERCISE 3. (Lack of Self-Discipline to Listen) Reflect on your listening behavior in the past. Recall those events during which the lack of self-discipline caused you to stop listening. Think of the topics about which you failed to get needed information. How were you handicapped? Has this caused a job-performance problem? Record the data in your Listener Log.

EXERCISE 4. (Listening With Your Power-Centered Brain) Listening occurs between the ears — in the brain. Major parts of the brain perform certain tasks enabling us to listen. In the Listener Log list any five structures of the brain. Using major words, note where each part is located in the brain (place your hands on your skull to learn the approximate location of each part). Write the particular function of each structure and relate it to the complex process of listening.

EXERCISE 5. (Listening With the One–Process Brain) Contact a colleague, friend, or relative. Briefly explain the one–process brain concept: We can concentrate on only one activity at a time. Ask these people to *read* a poem while *writing* their names. Did the people pass or fail? Did the test demonstrate the operation of the one–process brain? Give another test to the same person using two activities other than reading and writing. Discuss and record the results.

EXERCISE 6. (The STTD Extra Listening Time) Write in the Log or share with your colleagues five facts that you have learned about the STTD concept. Also be prepared to write or discuss the answers to these questions: What does STTD mean? Why do we have this valuable resource? As a perceptive listener, which tasks should or should not be performed during the extra listening time? What other insights have you gained from this exercise?

EXERCISE 7. (Worry: The Most Useless Human Activity) In the Listener Log prepare a worry chart.

THE WORRY CHART				
Date	Problem	Starting Time month/year	Place	Worry Time (min.)

At the end of each day for a two-week period, complete the worry chart. At the end of two weeks, total the Worry Time column. Of that time, estimate the amount of listening time wasted. What have you learned about yourself from data in the chart? Are you a worrier? Do you worry more or less than you expected the chart to indicate? Specifically, what are your plans to offset worry? What are your plans to reinforce worry-free behavior? Has worry affected your level of listening competency? How? Report these findings in the Listener Log or discuss them with family, friends or colleagues.

EXERCISE 8. (Listener Self-Concept) Refer to Definition Box 3. On a scale of 1 (low) to 5 (high), assess how you perceive yourself as a listener in respect to:

self-image	( )	self-disclosure	( )
self-esteem	( )	self-improvement	( )
self-awareness	( )	self-discipline	( )

Consider your assessments. Specifically, what can you do to improve your listener self in respect to the concepts with lower ratings? How can the results of this exercise influence your self-concept at the next and subsequent listening events? Write a summary report in the Listener Log.

EXERCISE 9. (The Listener Behavior "D" Formula) Which of "the three D's" (DDOT, DMP, DD) do you engage in most frequently and least frequently? Reflect on past listening events. Which of the elements has wasted the most listening time? For each of the three D's, write in major words two behavior changes you plan to implement as you begin listening retraining.

EXERCISE 10. (Retraining Goals) Consider the overall content of this chapter: one–process brain concept, STTD, listener self-concept, motivation, and the listener behavior "D" formula. In projecting your goals to improve listening competency as a perceptive listener, which area needs your attention? Can you exercise the degree of self-discipline required to accomplish your goals? Find a quiet location and define your retraining goals via the self-communication process. For frequent referral, write them in an accessible area in the Listener Log.

NOTES

1. Guy R. Lefrancois, *Psychology* (Belmont, CA: Wadsworth, 1980), 39.
2. Joan Minninger, *Total Recall* (Emmaus, PA: Rodale Press, 1984), 2.
3. Lefrancois, 39–46. Also, see Joan E. Grusec, Robert S. Lockhart and Gary C. Walters, *Foundations of Psychology* (Toronto: Copp Clark Pittman Ltd., 1990), 70–80.
4. Minninger, 64.
5. Paul J. Kaufmann, *Sensible Listening* (Dubuque, IA: Kendall/Hunt, 1990), 61.
6. Kaufmann, 61–62.
7. Kaufmann, 62.
8. Ralph G. Nichols, "Listening Is a 10-Part Skill," *Nation's Business*, 45 (July 1957), 4; cited by Carol Allen, Caryl Brown, Martha Cooper and Charles Tucker, *Basic Listening Skills: Strategies, Readings and Exercises* (Dubuque, IA: Kendall/Hunt, 1989), 107; also cited by James J. Floyd, *Listening: A Practical Approach* (Glenview, IL: Scott, Foresman, 1985), 53.

9. Harry Goldstein, *Reading and Listening Comprehension at Various Controlled Rates*, Teachers College, Columbia University Contributions to Education, No. 821. (New York: Bureau of Publications, Teachers College, Columbia University, 1940).

10. W. D. Garvey, "Duration Factors in Speech Intelligibility," (Master's Thesis, Charlottesville, VA: University of Virginia, 1949).

11. G. A. Miller and J. C. R. Licklider, "The Intelligibility of Interrupted Speech," *Journal of the Acoustical Society of America*, 22 (March 1950), 167–73.

12. ———, "VSC Means Top Grades for Visually Impaired Freshman," *Technical Horizons in Education Journal*, 6 (January 1979).

13. Dale Carnegie, *How to Stop Worrying and Start Living: Time–Tested Methods for Conquering Worry* (New York: Pocket Books, 1984), 37.

14. Teri Kwal Gamble and Michael Gamble, *Communication Works* (New York: Random House, 1984), 35.

15. Judy Cornelia Pearson and Paul Edward Nelson, *Understanding and Sharing: An Introduction to Speech Communication*, 3rd ed. (Dubuque, IA: William C. Brown, Publishers, 1985), G-8.

16. William Morris, ed. *The American Heritage Dictionary of the English Language* (Boston, MA: Houghton Mifflin, 1974).

17. Lawrence B. Rosenfeld and Roy M. Berko, *Communicating with Competency* (Glenview, IL: Scott, Foresman, 1990), 183.

18. Ronald B. Adler and Neil Towne, *Looking Out Looking In* (Fort Worth, TX: Holt, Rinehart and Winston, 1990), 299.

19. Ibid., 300.

20. Joseph Luft, *Group Process: An Introduction to Group Dynamics* (Palo Alto, CA: National Press, 1964), cited in Bobby R. Patton and Kim Griffin, *Interpersonal Communication in Action: Basic Text and Readings* (New York: Harper & Row, 1977), 39.

21. Linda Costigan Lederman, *New Dimensions: An Introduction to Human Communication* (Dubuque, IA: Wm. C. Brown, Publishers, 1977), 71.

22. Ibid., 70.

23. Neil R. Carlson, *Psychology: The Science of Behavior*, 3rd ed. (Needham Heights, ME, 1990), 404.

24. Abraham Maslow, *Motivation and Personality* (New York: Harper & Row, 1954).

25. Charles U. Larson, *Persuasion: Reception and Responsibility*, 5th ed. (Belmont, CA: Wadsworth, 1989), 165–170.

26. James V. McConnell, *Understanding Human Behavior*, 3rd ed. (New York: Holt, Rinehart and Winston, 1980), 302–303.

27. Poem by Paul J. Meyer, President, Success Motivation Institute, Inc. (P.O. Box 7614, Waco, TX 76710, distributed by Wilcox & Associates, P.O. Box 118, Versailles, OH 45380).

PART TWO

LEARNING
TO LISTEN

CHAPTER 5

Five Kinds of Listening We Do

The ear trieth words as the mouth tasteth meat.
— Job 33:16

THESIS We listen to learn, to assess, to lift the spirit, to be perceptive of the feelings of others and to be aware of ourselves. We can learn to recognize each kind of listening and employ specific strategies to improve each.

CHAPTER OBJECTIVES

1. Realize that message senders have specific goals in terms of a specific kind of listener response; be aware that each kind of message sent demands a specific kind of listener response.
2. Know the five kinds of listening and the specific strategies a listener can use to improve each.
3. Be aware of special situations where listening can enhance physical and emotional healing.

CHAPTER PREVIEW

- Discriminative listening goals and strategies.
- Evaluative listening and the persuasive speaker.
- Appreciative listening and the pleasurable message.
- Empathic listening: the mind-body connection.
- Self-listening and its functions.

When we send messages, we usually know the kind of message we intend to send — informative, persuasive, pleasure-giving or relief-seeking. We also have in mind the kind of response we seek. Before teen-agers wheedle their parents into lending them the family car, they know their messages must be persuasive, and they hope their parents will hand over the car keys. Before instructors begin retraining sessions, they plan to share information and hope that their listeners will learn something. The life of the party tells stories, believing they are entertaining, and expecting laughs. Before our friends tell us their troubles they know that they seek relief and hope for understanding responses that will restore their self-esteem. Whenever we sit down to think through a problem, we know we are seeking the best solution.

Unfortunately, when we listen we often have no plan at all. Graham Wallas, a British philosopher, observed, "Our mind is not likely to give us a clear answer to any particular problem unless we set it a clear question."[1] We may be aware that, as speakers, we set ourselves precise questions and have goals in mind, but, too often, when we're on the receiving end, we suppose we're "only listening." Therefore we float through the communication process without goals. Unless we also identify what we seek from the speaker's message and identify the kind of listening we do, we will listen aimlessly.

In this chapter we define five kinds of listening, each serving a different end. We do *discriminative listening* to informative speech in order to increase our knowledge and store ideas and information received for possible utilization later. We do *evaluative listening* to persuasive messages to improve our assessing ability as we carefully weigh the strength of the speaker's argument and evidence. We do *appreciative listening* to any kind of stimuli that is gratifying to our senses. We do *empathic listening* to a speaker who vents innermost feelings or who seeks a caring response. We do *self–listening* to the messages from our bodies and minds which can provide understanding, healing, and strengthening of our self-concept.

Four kinds of listening — discriminative, evaluative, appreciative and self-listening — are basically intrinsic operations. That is, we listen for personal gain or profit. The other kind, empathic, is an extrinsic operation, which we do primarily for the personal needs of another, the speaker.

In this chapter we show the speaker's and listener's roles and the interdependence of each in the communication process. We also show various special functions of each kind of listening, and strategies to assist the listener who seeks to improve this competency.

Many combinations of different kinds of messages are possible. But one of the five kinds (informative, persuasive, pleasure-giving, esteem-seeking, or self-talk messages) can be identified as dominant in any given situation. The skillful listener will make the identification early and adjust receptive activity accordingly to acquire information, to evaluate, to appreciate, to empathize, or to self-listen.

1. DISCRIMINATIVE LISTENING

We use the word *discriminative* to describe listening to informative messages. As we interpret the message sent to give us knowledge, we distinguish the excellent, appropriate, or true. We then re-create the information and add it to our previous experience. We listen discriminatively to add to, refine, reorganize, or enhance that experience. When we listen to instructive or informative speech, we expect to extend our previous experience to include the messages received and to distinguish that which we can use. We do this to acquire material that will be of future value to us or that we deem to be of future value. We do this in both formal and informal settings.

Formal discriminative listening is the kind we do when we come to a particular place for the purpose of listening to learn. We practice it during lectures, training sessions, and reports. We act as informal discriminative listeners in dozens of daily encounters: When an insurance agent explains policies, an accountant shows which deductions to take for federal income tax, a mechanic reveals what's wrong with our car.

We can profit by considering each kind of communication from both the speaker's and the listener's goal. By *goal* we mean the conscious end or objective toward which both the speaker and listener aim.

The Informing Speaker's Goal

The informing speaker's goal is defined in terms of sharing knowledge through teaching or explaining. Informative or expository speaking is thought to be the most common kind of message sending, a process in which a speaker creates and transmits messages to receivers so as to be understood and to develop shared meanings.[2] Whether in formal or informal sending, the speaker explains what something is, why it happens, or how it works. The speaker aims the message toward helping listeners to understand it, to learn and benefit from it, and to expand their thinking.

Informing speakers identify goals in terms of the ultimate behavior they expect in listeners and formulate their goals in terms of the listeners: They will know how to make a quilt, understand why an automobile engine knocks, or know what is expected of them on a committee.

The speakers also look for both verbal and nonverbal feedback showing that the listener has indeed understood. They may expect an enthusiastic smile or nod, a comment such as, "That made things clear for me," or "I learned a lot."

Just as speakers identify their goals as information senders, we are wise to identify our goals as discriminative receivers.

The Discriminative Listener's Goals

The discriminative listener's goals will correspond to those of the informing speaker.

When we listen to gather information, we wish to understand the material we gather, to learn something from it, and to extend our experience by using it. We expect that after listening we will know how to do something, will understand more clearly how something works, or will understand more about why something has occurred. We expect to recognize differences or similarities among ideas, to compare the speaker's ideas to our own, or to define totally new concepts.

Four Strategies for Improving Discriminative Listening

1. **Identify the main idea of the message**. Identifying the main idea is a crucial first step in discriminative listening. Everything in a message, whether it is formally or informally presented, focuses on a central idea or thesis statement.

2. **Identify key ideas and key words**. In focusing on each point developed from the main idea, we can identify one or two key words. It is easy to become sidetracked by the examples, anecdotes, or statistics that both public speakers and interpersonal communicators use to support an idea. However, in order to listen for ideas, we must learn to recognize the main idea our co-communicator wishes to send.

3. **Identify the speaker's pattern of organization**. Otis Walter and Robert Scott have identified several logical patterns a speaker might use to adapt material to a specific subject and goal. They suggest that speakers often arrange material into one of these traditional patterns: time sequence, spatial relations, problem solution, cause and effect, topical sequence, and climactic and anticlimactic.[3]

Speakers use the time-sequence pattern whenever chronology is important. They use it to examine the past, present, and future of an idea or an issue. Speakers also find it useful when they tell us how to do something in which steps must be taken in a specific order.

The spatial relations pattern is used when speakers develop messages in relation to space or placement. When we listen to presentations about attractive wall covering for the kitchen, we can often recognize spatial-relations patterns. The sectional location of different cars on a car lot also exemplifies the spatial-relations pattern of organization.

Listeners recognize the problem-solution pattern when they evaluate a speaker's position on an important issue and also a suggested remedy.

In cause–effect patterns, we listen to learn of the problem's ramifications or effects. For example, we may listen to two thirds of a speaker's message that the cost of manufacturing goods is increasing steadily. The ramifications (consumers will pay higher prices) may require only one third of the message. Conversely, we may listen to a shorter segment of the message defining the cause, and a longer segment explaining the ramifications or effect.

The topical–sequence structure creates divisions or subdivisions of the topic in a manner similar to the traditional outline. For example, a vocal instructor uses the topical sequence when explaining the four properties of the human voice (quality, volume, pitch, and tempo).

Listening to a message containing fewer supportive data at the beginning and the most supportive material toward the end indicates that the speaker has used the *climactic pattern* of organization. When the reverse is true, the strongest and most supportive evidence appearing early in the message followed by the less supportive material, the speaker has used the *anticlimactic pattern* of organization.

What kind of messages tend to follow the climactic and anticlimactic patterns? Paul Nelson and Judy Pearson use an excellent example of the climactic pattern: "The Institute for Social Research at the University of Michigan indicates that 80% of the freshmen students want a good marriage and family life, . . . But only 4% of the women expect to be full-time homemakers at the age of 30."[4] An example of the anticlimactic pattern is for the speaker to say, "Warning: The Surgeon General has determined that cigarette smoking is dangerous to your health," as part of the introduction to an anti-smoking message. This is followed by supportive data on the harm cigarette smoking imposes on the body.

4. **Review the information received**. We can review the information we receive by identifying the message, main points, and pattern of organization to separate the important from the unimportant during a message to inform. However, sometimes it will be useful to ask ourselves three crucial questions to fully assess discriminative messages: (1) Did I understand the speaker? (2) Is what the speaker said true? (3) Does the speaker's interpretation lead to the conclusion reached?

Retraining: Guidelines to Improve Discriminative Listening

1. Learn to recognize informing messages and then take care to follow discriminative listening strategies.

2. Whenever you recognize a discriminative listening situation, recall (or formulate) your own goals as a discriminative listener and, if possible, write them down for reinforcement.

3. Prepare for discriminative listening by setting aside time to learn all steps in identifying main ideas, key words, and patterns or organization.

4. During discriminative listening, make use of the speech-thought-time differential (STTD) to apply all prescribed strategies for improving that listening.

5. During listening, take notes identifying the main idea, key ideas, key words and specific pattern of organization used by the speaker.

6. Always review the truth and logic of each informational message.

2. EVALUATIVE LISTENING

Evaluative listening is what we do when listening to a speaker who intends to persuade or convince. Whether the process involves parent and child, doctor and patient, dictator and subjects, it constitutes someone's attempt to influence the attitudes, beliefs, or actions of another.

The persuasive process is varied and complex. Winston L. Brembeck and William S. Howell define persuasion as: "communication intended to influence choice." They explain:

> The word *communication* denotes that this phenomenon is symbolic and interactive, the word *intended* suggests that the persuasive attempt has a predetermined goal, and the word *influence* suggests that a behavioral change of some sort is sought and the word choice reflects the view that the receivers have options open to them.[5]

Brembeck and Howell's definition can be said to include argumentation (essentially reasoned discourse using evidence), motivational appeal (aimed at our wants and needs), emotional appeal and suggestion.

Our receiving role in responding to persuasive messages through one of these approaches is *evaluative listening*. When we evaluate, we weigh and ascertain or fix the value or worth in terms of something already known. Therefore we can describe our participation in the process of persuasion as assessing the value *to us* of the reasoning, evidence, suggestions, and motivational appeals used by a persuader before we make a decision. We weigh all and then may or may not modify our attitudes or behavior.

The Persuading Speaker's Goals

The individual who sets out to talk people into changing their thoughts or actions becomes a persuasive speaker. Because many believe that persuaders attempt to manipulate behavior for their own selfish reasons, they tend to respond negatively. Therefore persuasive message senders choose with care the steps they take in order to produce a desired effect.

Authors Ernest Bormann, William Howell, Ralph Nichols, and George Shapiro describe four key steps which most persuaders follow in order to produce a specific response.[6]

1. Gain the listener's attention and keep it.
2. Discover what the listeners want that can be related to the speaker's own purpose.
3. Show how a specific speaker recommendation will serve the listener's purpose.
4. Encourage a specific response by suggesting particular ways the listener can get started.

Persuaders aim these steps toward an observable effect — that of changing listener opinion so that they either start or stop doing something the persuader suggests. These goals have been called *adoption* and *discontinuance*.[7]

Speakers aiming toward a goal of adoption urge us to accept a new idea or belief. Persuaders who attempt to convince us that we should stop doing something aim toward discontinuance.

The Evaluative Listener's Goals

Persuasion is not something speakers do to listeners. It is a process wherein listeners and speakers communicate. A listener's response or lack of response to a message signals possible success or failure, but the process of persuasion has to come before the listener's reaction occurs.

Once we recognize that the message coming to us is persuasive, we normally attempt to identify our specific goal as evaluators. As we begin to do this, we are wise to assess our own resistance to persuasion. Because of some ethically questionable practices in persuasion, some listeners condemn all persuasion. Brembeck and Howell caution against this dangerous practice by reminding us: "A free society cannot survive by condemning the free exchange of ideas, however distasteful some of these ideas may be. Our methods frequently need refinement, and our ethical codes need to be sharpened, but let us not discard the system."[8]

Therefore, we often take the first step in identifying our goal as evaluative listeners by agreeing to take part in the persuasion process. The second step quickly follows. We determine whether we can most effectively appraise the evidence immediately or if it would be wiser to delay that appraisal for a definite time interval.

Necessary as it is, immediate appraisal of main points may not be sufficient to achieve truly evaluative listening. Often significant persuasive messages defy quick evaluation. Also, we may not have adequate time for an in-depth appraisal during the immediate listening situation. In such instances a delayed analysis of the evidence presented becomes imperative.

Rabbi Harold Kushner wrote *Why Bad Things Happen to Good People* in examination of his reaction to his son's life and death as a victim of progeria, the rapid–aging disease that causes young children to die of old age. Kushner recounted the process he went through in persuading himself that there was an acceptable explanation for why he and his family had to suffer as they did.[9] He struggled for over 14 years evaluating all possible explanations for his emotional burden. He finally changed his attitude toward suffering — indeed, was able to define a way to survive suffering by this delayed analysis.

Most of us will not require that much time to evaluate the persuasive messages we receive. However, we are wise to set aside some time each day to weigh and judge with care the most significant messages to which we have listened during that day. We recognize that we often seem to change our attitudes very quickly. We realize upon further consideration that we have not changed our fundamental beliefs.

Delayed appraisal can help us evaluate large decisions that affect our very life style as well as small decisions, such as whether to attend a party or buy a new suit. When we verbalize our goals as evaluative listeners, we state them in terms of the end result which we believe the speaker aims toward and the immediate or delayed response which is our aim; we express them in terms of our listener behavior.

Whether we appraise evidence immediately or delay until later, four strategies can help us evaluate objectively.

Four Strategies for Improving Evaluative Listening

1. **Learn to recognize strategies used by persuaders**. Generally, persuaders use logical procedures such as reasoning and evidence, and procedures that are not logical, such as suggestion and motivational appeals.

2. **Evaluate persuasive evidence**. When speakers present ideas, we expect evidence to support them. If they present no evidence, evaluative listeners suspect the idea and judge it to be weak.

3. **Learn to identify commonly used fallacies and propaganda techniques**. Many times persuaders make hasty extrapolations or deliberately use fallacious reasoning and propaganda in attempting to elicit change. Three common

fallacies are the "always has, always will" fallacy, the hasty generalization, and the hidden variable. "Always has, always will" refers to the false reasoning that because something has existed unchallenged in the past, it is good and ought to be continued in the present and future. The hasty generalization describes conclusions reached from considering only a few cases. And, when persuaders suggest that when two things follow in sequence one is somehow responsible for the other, they exhibit the fallacy of the hidden variable.

Propaganda may be used in any attempt — good or bad — to change opinion. We do not suggest that it is universally unfair; however, it is often used unfairly in persuasion. Propaganda makes use of such approaches as name calling, glittering generalizations, testimonial, and bandwagon appeals.

4. **Identify any changes in belief or attitude**. During delayed appraisal, each day, we can consider and evaluate any changes we perceive in our own beliefs and attitudes that result from listening to persuasion. We can often facilitate this process by asking ourselves: What was my original position? To what did I respond? Was I objective? Was I persuaded?

Remember, persuasion is a process. Evidence and reasoning should combine to explain why we should change or cooperate. We should agree or disagree as a result of our own reasoning. When we listen to evaluate, we are wise to use every second to put into practice both discriminative and evaluative listening strategies.

Retraining: Guidelines to Improve Evaluative Listening

1. Recognize the complexity of persuasive messages and pay attention to persuaders' goals.
2. Take time to determine when a message is persuasive and then listen by using evaluative listening strategies.
3. Whenever possible, use immediate evaluation of a message. When this is not possible, resolve to take as much time as necessary for delayed evaluation of the message.
4. Take time to learn the strategies used by persuaders and how to evaluate evidence, common fallacies, and propaganda techniques as preparation for evaluative listening.
5. During evaluative listening, make use of these strategies to achieve perceptive evaluative listening.

3. APPRECIATIVE LISTENING

We listen appreciatively when we enjoy that to which we listen, value it for its aesthetic stimulation or otherwise find excellence in it. William Waack said "appreciative listening is aesthetic listening."[10]

Of course, it is possible to listen appreciatively for several reasons in addition to the aesthetic. Charles Hoffer, of the University of Florida, points out five reasons why he believes we might choose to listen to music:[11]

1. To promote feelings of unity
2. To reach deep feelings
3. For recreation or diversion
4. As "sonic background" to accompany another activity
5. For intellectual and psychological satisfaction

We believe these reasons for listening to music can also be thought of as reasons for other appreciative listening. We believe this unity, depth of feeling, recreation and intellectual stimulation comes from several formal and informal listening situations.

We enjoy formal appreciative listening during planned performances when people assemble to listen to concerts, movies, plays, speakers, comedians.

We find pleasure in informal listening for appreciation in more ways than we will recount on these pages. When we choose to listen to our favorite music on records, tapes, or radios, chat with a friend, listen to children at play, or walk through the woods to listen to the wind in the pines, we informally gain one of life's most profitable experiences — listening for appreciation. The growth we enjoy through appreciative listening can make deeply significant contributions to our lives. It can increase our pleasure in life itself, enlarge our experiences, expand the range of what we enjoy, and decrease the tension of daily living.

The Pleasure-Sending Speaker's Goals

The senders of a pleasurable message may be unaware they are doing so. Animal calls, rippling streams, crashing waterfalls, or whispering wind can provide listening pleasure although these sensations are not consciously generated for that purpose. Ecologist Sigurd F. Olson refers to such pleasure.[12] In *Listening Point*, he describes his reasons for choosing a wilderness hideaway:

> Wilderness sounds would be here, bird songs in the morning and at dusk. The aspen leaves would whisper and the pines as well, and in the sounds of water and wind I would hear all that is worth listening for. . . . I would come to listen and feel and to recapture for a little while the old joy I had known.

For him and countless other wilderness lovers, these sounds bring untold joy. Generally, however, when we discuss sender goals in this chapter, we mean only the goals of humans who consciously project messages meant to give pleasure.

A message sender (speaker, actor, comedian, musical performer) identifies goals in terms of audience behavior just as do speakers sending messages to inform or to persuade. When they send a humorous message, entertainers aim toward anticipated applause, laughter, or both, which feed back evidence that listeners have enjoyed it. When they send a tragic message, they aim for empathic responses such as tears, serious looks, nods, comments, or, once again, applause. In short, the speaker identifies the goal of significantly adding to the listener's pleasure and experiencing evidence of that pleasure.

The Appreciative Listener's Goal

Listeners often devote a great part of their day to appreciative listening, but often without a conscious plan. Often we allow all appreciative listening to become "sonic accompaniment" to daily living. When we identify a goal for appreciative listening we can begin a plan to enhance our lives.

We believe goal setting is the key to appreciative listening. Even on the level of "emotional" listening to influence a mood, we are more likely to be satisfied if we decide beforehand what we are looking for. It might be simply stated as, "I want to be more relaxed and in tune with myself after listening to this tape."

On another level, we can listen appreciatively to call upon memories, to rekindle or evoke former pleasures. Our goal might be stated, "I want to relive the pleasant experiences of childhood by listening to 'Peter and the Wolf' which I first loved as a child."

On still another level, we can plan to enjoy by concentrating on what is happening within an artistic creation. In music, we might concentrate on melodic line, tonality, and instrumentation. In drama, we might concentrate on characterization, voice, or tempo. In putting such a goal into words, listeners might say, "I want to appreciate this work of art by becoming aware of as many of its artistic qualities as possible."

When we identify our goals as appreciative listeners we can gather immeasurable rewards. We also can identify some strategies for improving that listening which can bring more opportunities and therefore more rewards.

Four Strategies for Improving Appreciative Listening

1. **Take time for appreciative listening**. Often, because we neither see nor measure the results of appreciative listening, we neglect taking time to do so. Aristides said serious listening "requires time—or, more precisely, repose," and Myra Hess believes, "For anyone wanting to think, listening to music gives them all they need; for anyone who wants to forget, it will give them that, too."[13] We recommend that listeners set aside time for appreciative listening. Schedule time for concerts, plays, and recitals; listen to tapes of books, musical favorites, or speakers while relaxing. Choose to set aside time for conversation with friends and family.

2. **Adopt a positive attitude toward listening for appreciation**. Once we have set aside time to listen, only we can decide to make the effort to listen. Only we can be tolerant toward the message coming to us. "Learning to listen is a matter more of wanting to understand . . . than of learning techniques for understanding. Without the desire and effort no amount of technique will succeed."[14]

3. **Concentrate on the main themes and artistic ideas in the work**. Although it is possible to enjoy music in a sensual manner by simply allowing it to "wash over" one, "doubtless missing its theme and the recurrence of the theme each time,"[15] we are far more likely to find joy in that which we understand. How do we identify the theme and artistic ideas? By mental preparation before the listening experience. If we read a play and one or two reviews before we see it, we will have a kind of self-designed study guide to follow during the performance. This preparation in order to find main themes and artistic ideas will help the appreciative listener find ever more pleasure in the experience.

4. **Prepare for and practice listening appreciatively**. Make a choice of material to concentrate on during the time you set aside for listening each day. Remember, the more you know about any work of art, the more you can appreciate and enjoy it. An instructor of music, Susan Floyd Germek, suggests that the listener, during this practice listening, focus on one element at a time — tonality, melodic line, voice, theme — and then layer one new element each time you listen.[16] When we know what has been done and why, we can truly be part of the appreciative listening experience.

Professor Harold Dalrymple, of Kent State University, suggests that careful preparation for theater performances can enhance all appreciative listening.

> When students are trained to listen for the theatre, they receive a great deal indeed. Appreciation of the theatrical performance is enhanced. Students learn to use a life-enriching experience more fully. They also develop social skills in listening which others, without training in listening for the theatre, do not have. The trained theatre listener realizes that we listen to our total environment and to emotional messages through nonverbal cues. Through training in listening for the theatre, students become better listeners in all situations.[17]

William Waack suggests: "Students of all ages need to spend more time perfecting their ability to use the fine senses. . . . In doing so, they will improve their competence to think, to listen and respond to others with great fluency, flexibility, and originality."[18]

Healing Function of Appreciative Listening

During the past several years, many people have become intensely aware of the mind-body connection and its role in healing the body or in extending quality of life. Hal Lingerman states: "Sound and light influence every area of life. How we respond to these two great universal forces will condition a large part of our health and happiness."[19] He suggests specific musical works to be chosen to meet specific emotional needs such as strength and courage, relaxation and reverie, clear thinking and mental power, and meditation and prayer.

Yale University surgeon Bernie Siegel suggests we listen to quiet music four to six times a day. He believes this interrupts your body with healing intervals of appreciative listening which refocus and give your body "live" messages. In his work with cancer patients, Siegel learned the need for healing listening at times of great stress. He suggests we create our own tape and play it whenever we are under stress, in addition to the regular four to six times a day. He further recommends we listen to this tape during surgery or whenever we are under anesthesia.[20] Deanna Edwards, who uses music as therapy for nursing–home patients, reiterates Siegel's belief that we not only hear when we are under anesthesia, but also can respond positively. When she played music for extremely ill patients, she discovered that even patients in a coma would respond verbally, by singing along with her, when she played a favorite hymn.[21]

Retraining: Guidelines to Improve Appreciative Listening

1. Take time for appreciative listening — both planned events and those that come unexpectedly.
2. Whenever possible, identify your goal for taking time to listen appreciatively: to relax, to relive pleasant memories, or to discover levels of art within a work.
3. Set aside time every day for at least one appreciative listening experience.
4. Before a scheduled appreciative listening experience, spend time in self-designed preparation for the event. Remember, the more you know about an artistic presentation, the more you can appreciate it.
5. Whenever you feel the need, give yourself a "live message" through planned or taped appreciative listening experiences.

4. EMPATHIC LISTENING

All of us need for others to listen to us. In fact, no matter what kind of message sending we do, we expect listeners to respond with the correct listening style (discriminative, evaluative or appreciative) and with genuine concern and involvement. This is one aspect of a very complex kind of listening which we call empathic listening and which means listening with empathy or perceptive feeling. Authors Ronald Arnett and Gordon Nakagawa tell us that the term "empathy" is the English equivalent of *Einfühlung* ("feeling into"), a concept which originated in 1909 with Cornell psychologist Edward Tichener.[22] Many communication specialists have attempted to define empathy as it exists in communication. Professor William Howell, of the University of Minnesota, offers a useful definition:

> Empathy is the ability to replicate what one perceives. . . . Empathy, then, is *not* feeling what another feels, or putting yourself in another's shoes, or projecting your consciousness onto another human being. It is rather thinking and feeling what you *perceive* another to be thinking and feeling. As the perceptions of two people witnessing the same event differ, so will their empathic responses contrast.[23]

We describe empathic listening as that listening during which we attempt to understand what we perceive speakers think and feel. It differs from the first three kinds because of our intent. We listen discriminatively, evaluatively, or appreciatively for intrinsic reasons. In one way or another, we expect to grow personally or to profit from it. We listen empathically primarily for extrinsic reasons. We reap several personal rewards from empathic listening, but we do it principally so that another person—the speaker—may grow and profit from being listened to. In both formal and informal roles, empathic listening is one of the most used listening styles and it is used in many settings. The therapeutic role of empathic listening is easily seen in formal counseling. We commonly arrange this with trained professionals in the helping professions. Other professionals, such as clergymen, teachers, general physicians, and lawyers, often listen empathically in formal situations. But if they are untrained in these skills, they may provide only frustration for their clients.

Empathic listening is not easy; it is perhaps the pinnacle of listening. It demands fine skill and exquisite tuning to another's mood and feelings. Presumably, only psychiatrists, psychologists, and counselors perfect it and possess the necessary training to help clients find curative power by talking. Unless we have the kind of intensive training that helping professionals acquire, we cannot presume to predict healing results from listening.

However, very few people go to psychiatrists with their problems. But many people take their troubles to close friends and relatives. We cannot offer our friends the help that a psychiatrist gives to a patient but we can become helpful empathic listeners. We can provide a listening ear to our friends in informal situations.

We listen empathically almost daily in informal encounters with friends, family, and co-workers who need someone to listen. When a friend calls to report feelings of rejection, when a co-worker stops to share feelings of inadequacy, when members of our family come home angry because they had frustrating days, we encounter opportunities for informal empathic listening. We cannot cure these problems by listening. However, these people are looking for neither therapy nor advice. They are looking for someone who is willing to sit still and listen. These speakers wish to talk freely and, by listening to their own thoughts as they put them into words, arrive at their own solutions or come up with their own advice.

Empathic listening must be an integral part of all listening—discriminative, evaluative and appreciative—and function in a special therapeutic role when we listen to each other.

Thomas Bruneau, Professor of Communication at Radford University, reminds us that Martin Buber first made reference to "mutual empathy or what also could be called 'interactive empathy' where both listen and speak empathically to one another resulting in a very positive intimate sharing." He cautions: "Empathy in interpersonal and public contexts . . . appears to require different kinds of empathic communication skills. The difference is mainly found in the degree of interaction expected and the kinds of feedback operable."[24] The special "interactive" empathy occurs, we believe, in therapeutic person-to-person empathic listening encounters and the second kind in a day–to–day business, social, and professional communication situations.

The Empathy-Seeking Speaker's Goals

When speakers aim for therapeutic help from empathic listeners, they explain inner feelings about something. If the speaker puts a goal into words, it might be, "I want to talk about my fears about my mother's illness," or "I want to talk about how I feel about my son's leaving home." The purpose centers around the speaker's own feelings about the subject.

Because speakers identify goals in terms of listeners, they focus on anticipated results. They hope listeners attempt to perceive not only what they say but how they feel about it. Speakers may also expect to observe both verbal and nonverbal indications that the listener understands. They may watch for eye contact, nods, or even comments that communicate that the listener empathizes.

The Empathic Listener's Goals

The empathic listener gathers information, but the process differs from discriminative listening. We attempt to understand both the verbal and the nonverbal messages the speaker sends, and also attempt to comprehend the speaker's feelings about it.

We ultimately aim toward not only understanding the message and the feelings about the message, but also toward communicating this understanding to the speaker. We must add this dimension — of letting the speaker know — to our goal.

Four Strategies for Improving Empathic Listening

1. **Be aware of feedback to the speaker**. In Chapter 2, Listening Power Generates Knowledge, we defined feedback as verbal and nonverbal responses from the listener and speaker that are received, interpreted and transmitted. We consciously send feedback so perception errors can be corrected. Bormann et al have compared the way feedback works to the way a thermostat controls the level of temperature in a room:

   Someone decides upon the desired level of temperature and sets the thermostat at that level. The thermostat takes a continuous reading on the actual level and feeds the information back to the furnace when the temperature departs from the desired level. This information causes the furnace to modify its behavior and turn off or on depending upon the information it receives from the thermostat. In this way the actual level of the temperature is brought on target to approximate the desired level. In the same way, the source of a message should take a reading on its effect on the receiver and modify subsequent stimuli.[25]

   Our listener feedback helps the speaker take a moment-to-moment reading of the effects of a message. As we listen we must be aware of the amount and kind of feedback we send. To assist this aspect of empathic listening, we can ask ourselves the following questions and look for positive responses:

   • Am I giving the speaker eye contact?

- Am I communicating that I am interested in the message and that I attempt to discern the feelings behind it?
- Am I standing or sitting in a manner that indicates alert attention?
- Am I standing or sitting at a distance that allows the speaker to remain comfortable?

Responses to these questions should help us remember to send positive feedback while we listen. Positive feedback does not mean showing that we agree but does mean showing that we are interested. This helps keep channels of communication open.

2. **Avoid judgment or signaling judgment**. Most of us have a natural tendency to pass judgment on the world around us. However, such evaluation interferes with empathic listening. Making judgments about what we receive places us outside the message; figuratively, we stand back and look at it. This limits us to considering the content of a message rather than considering how the speaker feels about it.

We cannot help a speaker experience being understood while we provide the experience of being judged. If we judge, we force speakers to do one of two things. First, we place them in the position of defending and justifying what they said, in which case they are no longer aiming toward their goal. Second, when speakers realize we communicate no empathy they often end the conversation.

All of us have experienced critical evaluation almost from birth. When we are babies, our parents evaluate our physical progress by comparing us to the neighbor's baby. In school, our teachers give us report cards that evaluate our progress by comparing us to others in the class. On the job, our superiors evaluate our work by comparing it to what someone else has done. Most of us are judged and found wanting during most of our lives. It is no wonder that when speakers find a listener who empathically listens and does not judge, they often feel as if they could talk all day. Indeed, they often do a better job as a result of having been listened to empathically.

3. **Give the speaker time**. We must allow the speaker time to tell the entire story. When people come to us because they want to talk, they want us to allow them to proceed without interruption and arrive at a clearer understanding of their own feelings and perceptions.

We suggest that empathic listeners in the therapeutic role limit responses to three kinds only. First, as the talker proceeds, the listener may employ a series of eloquent and encouraging grunts. "Hmmm," "Oh," or "I see."

Second, if the talker becomes wild and unreasonable, the listener should restate what has just been said, putting it in the form of a question. We might say, "You really think, then, that all middlemen are dishonest?" or "You believe your mother-in-law is deliberately trying to ruin your marriage?" In no case should we give relief-seeking speakers advice—even when they request it.

Third, if the talker pauses momentarily, we should remain silent, continuing to make eye contact, perhaps nodding to indicate understanding. Silence is an important part of empathic listening. Speakers who are not interrupted by questions can concentrate on sorting out the parts of the message they wish to send. They are not forced to respond to our message, thereby are not forced to diffuse their focus.

4. **Focus on the speaker**. The extrinsic nature of empathic listening suggests that we do it primarily for the benefit of another. Therefore, as we listen, we must remember to focus attention on the speaker no matter how tempting it may be to draw a parallel between that situation and our own life.

Truly empathic listeners attempt to set aside their own worries in order to see from the viewpoint of another. Speakers who need to talk through a problem have chosen us to be empathic listeners. The speaker who does so believes that we are sensitive and capable of accepting trust. At that moment speakers do not care at all about our problems or our point of view. They only want us to accept them and listen.

A Special Function of Empathic Listening

The mind-body connection discussed in appreciative listening is also eminently advanced by use of empathic listening and specifically by making use of the four strategies just described.

When empathic listening is employed in self-help groups, it can produce dramatic results. Gayle Cluck and Rebecca Cline call these groups "circles of others" and believe they substitute for the one-on-one interaction which is often difficult to find.

They tell us that these groups become the "gatekeepers and doorkeepers of the heart."[26] A longitudinal study of women with breast cancer conducted at Stanford University School of Medicine showed that, of 86 cancer patients in the study, 36 (the control group) received standard treatment only and 50 (the experimental group) participated in support groups. Those taking part in the support groups were less fearful and fatigued, had better coping skills, and *lived twice as long* as those in the control group.

Dr. David Spiegel, who conducted the study, believes that increased ability to fight disease came from the development of powerful personal bonds among members of the group.[27] In short, members of the self-help groups became skilled empathic listeners who avoided judgment, gave each other time, remained silent when necessary, and focused on each other.

Retraining: Guidelines to Improve Empathic Listening

1. Resolve to listen empathically whenever you practice discriminative, evaluative, or appreciative listening.

2. Recognize when a speaker's message appears to call for the therapeutic role of empathic listening.

3. Realize that we make a conscious decision to listen empathically. Remember

that if you make that decision you must follow through with *genuine* concern and caring. Empathic listening can never be "faked."

4. Resolve to learn each strategy for improving empathic listening so you can use it during the actual empathic listening encounter.

5. SELF–LISTENING

Much writing about the power of our thoughts and the strength of "self-talk"[28] suggests that listening to that talk is a special kind of listening which we will call self–listening. This communication with ourselves affects how we communicate with others. Listening to our feelings about ourselves may indeed be a key to listening to others. Our own self-esteem and self-image often contribute to our willingness to listen, our attitude toward listening, and our level of empathy in listening.

Paul Kauffman, of Iowa State University, has described "listening to ourselves" in relation to organizational self–listening.[29] Kauffman states:

> If listening is the core ingredient to the effectiveness of a professional organization, it is also central to effectiveness on an individual level. . . . Just as in an organization, on an individual level, appropriate listening responses to others can take place only after listening and responding internally to ourselves. In short, we have to be secure and comfortable with ourselves before we can be secure and comfortable with others.

Daniel J. Anderson, president emeritus of the Hazelden Foundation, a nonprofit agency in Minneapolis which provides help for chemical dependency, believes self-listening is vitally important in changing self-talk messages from negative to positive. He discusses self-listening in relation to Albert Ellis's rational-emotive therapy (RET), which posits that people become distressed not because of external events — impending deadlines, a stock market crash — but because of their beliefs about such events.[30] Thus, the way we talk to ourselves and the way we listen to that talk can echo the words of Edmund Spenser:

> It is the mind that maketh good or
> That maketh wretch or happy, rich or poor.

Some Functions of Self–Listening

Self–listening can function in the role of changing self-image. RET suggests that we identify negative self-messages and replace them with positive messages. Similarly, Shad Helmstetter's "self-talk" regimen recommends creating a "self-talk script"[31] in which we repeat positive statements to ourselves over a period of time until our minds accept these positive messages as statements of who we are. Our minds can then make us "good, happy and enriched" if that is what we have told ourselves. In *Anatomy of an Illness* and *Head First*, Norman Cousins discusses the role self–listening played in his dramatic recovery from a rare disease of the connective tissues — and in those doctors and patients with whom he interacted during his years as a special consultant at a medical school.[32]

Bernie Siegel also has documented the power of self–listening in his work with cancer patients.[33] Siegel discovered that some patients lived in spite of all medical predictions to the contrary and sought to discover why. He learned that these patients told themselves they would or had to survive and *listened to the message*. He then set out to teach others what he called imaging and guided imagery, to help them create similar messages and to listen to them. Imaging involves making a taped message in which we describe ourselves in positive situations and then listening to it at regular intervals. Guided imagery uses a similar tape made by someone else — typically an expert in imagery — and listening to it.[34]

Helmstetter states:

> Far from being vague "nothings that go nowhere and do nothing," neuroscientists have learned that thoughts are electrical impulses that trigger electrical and chemical switches in the brain. Thoughts are not just psychological in nature, they are physiological — electro–chemical triggers that direct and affect the chemical activity in the brain.[35]

What are some steps we can take to become more aware of these electro–chemical impulses and to make use of them to improve our listening? Let us consider these.

Four Strategies for Improving Self–Listening

1. **Listen to our bodies**. How well we listen to our bodies depends upon how aware we are of our self-talk. In addition to the messages sent by our minds, we also receive messages from our bodies. Communication trainer Sandy Stein believes that our physical bodies regularly send messages which, if listened to, can save our lives. Shortly after surgery, she realized, listened and reported that her foot "felt like a meat loaf." In spite of such nontechnical description, her physicians listened to her and discovered a life-threatening blood clot.[36]

   Often we are sent messages from our blood vessels, heart, or lungs to which we do not listen. Dangers are discovered by listening to the messages our bodies send us.

2. **Reverse negative self-messages**. We can recognize negative self-messages and then deliberately change them to positive messages. Helmstetter believes self-talk (and, we believe, the corresponding self–listening) encompasses five levels.[37] Starting with the least beneficial, they are: (1) negative acceptance, (2) recognition of need to change, (3) decision to change, (4) "the better me," and (5) affirmation.

   As we perceptively listen to each level of self-talk, we can, at the response level, suggest the next level of achievement.

3. **Let self-listening lead to more perceptive listening to others**. If self–listening can lead to higher self-esteem, it can lead to better listening to others.

This level of self-esteem can be raised by practicing the preceding strategies. The listener whose self-esteem is high also can project respect for the message sender.

Just as empathic listening to a message sender can improve that sender's communication, we believe that empathic listening to ourselves can improve every level of our own communication.

4. **Set up self–listening practice programs**. We can tape positive self-messages — similar to Siegel's or Norman Cousins's — and listen to them every day, focusing on the positive elements of each. Karl Menninger said: "Listening is a magnetic and strange thing, a creative force. The friends who listen to us are the ones we move toward, and we want to sit in their radius. When we are listened to, it creates us, makes us unfold and expand."[38] We would add, self–listening also makes us unfold and expand.

Retraining: Guidelines to Improve Self–Listening

1. Recognize the role played by self–listening (intrapersonal listening) to self–talk messages.
2. Resolve to put effort into using self–listening strategies to change self–talk from negative to positive.
3. Take time to become aware of your body and become attuned to the messages it sends.

Listeners Determine the Kind of Listening

We determine the kind of listening we do based on the kind of message sent plus our own goal or purpose for listening. If we listen to a concert, we recognize that the performers intend to convey pleasure to the listeners. Most of us would listen for appreciation. However, listeners' goals may lead them to a different kind of listening. A student of music appreciation might be a discriminating listener who expects to learn enough from the performance to pass an examination. A music critic might be an evaluative listener wishing to appraise the performance for the morning edition of a newspaper.

Sometimes we decide not to listen at all. This is acceptable. When we consciously decide not to listen, we may miss a great deal in life — knowledge, a new point of view, pleasure, or the opportunity to help another. However, we miss these things by choice, and we must be willing to accept the fruits of that choice. The danger is to have meant to listen and then not to have done so, or to have responded to a speaker's message with inappropriate listening.

Generally, however, listeners will attempt to respond to the message with the corresponding listening role. If we do not, we can short-circuit the communication process. For example, if an instructor presents new ideas and we respond by listening for appreciation, we can be pleased but have learned very little. If a co-worker reveals personal difficulties and we respond by weighing evidence, drawing conclusions and making judgments, the speaker will be certain that we didn't listen at all.

We can avoid much of the well-publicized breakdown in communication by giving attention to the kinds of listening we do.

WRAPPING IT UP: A SUMMARY

We have identified five kinds of listening: discriminative listening to informative messages, evaluative listening to persuasive messages, appreciative listening to pleasurable messages, empathic listening to others' concerns in a variety of messages, and self–listening to our own minds and bodies.

Speakers identify the goal they intend to achieve with each kind of message sent. Listeners must likewise identify the goal they aim toward in each kind of listening they do.

Just as speakers employ specific strategies to ensure achieving their planned goal, so must listeners employ strategies. Such procedures can improve the quality of each kind of listening and increase the likelihood of attaining our goal in discriminative, evaluative, appreciative, empathic, and self–listening.

DISCUSSION AND STUDY GUIDES

1. Have you ever been involved in a communication situation that was not working because you made an inappropriate response to the speaker's purpose? What was the result?

2. Can you identify, in your own life, penalties of failure to identify your goal as a listener, such as poor performance reviews, accidents, broken friendships, family misunderstandings, boredom, buying something you neither wanted nor needed?

3. When you listen to persuasion do you evaluate the message by examining and determining its value to you, or do you set out to prove that the speaker's argument is ridiculous?

4. Can you remember a situation where you wanted an empathic response from another but the person did not seem to be listening? Describe your reactions.

5. When someone listens to you, does that person's listening skill influence how you feel about yourself? Explain.

LISTENING EXERCISES THAT WORK

EXERCISE 1. (Identifying Goals and Choosing Listening Strategies) During a period of one week, choose one of each kind of listening situation — discriminative, evaluative, appreciative, and empathic — and determine for each: What result did the speaker anticipate? What steps did the speaker take to achieve this goal? What result did you anticipate? What steps did you take to accomplish this goal? What rewards did you gain as a result of this goal identification?

EXERCISE 2. (Reaching Goals Through Appreciation) The next time you anticipate a demanding mental, emotional, or physical exercise, prepare for it by appreciative listening. Choose the aural stimuli you like best. Listen for as long as it takes you to reach a calm state of mind.

EXERCISE 3. (Using Silence to Communicate) Choose a "silent day" when you attempt to remain silent instead of speaking during several communication processes. Maintain eye contact but do not speak. Analyze the results. Do you think you made good use of silence? Do you think you could make better use of silence in the future? Identify specific areas where remaining silent at crucial times could enhance your listening performance.

EXERCISE 4. (Identifying Role of Self-Help Group) Arrange to visit a self-help group (Al-Anon, Children of Alcoholics, I Can Cope, etc.). Answer: What kind of empathic listening strategies can you observe? How do members appear to relate to each other? Do you think the members experienced enhanced self–esteem? Explain.

EXERCISE 5. (Identifying Communication Problems) Identify a major communication problem which you experience in your job. Be specific. Name the problem, the kind of listening you believe can best be used to deal with the problem, and give some suggestions for incorporating specific strategies for this kind of listening.

EXERCISE 6. (Using Empathic Listening) During the next two weeks, identify two situations where use of empathic listening skills improved communication. Without divulging names or personal details of the speaker's message, analyze and document what you did as an empathic listener. Include the speaker's goal, your goal, kind of nonverbal feedback used, way in which you used silence and in which you used questions, and analysis of what you did well. What could you have improved upon? Write a description of final results.

EXERCISE 7. (Reversing Negative Self-Image) Choose a communication skill which you believe you practice poorly and would like to improve. Write the statement of this skill in four separate sentences. Each of the sentences should fulfill one of these levels: negative self-acceptance, recognition of need to change, decision to change, and "a better me."

EXERCISE 8. (Improving Appreciative Listening) Choose an appreciative listening experience (play, concert, talk). Read as much as possible about the author, performer, and work of art. As you listen, decide: What is the most important thing happening in this work? What were some signals that this would be happening? Document whether you listened with your ears, eyes, spine, brain, heart.

EXERCISE 9. (Identifying Kinds of Listening) For a period of one week, identify as many listening situations as you can by designating each as discriminative, evaluative, appreciative, empathic, or self–listening. At the end of one week, analyze your results. Include: What kind of listening occurred most often? What difficulties did you encounter in deciding upon an appropriate listener response?

NOTES

1. David Kileffer, *How Did You Think of That? An Introduction to the Scientific Method* (Garden City, NY: Doubleday, 1969), 9.
2. Gordon I. Zimmerman, *Public Speaking Today* (St. Paul, MN: West, 1979), 224.
3. Otis M. Walter and Robert L. Scott, *Thinking and Speaking: A Guide to Intelligent Oral Communication* (New York: Macmillan, 1973), 66–75.
4. Paul E. Nelson and Judy C. Pearson, *Confidence in Public Speaking* (Dubuque, IA: Wm. C. Brown, 1981), 101.
5. Winston L. Brembeck and William S. Howell, *Persuasion: A Means of Social Influence*, 2nd ed. (Englewood Cliffs, NJ: Prentice-Hall, 1976), 19.
6. Ernest G. Bormann, William S. Howell, Ralph G. Nichols and George L. Shapiro, *Interpersonal Communication in the Modern Organization*, 2nd ed. (Englewood Cliffs, NJ: Prentice-Hall, 1982), 42.
7. Judy Pearson and Paul E. Nelson, *Understanding and Sharing: An Introduction to Speech Communication* (Dubuque, IA: Wm. C. Brown, 1979), 290–91.
8. Brembeck and Howell, 20.
9. Harold S. Kushner, *When Bad Things Happen to Good People* (New York: Schocken, 1981).
10. William Waack, "Appreciative Listening: The Aesthetic Experience," *Journal of the International Listening Association* 1 (Spring 1987), 80.
11. Charles R. Hoffer, *A Concise Introduction to Music Listening,* 4th ed. (Belmont, CA: Wadsworth, 1988), 2–3.
12. Sigurd F. Olson, *Listening Point* (New York: Knopf, 1958), 7.
13. Aristides, "The Ignorant Man's Guide to Serious Music," *The American Scholar* (Winter 1991), 8, 16.
14. Hoffer, 8.
15. Aristides, 8.
16. Susan Floyd Germek, Instructor of Music, Vermilion Community College, Ely, Minnesota, personal interview, December 1990.
17. Harold R. Dalrymple, "Theater as a Listening Laboratory," *Communication Education* 36 (July 1987), 283–86.
18. Waack, 83.
19. Hal A. Lingerman, *The Healing Energies of Music* (Wheaton, IL: Theosophical Publishing House, 1983), 79–81.
20. Bernie Siegel, *Love, Medicine and Miracles* (New York: Harper & Row, 1986).
21. Deanna Edwards, *Music Brings My Heart Back Home* (Salt Lake City, UT: Shadow Mountain Press, 1988).
22. Ronald C. Arnett and Gordon Nakagawa, "The Assumptive Roots of Empathic Listening: A Critique," *Communication Education* 32 (October 1983), 369.
23. William S. Howell, *The Empathic Communicator* (Belmont, CA: Wadsworth, 1982), 108.
24. Thomas Bruneau, "Empathy and Listening: A Conceptual Review and Theoretical Directions," *Journal of the International Listening Association* 3 (1989), 9.
25. Bormann, Howell, Nichols and Shapiro, 224–26.
26. Gayle G. Cluck and Rebecca J. Cline, "The Circle of Others: Self-Help Groups and the Bereaved," *Communication Quarterly* 34 (Summer 1986), 3–8.
27. Marvel Patton, "Meeting Together," *Herald of Hope* 13 (January 1991), 6; and Vickie Brower, "Facing Death and Living Longer: Support Groups that Deal with Dying Enhance — and Prolong — Death," *American Health* (May 1990), 40.
28. Shad Helmstetter, *What to Say When You Talk to Yourself* (Scottsdale, AZ: Grindle Press, 1989).
29. Paul J. Kauffman, *Sensible Listening* (Dubuque, IA: Kendall/Hunt, 1990), 49.
30. Daniel J. Anderson, "Changing Irrational Beliefs and Negative Self-Talk Is a Powerful Tool for Recovery," *Minneapolis Star and Tribune* (Tuesday, June 4, 1991), 7-E.
31. Shad Helmstetter, *The Self-Talk Solution* (New York: Simon & Schuster, 1987).

32. Norman Cousins, *Anatomy of an Illness* (New York: Norton, 1977), and *Head First*: *The Biology of Hope* (New York: Dutton, 1989).
33. Siegel, *Love, Medicine and Miracles*, and *Peace, Love and Healing* (New York: Harper & Row, 1989).
34. In addition to the works of Siegel and Cousins, readers may consult: Stephanie Mathews Simonton, O. Carl Simonton, and James I. Creighton, *Getting Well Again* (New York: Bantam Books, 1978), and Norman Vincent Peale, *Positive Imaging*: *The Powerful Way to Change Your Life* (New York: Random House, 1982).
35. Helmstetter, 1987, 14.
36. Sandy Stein, "Self-Listening" (Program presented at the International Listening Association Convention, Phoenix, AZ, 1989).
37. Helmstetter, 1989, 60–67.
38. Karl Menninger, *Love Against Hate* (New York: Harcourt, Brace, 1942), 275.

CHAPTER 6

THREE BASIC CONCEPTS TO ENHANCE LISTENING COMPREHENSION

I know you believe you understand what you think I said, but I am not sure you realize that what you heard is not what I meant.

—Anonymous

THESIS We can improve listening comprehension by preparing ourselves to listen (self-preparation), by visualizing messages with pictures in mind (PIM) and by using appropriate note-taking systems.

CHAPTER OBJECTIVES

1. Understand the importance of performing physical, mental, and emotional self-preparation to listen.
2. Learn how to use PIM (Pictures In Mind) in the STTD (Speech-Thought-Time Differential) listening time.
3. Decide which of seven note-taking systems to use during specific listening events.
4. Start immediate retraining to listen by focusing on the three basic concepts in this chapter.

CHAPTER PREVIEW

- Preparation to listen.
- Pictures In Mind (PIM).
- Expedient note-taking systems to use while listening.

"I bought the super–chunk peanut butter. I didn't know you asked me to get the creamy-smooth kind."

"How soon did the salesperson say this suit would be marked down for the spring sale?"

"Where will the next financial planner conference be held? I didn't understand the announcement."

These comments were made by listeners who were unprepared to listen and who lacked the techniques and skills to listen comprehensively.

Listening Comprehension

Aristotle claimed "when we learn a thing by using the faculty of knowing, we are said to 'understand' it."[1] However, in order to achieve the highest level of comprehension, we should recognize that we may never hope to understand fully what we listen to so long as we think we already do. Even Aristotle fell prey to the fatal mistake of thinking he knew, when in fact he didn't. British philosopher Bertrand Russell claimed that Aristotle could have avoided the mistake of thinking that women have fewer teeth than men by mere observation.[2]

We face a challenging task when we attempt to become truly effective listeners because we must adjust to speakers. Within a single oral presentation the speaker may require us to listen in most or all of the different ways as discussed in Chapter 5, Five Kinds of Listening We Do. For example, consider a college professor who begins an informative lecture (discriminative listening) with a humorous anecdote (appreciative listening). Later the professor asks a blind student to identify the major problems of the blind (empathic listening). Listening to the blind speaker, we individually ask ourselves, "If I were deprived of sight, would I be as courageous and confident as the blind student?" (self–listening). Finally, the professor winds up the lecture by convincing the class to attend a visiting speaker's address on a class-related topic (evaluative listening). Note what has happened. In one lecture, five kinds of messages were presented requiring us to apply the techniques of the five kinds of listening we frequently need to do. Both the speaker and the audience benefit when the listeners quickly identify the changing character of the message being conveyed. The students are then able to utilize all five types of effective listening responses. Each response is made according to the context of the material being presented. And the speaker receives meaningful feedback as indicating the message is being processed and understood. This is what we mean by *listening comprehension*. When we employ it we vastly improve communicative efficiency.

Listening comprehensively is difficult when speakers deliberately play games with us to complicate messages. For example, some years ago when Joe Medwick was in his prime with the St. Louis Cardinals, he toured Europe with a group of entertainers. When they reached Rome, Pope Pius granted the troupe an audience and asked each the nature of his business.

"I'm a comedian," answered one.

"I'm a singer," replied another.

Then came Medwick's turn. With simple dignity he said, "Your Holiness, I'm a Cardinal."

Writer James Barber implies that, above all, the president of the United States should listen comprehensively. The president should listen *to* the people, not *in on them*. Franklin Delano Roosevelt was fond of listening to and then sharing with the cabinet the investigative reports on timely issues that were prepared by his wife, Eleanor. Politicians described Roosevelt as "a ganglion for reception, expression, transmission, combination, and realization."[3] He listened. Having listened comprehensively, he skillfully undertook the politics of persuasion about timely issues.

Other presidents showed a lack of interest or ability in listening comprehensively. For example, President Richard Nixon once remarked, "I had to build a shield around myself." Actually he wanted to keep away the overwhelming flood of information in which a president can get lost. Watergate witness John Mitchell stated that Nixon failed to listen or move to action when informed of political activities that might be fatal. Nixon earned the reputation of conducting meetings not to listen and learn, but to instruct.[4] Possibly, Nixon did not recognize the need to take time or prepare to listen comprehensively. He failed to reap the reward of understanding his constituents and the nation's problems and needs.

To listen comprehensively we can learn to apply three basic concepts: self-preparation to listen, PIM (pictures in mind), and expedient note–taking techniques.

CONCEPT 1: SELF-PREPARATION TO LISTEN

Performing Self-Preparation to Listen Comprehensively

An indifferent attitude toward the actual kind and amount of self-preparation required to listen comprehensively creates one of the most powerful deterrents to successful listening. Because we lack formal instruction in listening, most of us fail to realize the importance of *preparing ourselves* to listen. Many don't know how to prepare. But there is hope. Psychologists report that one way to achieve a habit is to behave as if we already have acquired that habit. To do so, we need to understand the concept. Let's begin by examining the terms in Definition Box 3.

DEFINITION BOX 3: Terms Relating to Self-Preparation to Listen

listening situation: the specific location, circumstances, or conditions in which the listening experience occurs

impromptu listener: one who unexpectedly assumes the role of listener and actively participates in the receptive process of listening to interpret the speaker's intended message

prospective listener: one who anticipates fulfilling the role of the efficient listener at some future time

self-preparation to listen: the overall analysis and modification of the prospective listener's physical, mental and emotional state for the accomplishment of a listening task

planned self-preparation to listen: the prospective listener's effort to prepare to listen competently during a particular scheduled event

on-the-spot listening: assuming the role of listener during an unexpected encounter or event

spontaneous self-preparation to listen: the impromptu listener's on-the-spot effort to prepare to listen competently during an unexpected listening episode

> **emotional masking**: repressing or falsely expressing feelings toward the speaker
> **aural masking**: withholding or concealing a genuine response to the speaker
> **cognitively structuring**: reinforcing patterns in the brain
> **dyadic encounter**: one-to-one communication
> **small group**: interaction of five to seven persons
> **public address**: one person speaking to an audience at a formal gathering

It is crucial that both impromptu and prospective listeners realize the benefits derived from self-preparation. The more extensive the self-preparation, the better the listening results.

Physical Self-Preparation to Listen Comprehensively

Basic physical preparation to listen comprehensively begins with our general health. The ability to listen is contingent upon our overall physical condition and level of energy.

Listening is exceedingly hard work. Efficient listeners experience increased heart action, faster circulation of the blood, and even slightly increased bodily temperature. By contrast, inefficient listeners often are unable to expend the energy required in a listening situation. They are unchallenged by the physical demands made upon them.

Exhausted Jim Lost Out. Jim, a top-notch sales rep of a Chicago data-processing equipment corporation, experienced the devastating results of being physically unprepared to listen. He had played poker, smoked, eaten, and drunk beer until 3:00 A.M. The following day he kept an important appointment with the processing manager of a large insurance company, his major account. Jim could barely keep his eyes open as he tried to listen to his client explaining a problem arising from an auxiliary memory storage unit purchased from Jim's corporation. Noting Jim's bleary-eyed expression and persistent yawns, the manager finally asked, "Am I boring you?" Unfortunately, Jim, too exhausted to listen, was unprepared to answer. He continued to transmit a series of nonverbal messages that his customer mistakenly interpreted to mean, "Look, Sam, I'm tired of filling your order. Why don't you take your business elsewhere?" Within a matter of minutes, the irritated corporate manager decided to return the storage unit. It was the last order that Jim ever wrote for that customer. Jim learned an important lesson too late. A body physically unprepared to listen houses a brain unfit for listening.

Jim ignored several of the following suggestions for physical self-preparation to listen.

Suggestions for Physical Self-Preparation to Listen

Carole Grau, an educator and active member of the International Listening Association, offers the following suggestions for physical self-preparation to listen:[5]

- Settle down to the projected task and seat yourself comfortably (not overly so) where you can easily hear and see the speaker.
- Organize yourself (have writing and other required materials ready).
- Reduce distractions through environment control: adjust for lighting, vision, room temperature, and sound level.
- Be fully rested.

Health experts across the country say that Americans are cramming too much into busy schedules and not getting enough sleep. Note the following results of sleep deprivation research and consider the far-reaching effect on listening comprehension.

- In Detroit, a 1988 study of 130 people from 21 to 35 years old found that 40 percent were not getting adequate sleep and were sleepy during the day; 16 percent were "seriously sleepy."
- In California, two studies involving 3,000 students at San Jose State University found that the number of hours students spend sleeping dropped from 7.3 in 1978 to 6.8 in 1988.
- In Rhode Island, a study of 3,000 high school students in the 1988-89 school year showed that 58.7 percent of them worked parttime jobs which — along with extracurricular activities — were regularly robbing many of them of sleep. Scores of students reported falling asleep in class.[6]

Dr. Jane Fry, director of the Sleep Disorders Center at the Medical College of Pennsylvania, said, "The sleep problem is probably much worse than anyone realizes or knows. This is not an illness. This is a self-inflicted problem that is quite dangerous. . . . Probably half of the occupational accidents are caused by sleepiness and decreased alertness and concentration."[7]

Timothy Roehrs, research director at the Sleep Disorders Center at Henry Ford Hospital in Detroit, claims there is a cultural attitude that it's macho to decrease the hours of sleep and that the people who do so are the people who are successful. Mary A. Carskadon, director of chronobiology at the E. P. Bradley Hospital in Providence, Rhode Island, said "a casual approach to sleep is learned early on. So teen-agers don't really plan for sleep in their schedule."[8]

Sound-Sleep Advice for Snoozers and Prospective Listeners

Kevin Huban, a clinical psychologist and sleep specialist, explains, "People need to realize that sleep is a physiological need just like food and drink, and they need to put it as a priority in life to maintain performance." Consider the following sleep-inducing tips to dreamland:

- Limit yourself to one or two cups of coffee a day; quit drinking it 12 hours prior to bedtime.
- If you drink alcohol, limit yourself to one or two drinks a day; stop three hours prior to bedtime.

- Go to bed only when really sleepy in a bedroom with a temperature of 64°–66°F.
- Don't use your bedroom as an office. Spend no more than 20 minutes in bed without sleeping, then get up and do relaxing activities (read, watch TV, listen to soothing music) until feeling sleepy, then return to bed.
- Don't perform stressful activities in bed (paying bills, watching suspenseful TV programs, working on reports).
- Refuse to worry about falling asleep once you go to bed; instead, try to relax with special kinds of exercise (see next section).
- Remember to use falling-asleep-time to daydream and reinforce your goals (see Chapter 4, Five Power Tools of Listening).

We who are retraining to perform as holistic perceptive listeners (those who use *both* hemispheres of the brain to decode verbal and nonverbal messages) must realize the effect of sleep deprivation on self-preparation to listen and overall listening behavior. In addition to adequate sleep, exercise is a beneficial activity to use in self-preparation to listen.

Impromptu Exercises for Self-Preparation

A type of exercise providing added energy in preparing to listen is what your authors refer to as impromptu exercises. These can be performed unobtrusively in any listening setting while providing stimulation and extra energy for the listening act. This added energy induced by mental and physical activity can help to reduce stress and brief periods of depression that disrupt the listening process.

- Finger-Toe: While standing or sitting, form a tight fist then open the hand wide stretching the fingers. At the same time, tightly curl the toes under then stretch outward. Coordinate the finger-toe movements. Repeat ten times.
- Tighten-Hold-Release: Keeping the heels of the feet flat, lift both feet as high as possible inside the shoes; hold for five seconds then lower the feet. Repeat five times. Concentrate to tighten the calves; hold for five seconds and release. Repeat five times. Follow the same procedure for the thighs, buttocks, abdomen, and chest.
- Shoulder-Roll: Bring shoulders inward and to the front. Holding the front position, raise shoulders as high as possible. Holding the front-high position, move shoulders straight back. Holding the high, straight back position, lower the shoulders. Repeat the shoulder roll five times.
- Abdominal Breathing: Looking down, inhale deeply and watch as you push out the abdominal area; hold the breath for three seconds. Slowly exhale and watch the abdominal area retract. Repeat five times.
- Posture: Frequently straighten the spine and, with chin inward, imagine the top of the head pushing toward the ceiling. Repeat the straightened, upward position until it becomes a permanent sitting and standing position.

Design other exercises you can perform unobtrusively on the job to generate added energy. And at home immediately before retiring, practice the following relaxation exercises to induce restful sleep.

Relaxation Exercises to Induce Sleep

- Clear the Brain: Lie in a darkened room and listen to soft, soothing music. Close your eyes. Imagine that you are placing each unresolved problem or concern in a large box. Tape the lid closed and toss the box into outer space. Remember the good things that happened to you last year, last month, last week, and today (if any). Reflect on these events. Then whisper repeatedly, "I intend to fall asleep reflecting on these memories."

- Abdominal Breathing: Remove pillows from the bed and lie flat on your back. Feel your body nestle against the mattress. Close your eyes. Pretend you are gliding on the surface of smooth, warm, blue water. Place your hands on your abdominal area. As you slowly and deeply inhale, feel your hands rise as you extend the abdomen. Hold your breath for three seconds. Slowly exhale as the hands are lowered with the abdomen. Repeat five times.

- Relaxed Body: Continue with deep abdominal breathing. Close your eyes. Concentrate on the top of your head, forehead, and eyes. As you do, slowly repeat, "Relax, relax, relax." Concentrate on your nose, mouth, and bottom half of the face. Again repeat, "Relax, relax, relax." Repeat the same routine for the shoulder, arms, and chest; the abdominal, pelvic, and hip areas; the thighs, knees, and legs; and the ankles and feet. Be sure to feel the relaxation before moving to the next body area. Conclude the exercise by whispering, "Relax, sleep, relax, sleep."

Now let's examine mental self-preparation to listen comprehensively.

Mental Self-Preparation to Listen Comprehensively

The prospective and impromptu listener can use either extended (planned) or brief (on-the-spot) self-preparation time. We use it to reinforce our determination to be attentive and to concentrate only on the speaker and the message in each encounter. However, an important part of self-preparation to listening in any situation consists of steadily increasing our mental capacity to do so.

Increasing Mental Capacity to Listen

In addition to controlling the thought patterns of the mind, we can prepare ourselves to listen by increasing our mental capacity. This can be achieved by: (1) increasing our vocabulary, (2) broadening our life experiences, and (3) studying and attempting to understand human nature.

By adding to our vocabulary, we increase the number of cognitions stored in the brain and thus expand its cognitive structures. Daily we come into contact with thousands of the estimated 500,000 words in the English language. However, we use relatively few words in spite of the fact that language is the one art experience that most humans share. Pocket dictionaries usually cite more than 50,000 words, of which only 20,000 are commonly used. Unfortunately, few of us work diligently to increase our vocabulary. Yet by *cognitively structuring* (reinforcing patterns in the brain) word meanings, we refine the communication skills of reading, writing, speaking, and listening. We increase our capacity to listen. Also, we are involved in preparing ourselves to listen more comprehensively.

We also can increase the mental capacity to listen as we broaden our life experiences by traveling, reading, writing, speaking, listening, and getting involved in challenging and innovative experiences. One who has completed a basic course in computer science or who has visited a computer center can listen with keener understanding to messages including such words as *input, output, terminal, memory core*, and *floppy disks*. By perceiving intently and participating enthusiastically in daily events, we add to our storehouse of knowledge. We increase our capacity to listen.

Finally, we can increase our intellectual capacity to listen by studying and gaining further insight into human nature. Human behavior is predictable. Acquiring a broad spectrum of knowledge from the study of anthropology, psychology, sociology, theology, and communication better prepares us to listen to and understand each other, to resolve problems, and to live harmoniously. One of the most valuable aspects of the Olympic Games is that competitors represent the many nations and different cultures of the world yet exemplify the universal nature of humankind. Realizing this in the light of our own nature and behavior, we become able to reach out and communicate with greater understanding and empathy.

Let us examine each of five useful tools available to the person preparing to listen.

Tools for Self-Preparation to Listen

Expected and unexpected listening acts occur in a hodgepodge of situations. This complicates the task of preparing for the process. However, we can clarify the focus and direction of preparing to listen by considering five questions. *Why* prepare to listen? *What* do we prepare beforehand? *How* do we prepare? *Where* do we prepare? *When* do we prepare? These familiar queries can help us to prepare for productive listening. Listening episodes may be brief or extended, casual or serious, and personal or impersonal. They may occur as we listen alone and during dyadic interactions, small group discussions, and formal public presentations.

Why Prepare to Listen?

Anthropologists, psychologists, communication specialists, and professionals in related disciplines agree that communication is a fundamental human need. The quality of listening, the communicative skill used most frequently throughout our lives, affects the end results of oral–aural communication in any situation. It is obvious why responsible individuals feel an urgency to prepare themselves for the process. To the familiar cliché, "Talk is cheap," we should add, quite truthfully, "But listening is priceless."

Without willing listeners who prepare to attend and respond to the speaker's intended messages, the fundamental need of humans to communicate orally remains mostly unanswered. We use language to fullfill most of our basic needs and creative drives. Therefore, we expect competent persons to prepare to listen in a miscellany of foreseeable and unforeseeable situations.

What Do We Do to Prepare to Listen?

Two vital components in the listening experience comprise *what* to include in self-preparation to listen: the *listener* and the *listening environment*.

The productive listener fulfills the primary obligation to maintain and safeguard physical and mental health. Nevertheless, both impromptu and prospective listeners enjoying excellent physical and mental health are wise to spend time in self-preparation. Both should examine and, if necessary, adjust their attitudes and feelings toward those with whom they communicate.

The second important facet of what we do to prepare ourselves to listen is the anticipated or predictable listening environment. The medium through which messages are transmitted is an essential part of that environment. We most commonly send oral–aural messages through air waves at home, in the classroom, at the plant or office, and for electronic transmission by radio and television.

How Do We Prepare to Listen?

Competent listeners prepare themselves by anticipating how the role of listener might be affected according to the different contexts or specific situations of the listening experience. We prepare ourselves differently when we anticipate listening alone. Most of us will then be in control of the immediate environment.

Advanced technology in radio transmission has increased the number of lone listeners. Dr. Jack C. Rang, Professor of Communication at the University of Dayton and media expert, notes that in the 1980s the 50 top radio markets in the United States listed "easy listening" or "beautiful music" as the most frequently chosen radio programs. Today's hottest radio program features "adult contemporary music" attracting the "baby boomer" adults who enjoy listening to popular music of the '60s, '70s and '80s. Rang indicates that radio will continue to function as a lifelong learning tool by broadcasting the news and special features of timely topics.[9]

How we prepare to listen alone differs dramatically from how we prepare to listen during dyadic or person-to-person encounters, the most common mode of communication. In this structure, the listener expects the perception of aural stimuli to be affected by the presence of and interaction with another person, the personalized transmission of unexpected verbal and nonverbal messages, and less stringent control over the situation itself.

We prepare ourselves to listen during a dyadic encounter to understand and interact with our best friend, an employer, a minister, or a sales clerk. Thus we need to anticipate the other person's physical, psychological, and intellectual needs.

When we anticipate listening and interaction in a small group, we focus a major part of our self-preparation on acquiring an understanding of the unique process of small–group communication. The group process of making decisions remains one of the most potent tools of communication in our society. Perceptive listening is a dominant factor in its success. In his book *Small–Group Communication in Orga- nizations*, H. Lloyd Goodall, Jr. defines "small group" as five to seven persons interacting regularly in a specific context with a set agenda to accomplish a goal. The size in organizations can vary with the nature of the task. Quality circles, for instance, may include as few as four or as many as fifteen group participants. Goodall predicts: "Organizations will increase the use of small groups and thus need more and better trained small group communicators to meet the demands of technology and decision-making in the future. . . . How you learn to communicate to achieve cooperation, consensus, and participation will determine how the future unfolds and affects you."[10]

We have barely touched on the broad spectrum of group dynamics theory.[11] Our purpose has been to encourage prospective listeners to prepare themselves for holistic listening and acquire a "get–set feeling" for each group session.

Finally, we must plan to prepare to listen during public address, a mode of communication during which the speaker presents a prepared message for a sus- tained time to a sizable number of people. Unlike listening alone or in dyadic and group structures, the participants do not become involved in the speaker–listener reversal of roles. There is limited nonverbal exchange — eye contact, head nods, frowns, or applause — however, listeners remain listeners, and speakers remain speakers. Occasionally a prearranged public address format permits members of the audience to interrupt the speaker to ask pertinent questions. However, this is the exception rather than the rule.

When and Where Do We Prepare to Listen?

The time and place for preparing ourselves for listening differ with each person and each anticipated event.

Naturally, the quality and extent of either planned or spontaneous self- preparation affect the outcomes of all listening experiences. Time schedules regulate most of our activities, including listening. We note on our desk calendar the time of a special community meeting. There concerned taxpayers may listen and partici- pate in discussion of a controversial tax-levy proposal. As part of our self-prepara- tion to listen, we should arrange adequate time to read about the proposal. We should inquire about the speakers who will support and oppose the debatable levy. We prospective listeners often can plan and accomplish self-preparation at our convenience before the event itself.

Many listening experiences cannot be planned. They may be entirely unexpected. Under such circumstances, what can we do to enhance listening efficiency? At best, we revert to on-the-spot preparation by concentrating physical and mental energy into a state of readiness to permit good performance.

Emotional Self-Preparation to Listen

Emotional self-preparation to listen means "readiness to control anticipated feelings during a listening event." For example, Barbara prepares herself for an early morning meeting with a supervisor who will discuss Barbara's application for an upgraded position. She and six men are the only applicants.

During emotional self-preparation time, Barbara plans to control feelings of frustration and anger if she is not offered the position. Objectively, she will listen to the supervisor's reasons supporting such a decision. She will not ask herself, "Is the reason that I am not offered the position because of the supervisor's prejudicial attitude toward women and unfair assessment of my application?" Instead, Barbara will plan to ask for a specific explanation supporting the negative decision. She will listen objectively to learn how on-the-job performance can be improved to qualify her for an upgraded position in the future.

If Barbara receives the position, she will listen to learn how the performance record qualifies her for the position. Then she can plan for future development in her career.

Focusing on emotional self-preparation to listen enables us to empty our minds of thoughts and feelings unfairly directed toward an anticipated speaker or message. Psychologically we are unprepared to listen comprehensively if we are occupied with emotional self-listening stimuli that outweigh the speaker's message. But it is difficult to set aside personal anxieties and other immediate concerns.

How can we free the mind of anxiety? We can substantially achieve it during most listening episodes by making a prior analysis of our own practical and selfish motives for involving ourselves in the situation. What was our original motive in being involved? Does it still hold true? What do we stand to gain or lose by striving for an open mind during the moments ahead? Do we have a real concern for the reactions of the speaker? All in all, do the gains outweigh the losses? If so, is there any doubt that putting our own house in order will enhance our capacity to perform as impromptu or prospective listeners? These questions deserve our careful attention.

Emotional Masking and Listening

Emotional masking means we repress or falsely express our feelings toward the speaker. Unfortunately, early in life most of us learn to use oral and aural masks which hide our true feelings.

Conversing with an old friend may be very enjoyable until she accidentally spills a cup of tea on an expensive couch. A host could suggest immediately cleaning up the tea to prevent a permanent stain. However, an insecure host might be tempted to revert to *oral masking* by saying, "Oh, don't worry; it's no problem; I'll remove the spot later." At this point, the host masks feelings of frustration and anger over the possibility of the best piece of furniture being marred. The conversation is being filtered through the aural masks of the concerned host.

Aural masking is a form of dichotic or "two-ear" listening. The host uses one ear for listening to the conversation. But the other ear is used for intrapersonal (inner) listening to frustrated thoughts: "Anyone should be able to drink a cup of tea without spilling it" or "Will she ever leave so I can remove the stain before it dries?" The initial warmth of the conversation between the two friends melts away. Unable to understand the oral and aural masking in the conversation after the spilled-tea incident, the friend departs, bewildered by the sudden change in her good friend's behavior.

We project a great deal of oral and aural emotional masking in the home. When asked to sweep the garage, cut the grass, or do the dishes, a child might decode messages with aural masks. "Why always *me* and not Sam?" "I *hate* sweeping the garage, cutting the grass, and doing the dishes." Quickly, the child conceals true feelings with an oral mask. "Gosh, Mom, I can't do those jobs now; I have tons of homework to do for tomorrow." All of us — parents, children, peers, managers, workers, and professionals — need to prepare ourselves to try to communicate without making or falsifying our true feelings.

Retraining: Guidelines for Self-Preparation to Listen

- Recover from an unexpected encounter quickly. Get to the job of listening.
- Use the few seconds of self-preparation time wisely. Activate the left and right hemispheres of the brain immediately by concentrating on decoding the speaker's verbal and nonverbal messages.
- If you decide to participate in the spontaneous dyadic or small–group interaction, do so sincerely. Half-hearted attempts at listening degrade speakers.
- If possible, end spontaneous listening events on an upbeat note for yourself and the speaker.

For the Prospective Listener During Planned Listening Events:

- Arrange for self-preparation listening time in accordance with the nature and complexity of the listening event. Learn in advance as much as possible about the topic, speaker, setting, and the professional, social, or academic listening event.

CONCEPT 2: PICTURES IN MIND (PIM)

Terms commonly used in reference to PIM (Pictures In Mind) are mental images and imagery, visual images and imagery, and visualization. In order to understand the PIM concept, we need to learn the related terms listed in Definition Box 4.

DEFINITION BOX 4:   Terms Relating to PIM as Used in the Process of Listening

create: bring into being in the mind — listening to and visualizing a description of a brick ranch house

re–create: to make anew — listeners mentally write, draw, or paint designs representing major words of the speaker's message

visual: the sense of sight — listening to clarify the interpretation of messages by observing the speaker's observable behavior

visualization: a mental image or design — learning to apply PIM as an integrated part of the listening process

image: a reproduction of the appearance of someone or something — visualizing the speaker's message

mental image: an in-the-mind picture of something not real or present — listening at a memorial service and recalling the face of a loved one

imagery: using vivid descriptions in speaking to produce mental pictures — listening to details of a violent murder

imagination: the ability to deal creatively with reality — thinking of ways to shorten the search for a "sharp" corporate chief executive officer

productive or creative imagination: the mental power to form concepts beyond those derived from external objects — listening to projections of living conditions on a space station of the future

reproductive or re–creative imagination: using the mind to form images or concepts of external objects — visualizing the new car you'll be driving on Monday

fantasy: an imagined event or condition fulfilling a wish — listening to a travel agent's suggestions for an exciting vacation and longing to go despite the prohibitive cost

PIM (Pictures In Mind): a concept enabling the listener to mentally re–create an intangible into a tangible — and any abstraction (the speaker's "created" message) into a meaningful mental image written, drawn or painted by the "fantasy artist" in the brain.

Author Ernest Parker Mills reminds us of the basics of communication: the ability of both the speaker and listener to form the same picture in their minds — to share an idea understood in the same perspective by both parties. Imagery enables listeners to transfer words into colorful images. The process requires conscious effort. The elderly may be more word-oriented and find it difficult to visualize bright, clear images without words.[12] Having been taught to use the word-oriented left hemisphere of the brain, your grandparents may have difficulty designing pictures in the mind, the type of thinking processed by the right hemisphere of the brain.

Author Earl Koile says that, for him, listening to someone becomes visual. He sees pictures as he hears words, as he believes most people do.[13] For example, listening to a friend describing Mount Vernon or the Tower of London, one visualizes the serenity of the plantation or the heavily guarded crown jewels displayed in the Tower. Each listener creates a unique PIM to decode and interpret the message.

To successfully use PIM while listening, we need to extend our brain power not by accident, but by design. Jacquelyn Wonder and Priscilla Donovan indicate this can be done — that *you can think how you think*. In addition to the split-brain functions charted in Chapter 4, Five Power Tools of Listening, we can recognize the following thinking activities to develop more right-brain processing of PIM.[14]

Split–Brain Activities for PIM

LEFT TO RIGHT	RIGHT TO LEFT
shift phone to left ear (controlled by right brain) for holistic listening	shift phone to right ear (controlled by left brain) for analytical listening
singing, humming, joking, chuckling	asking questions, making puns
drawing, coloring, or printing via PIM	working with outlines, solving math problems
breathing deeply until relaxed	doing calisthenics for a prescribed time
being aware of surrounding aroma, color, sound, etc.	valuing precise efforts and behavior
visualizing green for freedom to glide and soar	thinking amber or yellow to slow down

As Fritz Perls, founder of Gestalt therapy (a unified physical, psychological and symbolic treatment) explains: "The pictures of the world do not enter us automatically, but selectively. We don't look for, search, or scan for something. We don't hear all the sounds of the world — we listen."[15]

As we become more skilled in directing whole–brain thinking in performing holistic perceptive listening, we can use PIM to overcome a common weakness — the inability to remember names.

Using PIM (Pictures In Mind) to Listen to and Learn Names

Using PIM to listen to learn names has evolved from memory systems dating back to antiquity. Early Greek and Roman orators relied on trained memory to deliver lengthy speeches with unfailing accuracy. Actually, they used a form of PIM by associating different parts of a speech with parts of their homes (called *loci*). The speech introduction might be the front door; the second thought, the foyer; the third thought, a piece of furniture in the foyer, etc.[16]

Centuries ago Aristotle claimed that the mind never thinks without a mental picture. As we listen to the words, "tennis shoes" and "fax machine," a mental picture of each item flashes in the mind for a split second — provided these tangible items are in our realm of experience.

Memory experts Harry Lorayne and Jerry Lucas remind us that we recognize faces more readily than names. Seldom do we say or listen to, "Oh, I know your name, but I don't recognize your face." Rather, it is the reverse, "Oh, I know your face but can't remember your name." Using the PIM concept we can rely on the speaker's face to tell us the name.

Seven basic rules of the Lorayne–Lucas Memory System should be applied when listening to learn names with PIM. These are noted in Concept Box 1.[17]

We have applied a workable memory system to learn and remember the name of Ben Bentavania, which we classify as an N-P (Nonexisting-PIM) name. Names labeled E-P (Existing-PIM) are those with PIM contained in the name.

CONCEPT 1: Using PIM (Pictures In Mind) to Listen to and Learn Names

Original Awareness: Anything we wish to learn and remember must be observed; anything of which we originally are aware *cannot be forgotten*. Mostly, we fail to direct attention to observe and listen to learn names as they are spoken. Rather, we permit them to flit by the mind's ears unobserved rather than to focus attention on Mr. Bentavania whom we've just met.

Association: We can remember any new piece of information if it is connected to something we already know or remember. We associate two words with Mr. Bentavania's name (bent van) as our artist draws a picture of a van bent at the top.

Linking: By using the linking system, we connect PIM to a prominent feature of Mr. Bentavania's face—deep, excessive wrinkles. These are the roads traveled by the bent van.

Substitute Words: We use substitute words for data that seems abstract or intangible to us. We need to think of something that sounds like or reminds us of the abstract data to be pictured in the mind. Most names are intangible. For *Bentavania*, we substitute the words *bent van*. For his first name, *Ben*, we substitute the word *bends* typical of crooked roads highlighting the wrinkles in his face.

Out of Proportion: Make objects larger than life—in fact, extremely large or gigantic—and make the picture ridiculous. See a huge bent van riding on roads with extremely dangerous curves and bends on Ben Bentavania's face while listening to his initial comments.

Exaggeration: See the PIM items in excessive numbers—in hundreds or thousands. See hundreds of Ben Bentavania's deeply wrinkled faces with countless bent vans recklessly speeding down roads with hundreds of bends.

Action: Since action is easy to remember, fill the pictures in mind with action. The many bent vans are speeding at 500 miles an hour around thousands of bends in crooked roads embedded in a mass of facial wrinkles. Imagine the smell and sound of burning tires and screeching brakes.

E-P (Existing-PIM) and N-P (Nonexisting-PIM) Names

The amount of effort required to use PIM to listen to and learn names depends on two general categories of PIM: the E-P names with built-in PIM and requiring minimal recreative design; and the N-P names with no built-in PIM and requiring a unique, re–creative design, as our fantasy artists designed for Ben Bentavania.

Obviously the E-P names are easier to learn and retain in short-term memory than the N-P names.

Memory expert Chesley V. Young classifies names under different headings, five of which are: occupational, descriptive, names of things, names of places, and names of products.[18] These divisions automatically provide us with E-P names. Note the following examples of E-P names and the respective built-in PIM designs:

• Occupational E-P Names: Ms. Baker, Barber, Bishop, Brewer, Carpenter, Carter, Cooper, Tinker, Usher, Woodman, etc.

- Descriptive E-P names: Mr. Bold, Dark, Darling, Klinger, Long, Small, Stout, Short, English, Scott, Welch, etc.
- E-P Names of Things: The Rev. Fox, Lamb, Wolf, Crane, Dove, Crow, Ball, Bell, Bush, Cash, Diamond, Locke, Pitcher, Temple, etc.
- E-P Names of Places: Dr. London, Berlin, Fitch (Fitchburg, MA), Myers (Myerstown, PA), Gains (Gainesville, FL), Harmon (NY), Marion (KS), Barstow (CA), etc.
- E-P Names of Products: Mrs. Armour, Borden, Campbell, Dodge, Ford, Heinz, Hershey, Hertz, Hilton, Kellogg, Libby, Lipton, Morton, Post, Van Camp, etc.

While most bearers of these names do not reflect the name meanings, listeners can learn names by using the memory system to link the existing PIM with faces. For example, Ms. Baker's family and occupation are not connected with the baking industry, however, one ridiculous PIM linking the Baker name to Ms. Baker's face might be to focus on her large brown eyes: Rolling out of her eyes are millions of chocolate–chip cookies. Existing pictures in mind serve as handy tools of listening to learn names.

Listening to Learn N-P (Nonexisting-PIM) Names

Nonexisting-PIM or N-P names require the attention of our fantasy artists to expedite learning these names. The following are examples of N-P names with ideas for substitute words to link to faces.[19]

Substitute Words for Linking Names to Faces

Smolenski	smo-len-ski	a small lens camera skiing
Caruthers	car-u-thers	a car with udders
Pukczyva	puk-shiva	a hockey puck shivering
Esposito	es-po-si-to	expose a toe
Robinson	ro-bin-son	a robin and its son

Picturable equivalents are images generated by the sound of names and linked to the face.

Picturable Equivalents to Link Names to Faces

Petrocelli	pe-tro-cel-li	your pet rowing a cello
Chesnavich	ches-na-vich	chase no witch
Weidecke	wi-de-ke	wider key
Bartosiewics	bart-a-se-vitch	bought a savage
Hogan	ho-gan	whoa again

Once the word substitutes or pictorial equivalents have been identified, the imagination of the fantasy artist takes over. The data is linked to an outstanding feature of the person's face: lines in forehead; large nose; cleft in chin; bulging eyes; full cheeks; long, wide sideburns; high forehead; creases from nostrils to mouth; and thick lips.

Other suggestions for listening to learn names are:

- Listen to the name and immediately divide it into syllables; use PIM to see each syllable.
- Inwardly repeat the syllabized name three times (silent rehearsal).
- Use the name. After silent rehearsal of the name, say, "Mr. Bentavania, is there a Ben Bentavania family in. . . ?"
- Use the name at least two more times during the conversation.

While the PIM concept is a helpful tool to use when listening to learn names, health providers use the tool for healing and control of disease.

Using PIM (Pictures In Mind) in Medical Treatment

Marian Hall, director of psychology at Children's Health Center, Minneapolis, stresses the therapeutic value of using PIM for relaxation and pain control. She claims that mental pictures help children and adults organize experience, generate creativity, register and remember what is pleasant and exclude what is painful. PIM has a lot of "rehearsal value" allowing us to deal with conflict or other concerns on our minds.

Hall noted one heart patient unable to sleep at night for fear of not awakening in the morning. Hall asked the patient to use PIM and make an audio tape of his favorite place. As he described his grandfather's cabin by a lake, his fear of death subsided. Hall advised the patient, "Go to sleep thinking about this happy scene. When you awaken, you will be without fear and hungry for breakfast."[20] She encourages other staff members at the Center to use PIM as a tool for working with patients.

A nurse was troubled about how to respond to a gravely ill, 12-year-old boy. Not knowing how much the parents wanted him to know, the nurse began talking about their mutual interest in riding dirt bikes. After both had recounted exciting travels on their bikes, the boy finally said to the nurse, "What you're trying to tell me is the only way I can ride my dirt bike is in my imagination."

The shared imagery of the dirt bike in both brains created a feeling of acceptance and comfort. It was more acceptable and comforting for the dying boy to know he could ride his dirt bike in his imagination rather than knowing he probably had only a short time to live.

Hall is concerned that schools don't value or provide time for daydreaming and fantasy. This part of creative thinking generated in the right hemisphere of the brain (as discussed in Chapter 4, Five Power Tools of Listening) receives less attention than the perception-focused thinking of the left hemisphere of the brain. However, she cautions that we can't be sure that children or adults sitting passively are doing creative thinking.[21]

Physician Bernard S. Siegel suggests using channels of intrapersonal communication to send "live" messages to the body to promote healing:[22]

- Use Emotion to Stimulate the Immune System. Siegel tells his patients, "If you want to die, stay depressed; if you want to live, then love and laugh." Positive emotions like love, acceptance, and forgiveness stimulate the immune system.
- Use PIM by visualizing the healing process taking place in your body.
- Select symbols to represent the cancer cells and white blood cells. Siegel suggests thinking of the cancer cells as morsels of food and your white blood cells as birds, kittens, or any food-eating image you feel comfortable with.
- Close your eyes, quiet your mind, and play out the action in your mind. The action is imagining the white blood cells gobbling up the cancer cells. The more they eat, the stronger you become. In this way the disease becomes a source of personal strength and psychological growth.
- Repeat the exercise at least six times a day to maximize the healing effects. The PIM concept is effectively used by anyone fighting any disease or disability. And listeners also profit by using PIM.

Five PIM (Pictures In Mind) Scenarios

Scenario 1: The Fantasy Artist

You are attending a seminar on the art of listening. The seminar leader says, "Direct your fantasy artist to record all oral messages processed by the brain." What kind of PIM might your fantasy artist design to visualize this message?

While each listener's artist would design PIM unique to the listener's background and experience, the following design highlights the message: A properly attired artist with palette, brush, and canvas is swiftly painting the words floating in the air from the brain. This PIM reinforces the message, "Direct your artist to record all oral messages processed by the brain," as in Figure 6–1.

Scenario 2: A Rescheduled Meeting

Hurrying down the hall you pass by a colleague who quickly turns and says, "We have a last-minute change in plans. The meeting scheduled for Monday at 8:30 a.m. has been switched to Friday at 2:00 p.m. Pass the word."

As you continue down the hall you wonder: Was the meeting switched from Monday at 2:00 p.m. to Friday at 8:30 a.m.? Your fantasy artist could have made a PIM drawing of the message during the STTD (speech-thought-time differential) listening time, including a calendar of the week showing the canceled and the rescheduled meeting times, as in Figure 6–2.

Scenario 3: I Need a Ride

You receive a phone call from a family member who needs a ride from a friend's house. He gives these directions: "Drive south on I-75 to the third exit, Grant

FIGURE 6–1   Fantasy Artist

FIGURE 6–2   Rescheduled Meeting

Street. Exit and continue driving straight ahead past three traffic lights. After a mile past the third light, watch for a fire station on the right. At the next corner, Hubbel Street, turn right. I will be waiting on the left side of the street, at the front door of the second apartment building from the corner, 152 Hubbel Street." A PIM design, as in Figure 6–3, could show the route from I-75 to Hubbel Street.

Scenario 4: An Administrator's Request
The purchasing manager drops by your office and makes this request. "Tomorrow morning at 9:00 a.m., would you meet the AT&T Market Division Manager, Ann Shields, at the South Mariott Hotel? Bring her to a 10:00 a.m. meeting at Building 106 in Area B, Wright–Patterson Air Force Base, Fairborn, OH." The major details of the message are included in Figure 6–4.

FIGURE 6–3   Need a Ride

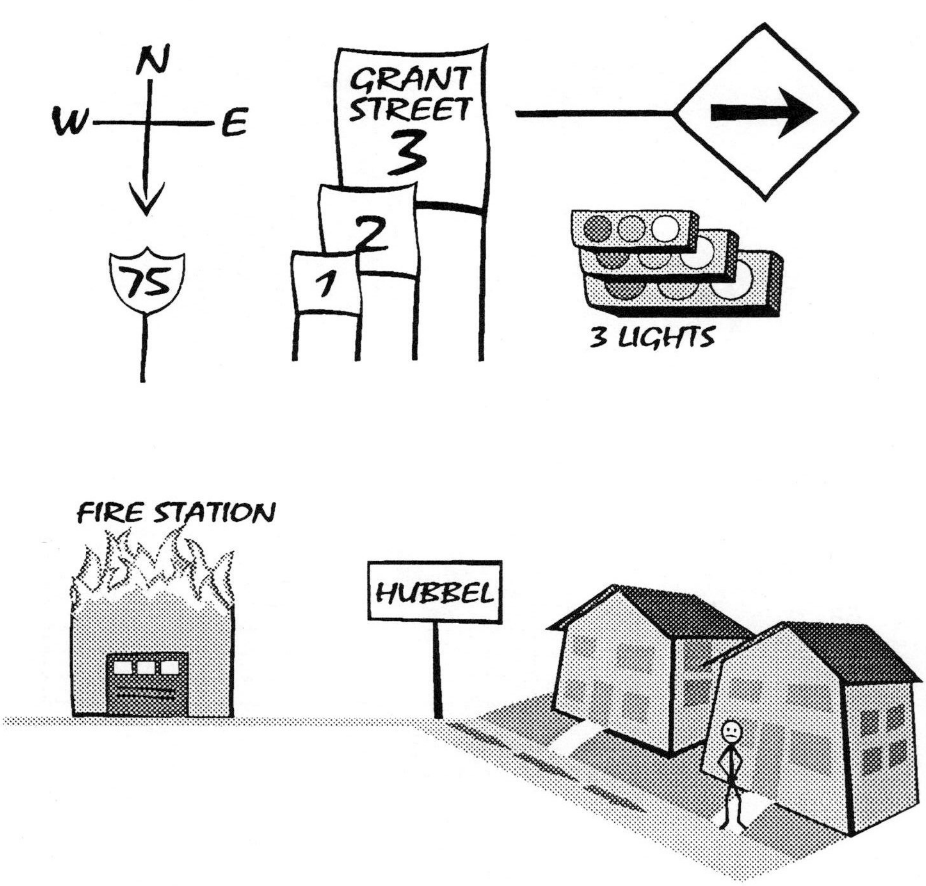

Scenario 5: Plans for a Graduation Weekend

Setting: You receive a phone call from a prospective graduate who explains plans for the special weekend: "Around 125 family and friends will gather at our home for a barbecue on Saturday at 1:00 p.m. At 8:00 p.m. we will go to dinner at Neil's Heritage. The weekend finale will be the graduation ceremony on Sunday at 10:00 a.m., at the University of Dayton Arena." The major details are included as in Figure 6–5.

As listeners, we benefit by processing speakers' messages via PIM. The more sensory cues we receive in decoding messages, the more processing we do in the right brain to "re–create" the speaker's "created" message. We can interpret and comprehend more accurately messages processed by both hemispheres of the brain: the left, for analytical data; the right, for creative thinking and sensory response. We refer to this as *holistic perceptive listening.*

FIGURE 6–4   Administrator's Request

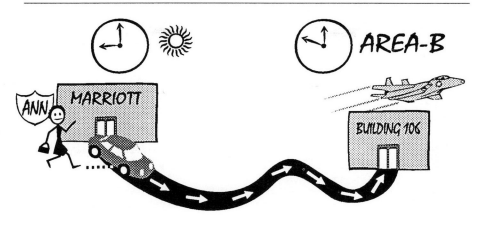

FIGURE 6–5   Plans for Graduation Weekend

Retraining: Guidelines for Using PIM (Pictures In Mind) in the Listening-Decoding Process

1. Use the "fantasy artist" in your mind. As an impromptu or a prospective listener, imagine that your fantasy artist awaits your command to write, print, draw or paint all messages processed by the brain. The PIM service is always available. Retraining to acquire skill in using PIM can greatly enhance listening comprehension.

2. When using PIM while listening to learn and remember names, plan to apply four of the seven basic rules advocated by memory experts Lorayne and Lucas: A. Original Awareness: Be attentive and concentrate on the speaker's first words. B. Out of Proportion: make PIM items "gigantic." C. Exaggeration: See "thousands" of an item. D. Action: Fill the pictures in mind with movement. These four rules can be successfully applied to PIM in all listening events.

3. Let your mind soar and design PIM to your liking. There is no right or wrong way to create and use PIM. Whatever we write, print, draw, or paint is our re–creation and requires no artistic ability.

4. Be assured that you have adequate time to implement the PIM concept. Use the STTD listening time for this task.

5. Do not become discouraged if you can't immediately flash a picture reflecting a speaker's message. Don't give up. Challenge yourself to activate your fantasy artist during every listening event.

CONCEPT 3: SELECTING AND USING EXPEDIENT NOTE–TAKING SYSTEMS WHILE LISTENING

Research indicates mostly positive effects from taking notes to retain data from aural messages.[23] Thus we buy millions of pads and notebooks each year to record notes during lectures, conferences, meetings, and discussions. However, taking notes without previous instruction and training in how to extract and record pertinent facts and ideas is of debatable value. Most educators readily confirm a phenomenon expressed by Ralph G. Nichols. He stated, "It is true that good students and good notebooks always seem to appear together."[24] But the pivotal cause–effect question, "Do good notebooks make good students?" or "Do good students make good notebooks?" generally remains unsatisfactorily answered.

After a two-year study of 1,200 freshmen students' listening habits at Michigan State College, Charles Irvin concluded that: (1) students who take notes are more consistent in comprehension and retention than those who do not, (2) students do not know how to take adequate notes of spoken messages, and (3) nearly 80 percent of the students wanted more training in note taking than they were receiving.[25]

Researchers believe there are two distinctive functions of note–taking: encoding and external storage. Encoding is creating a message mentally (planning what to say) or in writing (taking notes). As listeners we first decode or interpret the speaker's message before encoding messages. External storage is recorded data used to review and reinforce learning for transfer into long-term memory. Note–taking provides us with external storage. When we need to take notes, we encode or create messages in writing. Note–taking can cause increased attention, more elaborate processing, and better organization of the message.[26]

A review of the popular types of note–taking systems may assist prospective listeners to select and use those systems most adaptable to different listening experiences. We consider seven systems: (1) standard outline form, (2) précis or paragraph writing, (3) fact-principle notation, (4) the Cornell note–taking system, (5) annotative note–taking, (6) PIM mapping form, and (7) individualized note–taking. We discuss and then demonstrate seven note–taking systems in relation to a sample speech.[27]

The palest ink is better than the most retentive memory. — *Chinese proverb*

Sample Speech to Illustrate Note–taking Systems

Cigarette Smoking

"It is the most serious and most widespread form of addiction in the world. It is the foremost preventable cause of death in the United States." Dr. Richard Pollin, director of the National Institute on Drug Abuse, is not referring to alcohol or illegal narcotics, but rather to — cigarette smoking.

Don't smoke! It kills and may prevent you from getting that job you always wanted.

Among others, there are three reasons why you should not smoke: 1. health risks and adverse effects of smoking, 2. severity of nicotine addiction, and 3. lost job opportunities.

If you decide to become a smoker, the health risks are devastating. This habit kills more people in our country than any other cause of death. Four hundred thousand people every year die prematurely due to the effects of smoking cigarettes. *Smoking kills seven times more people each year than those killed in auto accidents. But unlike most auto deaths,* you *make the decision to smoke and assume the risk of a premature death. Are you willing to adopt a habit which, as noted in* USA Today, *increases your chances of contracting lung cancer by seven hundred percent? Dare you risk cancer of the mouth, throat, larynx, bladder, and other vital organs? Also, smoking drastically increases your chances of developing other potentially fatal diseases such as bronchitis and clogging of arteries leading to heart disease or heart attack. Some symptoms of damage to the body and mind due to cigarette smoking are jangled nerves, lower sex drive, a chronic cough, a husky voice, facial wrinkles, and an unrelenting physical-mental addiction to nicotine.*

It is amazing that so many people smoke today knowing these facts about the dangers of smoking. Why do millions of Americans still smoke? According to Dr. Richard Pollin, nicotine found in cigarettes is a pleasure-stimulating drug which is more addictive than heroin. Most of us would not consider trying heroin; but if you smoke, you may have the same or greater level of addiction as heroin addicts. The best way NOT to become an addict is to not even try that first cigarette. *Ninety percent of current smokers realize the health risks. They would like to quit but cannot because they are physically, mentally, and emotionally addicted to nicotine.*

One person who quit after only two years of smoking explains, "Talk about drug withdrawal symptoms! My nose dripped for a month. I had a constant sore throat. My eyeglass prescription changed. I had dizzy spells from breathing an unaccustomed amount of fresh oxygen instead of inhaling smoke. And talk about intestinal problems!"

Finally, as students who eventually will enter the job market, take heed. *The trend of companies today is to ban smoking in the workplace and, in some instances, not to hire smokers. According to* Industry Week, *the first company not to hire smokers was the USG Corporation in Chicago. They not only banned smoking in the workplace, but banned employees from smoking at home. Many other companies including Johnson and Johnson have followed suit.*

The State of Connecticut passed a law which mandates that companies must provide smoke-free work areas. This protects nonsmokers from inhaling smoke as passive smokers in contaminated work areas.

William Weis, a professor at Seattle University, notes that corporate maintenance costs for employees who smoke are upwards of $1,250 more per year than for nonsmokers. This is primarily because employees who smoke tend to have a higher rate of absenteeism and file more health insurance claims.

In addition to health risks, uncontrollable addiction and limited employment opportunities, the smoker has tar-discolored teeth and fingers, unpleasant breath and body odor, and has become isolated from society in general. Why put yourself in this position? Don't pick up that cigarette. Do you want to become a statistic? Don't Smoke! *

---

*This speech was researched, prepared, and delivered by David A. Klein, a sophomore majoring in physics, as an assignment for the Fundamentals of Oral Communication course taught by Instructor Kelly S. McNeilis, University of Dayton.

Standard Outline Form

In this system we indicate the main divisions of the message by Roman numerals (I, II, III), the main subtopics by capital letters (A, B, C), and other supportive details by Arabic numerals (1, 2, 3). An outline should distinguish between the major and subsidiary ideas and show how they are developed and supported. Depending on the nature of the data, we may use topical or short-sentence notes.

Educator Richard Kalish reminds us of two variations of the standard outline: (1) the decimal outline form and (2) the dash outline form. Instead of using Roman numerals, letters, and numbers, the decimal outline uses a decimal system (1.1, 1.2, 1.3, and so on). While the decimal system clarifies organization of data, listeners may have difficulty organizing information with the somewhat complicated decimal divisions. In the dash outline, organization is manifested through the use of the same pattern of indentation as in the standard and decimal outlines, with the dash replacing the Roman numerals, letters, and the decimal numbers.[28]

For further clarification of the three forms of outlines, see Figure 6–6.

Précis or Paragraph Writing

The word *précis* means "a precise summary of essential facts." Précis or paragraph writing involves a series of short sentences arranged into brief paragraph summaries of the message. The listener concentrates intently on the message for two or three minutes and then plans how to summarize the content.

We recognize several advantages of the précis or paragraph-writing system. Whether the message is developed *inductively* (reasoning from specifics to the general) or *deductively* (reasoning from the general to specifics), the listener can develop meaningful paragraph summaries about the message for future reference. This system also develops the listener's skills in summarizing, in thinking, and writing in sentence and paragraph form, and in detecting main and supportive ideas.

Possibly, the disadvantages outweigh the advantages of the précis system of note-taking. Listeners cannot apply the system to record lengthy lectures or reports related to mathematics. Nor is it practical to use for noting a series of formulas, axioms, and theories. Also, regardless of how skillfully we write the précis paragraphs, handwriting often cannot keep pace with the speaker's tempo. To examine précis note-taking of the sample speech, see Figure 6–7.

Fact-Principle Notation

To use this system, the listener draws two vertical columns on notepaper, and labels them *Facts* and *Principles*. During the discourse, we jot down a significant fact or principle in the designated column. We number the principles (a doctrine, law, rule, or generality) in Roman numerals, and the facts (an event, act, or statement accepted to be true) in Arabic numbers.

Listeners who use the fact-principle system learn to distinguish between principles and supporting facts, which can enhance listening and learning. Some persons

FIGURE 6–6   Standard Outline System of Note–taking

STANDARD OUTLINE TOPICAL FORM:

Cigarette Smoking

I. Introduction
   A. Dr. Pollin's claim
   B. Widespread, serious addiction

   C. Major cause of death in U.S.

II. Key Sentence
   Cigarette smoking kills.

III. Body
   A. Deaths: 400,000 per year

     1. Seven times more deaths than
       auto fatalities
     2. Largest number of U.S. deaths

   B. Smoking-related diseases
     1. Cancer: lungs, mouth, throat, larynx,
       bladder, other organs
   C. Why smoke?
     1. Nicotine addiction powerful

IV. Conclusion

DECIMAL OUTLINE SENTENCE FORM:

Cigarette Smoking

1. Introduction
   1.1 Dr. Pollin supports claim.
   1.2 Smoking is a widespread and
      serious addiction.
   1.3 Smoking is a major cause of
      death in the U.S.

2. Key Sentence
   Cigarette smoking kills.

3. Body
   3.1 Smoking causes 400,000
      deaths a year.
      3.11 Smoking causes seven times the number
         of deaths than from auto fatalities.
      3.12 Smoking causes the largest
         number of deaths in the U.S.

   3.2 Smoking causes serious diseases.
      3.21 Cancer strikes smokers in the lungs,
         mouth, throat, larynx, bladder, etc.
   3.3 Knowing the dangers, why do people smoke?
      3.31 Nicotine addiction is more powerful
         than heroin addiction.

4. Conclusion

DASH OUTLINE TOPICAL FORM:

Cigarette Smoking

- - Introduction
   - - Dr. Pollin's claim
   - - Widespread, serious addiction

   - - Major cause of death in U.S.

- - Key Sentence
   Cigarette smoking kills.

- - Body
   - - Deaths: 400,000 per year

     - - Seven times more deaths
       than auto fatalities
     - - Largest number of U.S. deaths

   - - Smoking-related diseases
     - - Cancer: lungs, mouth, throat, larynx,
       bladder, etc.
   - - Why smoke?
     - - Nicotine addiction powerful

- - Conclusion

FIGURE 6–7   Précis or Paragraph System of Note–taking

1. Cigarette smoking is a widespread and devastating form of addiction.
2. Smokers risk their health, develop a severe nicotine addiction, and lose out on job opportunities.
3. Every year 400,000 persons die of smoking-related diseases; that is seven times the annual number of auto fatalities.
4. Smoking causes bronchitis, emphysema, and clogging arteries leading to heart disease, heart attacks, and strokes.
5. Addiction to nicotine is at least as powerful, if not more so, as an addiction to heroin.
6. Cigarette smokers risk not being hired when applying for a position.
7. The annual corporate cost to maintain an employee who smokes is around $1,300 more per year than maintaining one who does not smoke.
8. Cigarette smokers are easily detected by their discolored teeth and fingers and by a strong nicotine odor on their breath, body, and clothes.
9. Since research shows that cigarette smoke forces others to smoke passively and jeopardize their health, more laws are being passed isolating smokers from the rest of society.

after transcribing the notes immediately following the discourse prefer to convert the data to an outline for future reference. Another positive aspect of this system is the minimal amount of writing required to record organized or unorganized messages. This allows more time for concentrated listening.

There are disadvantages in using fact–principle notation. Initially, the listener may have difficulty in distinguishing a principle from a fact while trying to understand the basic structure of the message. Furthermore, this system is not suitable for all subject areas, particularly the physical sciences. See Figure 6–8 for an example of this note–taking strategy.

Cornell Note–Taking System

This system was developed by Walter Pauk, director of the Reading-Study Center at Cornell University. The system is based on the five R's of note-taking.[29]

1. *Record:* During a lecture or speech write as many meaningful facts and ideas as possible in the *Record column* (a 6-inch-wide column on the right side of the paper).
2. *Reduce:* Immediately after the message note takers summarize the data in the *Reduce column* (a 2½-inch-wide column on the left side of the paper). The Reduce column data should be written as a series of short sentences or questions (note that in Figure 6–9, we use the short question). Place these cues adjacent to the relevant data in the Record column. This step reinforces

FIGURE 6-8   Fact-Principle System of Note-Taking

FACTS	PRINCIPLES
1. Dr. Richard Pollin, Director of the National Institute on Drug Abuse, supports the claim.	I. Cigarette smoking kills. (1, 2, 3, 4)
2. Cigarette smoking is the most serious and widespread form of addiction in the world.	(I didn't know that smoking cigarettes could cause so many deaths.)
3. The habit kills more Americans than any other cause of death.	
4. Smoking causes 400,000 deaths per year (seven times the number of auto fatalities).	
5. Smoking increases the chance of contracting lung cancer by seven hundred percent.	II. Smoking causes serious health problems. (5, 6, 7, 8)
6. Smokers risk getting cancer of the mouth, throat, larynx, bladder, and other vital organs.	(I've read about young people dying of heart attacks and cancer; I can't risk smoking.)
7. Smoking causes bronchitis, heart disease, and strokes.	
8. Symptoms of damage from smoking are jangled nerves, lower sex drive, chronic cough, husky voice, and facial wrinkles.	
9. The corporate trend is to banish smoking in the workplace; the number of companies not hiring smokers is increasing.	III. Smoking limits job opportunities. (9, 10)
10. Smokers cost employers about $1,300 more per year than nonsmokers due to absenteeism and health insurance claims.	(If I continue smoking, I may not be "hirable" for the positions I want.)

memory and helps students to prepare for examinations and those in the workplace to gain and store valuable information at meetings.

3. *Recite:* Cover the Record column. Use the cues in the reduce column to state the message in your own words as fully as possible. Periodically uncover the Record column notes to verify the recited message. Thus we are transferring data into the more permanent long-term memory.

4. *Reflect:* Record your personal opinion and reactions relevant to the message in a separate section of the notebook. These data should be classified and recorded in categories of knowledge acquired from taking notes primarily as a discriminative or evaluative listener during informal and formal listening events. Periodically it is wise to scan the data to keep them fresh in your mind.

5. *Review:* After note-taking, review the data immediately or within 24 hours. This helps us to retain most of what we have learned. Spend ten minutes every week or so in a quick review of all notes.

FIGURE 6–9   Cornell Note–taking System

QUESTION COLUMN	RECORD COLUMN
Who is Dr. Pollin?	Cigarette smoking--serious, widespread--U.S.--Dr. Richard Pollin--Director, National Institute--Drug Abuse. Three reasons not to smoke:
	1. health risks--adverse effects
What three reasons were noted for not smoking?	2. severity of nicotine addiction
	3. lost job opportunities
How risky is smoking cigarettes?	Health risks devastating--400,000 persons die each year--from smoking--7 times more than--auto accidents--700% chance--lung cancer; also get cancer of the throat, larynx, bladder, other organs.
Which diseases are typical of smokers?	Other diseases: bronchitis, emphezema, heart disease and attacks, strokes.
Why is nicotine addiction so powerful?	People get "hooked"--nicotine--more powerful addiction than heroin--smoking, a pleasure-stimulating drug--best way not become addict: don't take that first cigarette. 90% smokers--realize risk--want to quit--too addicted to nicotine.
What happened to the two-year smoker who quit?	A two-year smoker quits--severe withdrawal symptoms: drippy nose, sore throat, change in eye-glass prescription--dizziness from inhaling fresh oxygen instead of smoke--intestinal problems.
How can smoking hinder an applicant for a position?	Smokers looking for a job--TAKE HEED--corporate trend--ban smoking--workplace and at home--do not hire smokers--Johnson and Johnson and others--State of Connecticut: law passed--coporations provide smoke-free area--smoker costs company $1,300 more than nonsmoker--due to absenteeism--health insurance claims.
Why do companies perfer to hire nonsmokers?	
How does smoking affect one's appearance?	Smokers unattractive: discolored teeth and fingers--unpleasant breath, body odor--isolated from society.
What is the Key Sentence of this message?	Key Idea of Message: Cigarette smoking kills and limits professional growth.

In his book, *How to Study in College*, Pauk clarifies the design and use of several note–taking systems, including the Cornell system, to record different kinds of messages. Raygor and Wark recommend the Cornell system to listeners who need to gain greater confidence in taking valuable notes. The system requires intense and copious note taking with immediate review of notes. It assists those who have a difficult time taking notes.[30] To more clearly understand this strategy, again see Figure 6–9.

FIGURE 6–10   Annotative Note–taking System

"It's More Fun to be Healthy than 'Smoker Sick.'"

The continuing smoker has only sickness to look forward to and a body that is destined to deterioration of the lungs, heart, stomach and other vital organs—including the brain.

The "smoker sick" are depressed and down on the world. Life is drudgery. Smoke has robbed them of oxygen. The red cells are shortchanged, and so every cell in the body suffers. One feels dejected. Work suffers. One great interest remains—to get another cigarette. Smoking is a sickness, not a sign of success.

Like 2 colleagues at work

never thought of smoking this way

The sick smoker has a cloudy mind clogged and choked by nicotine. It is incapable of quick, creative thought. Memory is slow. Grades in school and on-the-job performance usually are mediocre or low.

Life is a song for the healthy nonsmoker. With rich red blood filled with oxygen circulating to every cell of the body, one feels vibrantly alive, ready for anything—problems, fun, success. Physical endurance is good. Bodily resistance is strong. Socially one is respected for clean living—admired for clean skin, hands, breath, and a healthy appearance.

Healthy people resolve problems better

I've met lovely people who smoke but they would be more enjoyable without the tobacco odor.

These are the negative aspects of smoking; it's sickness versus fun and health. We've got a good thing going when we stop smoking!

Yours for Life Without Nicotine, J. DeWitt Fox, M.D. [33]

Annotative Note-Taking

The word *annotative* means providing a critical commentary or explanatory notes. When a speaker explains or supplements sections of a text-book or a hand-out report, the listener writes major-word or short-sentence notes in the margin adjacent to the relevant textbook or report material. Some textbooks, workbooks, and reports have extremely wide margins or a part of the page left blank to accommodate annotation of the speaker's message. The listener develops a set of signals (asterisks, arrows, underlining, and others) to connect the annotative notes to the data being supplemented in a book or report. When studying for a test or to thoroughly understand a complicated report, annotative notes are invaluable. Using colored transparent ink pens to underline or highlight key phrases or sentences is an excellent annotative note–taking device. To review this system of noting data in textbooks or handouts, see Figure 6–10.

PIM Mapping System of Note-Taking

The PIM mapping method of note-taking is visually and graphically arranging data and re–creating the design on paper. To examine the PIM mapping example of note-taking as it relates to the sample speech, see Figure 6–11.

Walter Pauk offers suggestions for constructing concept maps while reading textbook passages.[32] We have adapted his suggestions to using the PIM mapping method of note-taking in the role of listener:

- Listen intently to the message to be mapped. Use nouns for key concepts and terms.
- Select the most important idea in the message and write it, at the top, or appropriate area of the paper, and other related concepts below it.
- Mentally rehearse by repeating the words along with the speaker. Identify the words that stand for key concepts by circling them on the paper.
- Rank the circled concept words according to importance in the message.
- Arrange the circle concept words on paper to reflect the direction and development of the message.
- Link the concept words by drawing lines showing the connections between and among them. When necessary, label the lines with a word or phrase.
- Review your PIM map, and add any other information.
- Write a précis summarizing the map.

There are many advantages to the PIM mapping note–taking system: It requires brief notes, is easy to design and file, shows relationships and ranks of importance, and can be used for both organized and disorganized messages. It uses the whole brain, and it develops creativity.

There are disadvantages to the PIM mapping system: Designing the map may distract the listener while taking notes. Also, note-takers need a high level of skill to

FIGURE 6–11   The PIM Mapping System of Note Taking

Title of PIM mapping speech: Cigarette Smoking

Key Sentence: Don't smoke—it kills and may prevent you from getting that job you always wanted.

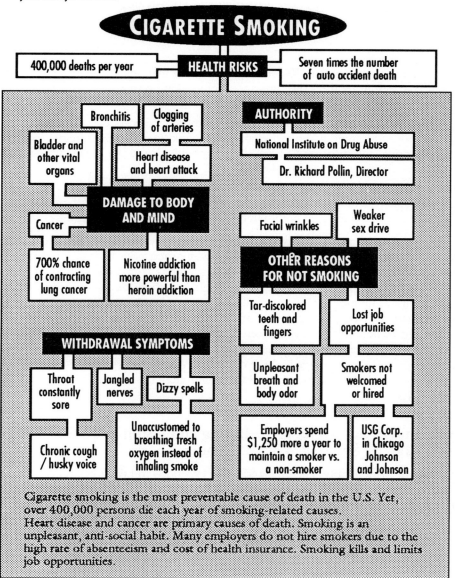

CIGARETTE SMOKING

| 400,000 deaths per year | HEALTH RISKS | Seven times the number of auto accident death |

Bronchitis **Clogging of arteries**

AUTHORITY
National Institute on Drug Abuse
Dr. Richard Pollin, Director

Bladder and other vital organs **Heart disease and heart attack**

DAMAGE TO BODY AND MIND

Cancer

Facial wrinkles **Weaker sex drive**

OTHER REASONS FOR NOT SMOKING

700% chance of contracting lung cancer Nicotine addiction more powerful than heroin addiction

Tar-discolored teeth and fingers Lost job opportunities

WITHDRAWAL SYMPTOMS

Throat constantly sore Jangled nerves Dizzy spells

Unpleasant breath and body odor Smokers not welcomed or hired

Chronic cough / husky voice Unaccustomed to breathing fresh oxygen instead of inhaling smoke

Employers spend $1,250 more a year to maintain a smoker vs. a non-smoker USG Corp. in Chicago Johnson and Johnson

Cigarette smoking is the most preventable cause of death in the U.S. Yet, over 400,000 persons die each year of smoking-related causes. Heart disease and cancer are primary causes of death. Smoking is an unpleasant, anti-social habit. Many employers do not hire smokers due to the high rate of absenteeism and cost of health insurance. Smoking kills and limits job opportunities.

identify the main and supportive ideas, the interrelationships and transitions of ideas in the message.

Individualized Note–Taking System
Changing the format of one or more of the note–taking systems automatically creates an individualized system. Listening and note–taking is a challenging task. Different types of speakers, messages, and settings create different types of listening, events. We need to adapt our individualized note–taking system to each listening event, as follows:

- A lecture or presentation: Recording notes in the margins of a textbook or a special handout requires the annotative note–taking system. A sheet of paper may be required to record additional notes.

- A speaker at a community meeting: An extemporaneous speaker expresses neighborhood opinion about the quality of drinking water. Because the speaker is emotional and disorganized, you might consider using the PIM mapping and the Cornell systems to record the message.

- A participant in a small–group session: Your colleague talks rapidly, inarticulately, and softly. To record the ideas, you partly use the fact-principle, précis, and individualized note–taking systems.

In addition to using a mixture of note–taking systems, we can use unique techniques and personal skills to create individualized note taking. For example, listeners may use common abbreviations and symbols; w/ for with, @ for at, a.m./p.m. for morning/afternoon, ≠ for not equal. Others develop unique word-shortening techniques of their own called short longhand: cmn for common, prep for preparation, char for character, mpr for empire, tchr for teacher.

It night be necessary to use all seven note–taking systems in order to decode and record one message. The greatest advantage of the individualized system is flexibility. The greatest disadvantage is abuse of flexibility. This occurs as note-takers create words and symbols that cannot be interpreted after the message. The notes are meaningless.

Retraining: Guidelines for Selecting and Using Expedient Note–Taking Systems While Listening

1. Write or print legibly. The time and effort expended to take notes is lost if we cannot decode or interpret the notes.

2. Take minimal, not excessive, notes. By concentrating to listen rather than to write excessive notes, we can include minimal notes in the STTD (speech-thought-time differential) time, as we rehearse and learn the message.

3. Review and clarify notes immediately or within 24 hours after the message. To store the data in long-term memory, glance over the notes frequently. "Cold notes" become meaningless and useless.

4. Create a setting conducive to note-taking. Do not use a tape or cassette recorder. Writing notes during replay time is wasting time. Position yourself near the speaker to hear and observe. Use a loose-leaf binder for easier rearrangement of notes. Use pens for easy reading and permanent filing.

5. Review notes before attending the next meeting or class. Copy the speaker's special terms.

WRAPPING IT UP: A SUMMARY

In this chapter we identify three basic concepts to enhance listening comprehension: self-preparation to listen, the PIM concept, and selecting and using expedient note–taking systems while listening. We stress the importance of preparing ourselves physically, mentally, and emotionally to listen. Efficient listeners apply five useful tools (why? what? how? when? and where?) to simplify self-preparation procedures. They do this when listening alone and during dyadic, small-group, and public communication.

We explain how to use PIM during the STTD listening time, directing our "fantasy artists" to write, print, draw, or paint messages processed by the whole brain. The PIM concept is used to listen, learn, and remember names, and also as a tool for healing and controlling disease.

We discuss seven note–taking systems: standard outline, précis or paragraph writing, fact-principle, Cornell, annotative, PIM mapping, and individualized.

DISCUSSION AND STUDY GUIDES

1. Define the following terms: impromptu listener, prospective listener, listening situation, and self-preparation to listen. Explain how planned self-preparation differs from on-the-spot or spontaneous self-preparation to listen. What is meant by listening comprehension?

2. Explain how each of the five analytical tools for self-preparation to listen can assist the prospective listener to prepare for a listening experience. List four kinds of listener roles and the self-preparation needed for each.

3. How well can you relate to having and using a fantasy artist in your mind? During past listening experiences, have you used pictures in mind to enhance comprehension of messages? Explain.

4. Specifically, how could you use PIM (Pictures In Mind) and the fantasy artist in the future while listening to lectures, reports, names of new acquaintances, and interpersonal conversation?

5. Which of the seven note–taking systems do you use most frequently? Why? What plans do you have for any changes during future listening–note–taking events? What do you consider the most valuable information you have received about note-taking?

LISTENING EXERCISES THAT WORK

EXERCISE 1. (The Prospective and Impromptu Listener) In the Listener Log label the one-half, vertical side of a page, *Prospective Listener* and the other, *Impromptu Listener*. In the appropriate section, number and list specific listening episodes during which you have assumed the role of either the prospective or the impromptu listener. After five minutes of reflective thinking and listing, review the results. Which section contains the greater number of listening episodes? Join a small group and discuss the following questions: Are the listed listening episodes typical of most persons' daily listening? Might you have portrayed a more competent prospective or impromptu listener if you had applied techniques of self-preparation to listen? After the group discussion, write a summary paragraph in the Log titled, "Self-preparation to listen as a prospective and impromptu listener."

EXERCISE 2. (Physical, Mental and Emotional Self-Preparation to Listen) In the Listener Log label three columns: *Physical, Mental* and *Emotional*. Review each listening episode listed in Exercise 1. In the respective column or columns, place the number of the episode followed by a brief notation of how you might have prepared yourself to listen before each listening episode. Can you use these suggestions to listen in the future?

EXERCISE 3. (Why Prepare to Listen?) An Analytical Instrument for Self-Preparation to Listen
Can you answer yes to any of these questions?

_____ 1. I walk out of the dentist's office wondering why I need to have a crown instead of another filling.

_____ 2. I forget the doctor's instructions before I get home.

_____ 3. Even after the school superintendent explains the need for a mill levy, I am still confused.

_____ 4. After my banker explains the interest rate carefully, I still am not sure why my payments are so high.

_____ 5. Sometimes I'm surprised by my repair bill even though the mechanic has explained it carefully.

_____ 6. I usually have a tax expert do my income taxes because I get confused when he explains deductions to me.

_____ 7. I know what I want when I go into a store, but often the salesperson convinces me that I really want something else or something more expensive.

_____ 8. I never did get good grades in that class; the professor is really hard to understand.

_____ 9. I can listen if I want to, but I'd go crazy if I listened to everything my wife (husband, friends, kids, boss) says.

——— **10.** Sometimes my co-workers get downright rude if I don't just stop everything and hang on their every word.

If you answered yes to any of these questions, can you estimate the loss you incurred in dollars, health, safety, good will, course or professional evaluations, and interpersonal relationships by not developing the techniques of self-preparation to listen?

EXERCISE 4. (Cost Assessment for Lack of Self-Preparation to Listen) What was the number of yes answers you recorded on the analytical instrument for self-preparation to listen in Exercise 3? Placing a $20 value on each affirmative answer, what is the financial loss you may have incurred from incompetent listening? Explain how you may have jeopardized important aspects of everyday living by not being prepared to listen. Try to assess your use of the self-preparation technique in the past. Using a scale (1, no self-preparation; 2, moderate self-preparation; 3, adequate self-preparation), write an assessment number by each affirmative answer indicating your use of the self-preparation technique in each listening situation. Specifically, what have you learned from this exercise?

EXERCISE 5. (PIM and Right-Brain Processing) Reflect back on the past two days. Think of the places you have been and with whom you communicated. Under the column heading, Right-Brain Processing, list those listening events and topics for which you used right-brain processing to decode messages.

EXERCISE 6. (Meeting Your Fantasy Artist) Close your eyes and visualize your fantasy artist. Write a brief paragraph in the Log clarifying these descriptive details of your artist: sex, race or nationality, height, weight, type of personality, kind of voice, design and color of clothes, education, and professional experience.

EXERCISE 7. (Learning E-P and N-P Names) List the names of four persons who have E-P names. After each, and in major words, write the PIM or image you associate with each name. Follow the same procedure after listing four N-P names. Share this information with a colleague or members of a group.

EXERCISE 8. (New Technique for Learning Names) Reflect on your past behavior when being introduced to a person. Using major words, list in the Listener Log the specific steps of the new technique, discussed in this chapter, that you intend to use in the future when meeting people. Which of these steps might require greater self-discipline to implement?

EXERCISE 9. (Using Other Note–Taking Systems) List the seven note–taking systems discussed in this chapter. Determine your present and future use of each system by placing, after each name, one of the following assessment symbols: FU (frequently used), SU (seldom used), NU (never used) or IU (intend to use).

Before a listening-note–taking event, glance over this list as a reminder to adapt your note–taking skills to improve listening comprehension.

EXERCISE 10. (The Use of Note–Taking Systems While Listening) List the seven common note–taking systems in the Listener Log. Allow ten lines for each to record data from the ABC, NBC, or CBS early evening news telecast. As a listening note taker, you are to: (1) quickly select the most efficient note–taking system to record the different news items, and (2) listen to and record the news. During the following class period, form small groups for each of the three networks' telecasts. Share and compare your data with other in your group. How does your selection of note–taking systems for the various news items differ or agree with your peer note takers? Which systems seemed to work or not work for special types of news reports? Who has correctly recorded the most data in your group? Discuss why this has happened. What do you think of your ability to take notes and listen? What difficulties did you experience? What can you do specifically to improve your listening and note–taking ability?

NOTES

1. J. A. Thomson (trans.), *The Ethics of Aristotle* (Baltimore: Penguin, 1953), 185.
2. Bertrand Russell, *Unpopular Essays* (New York: Simon and Schuster, 1951), 99.
3. James David Barber, "Tone-Deaf in the Oval Office," *Saturday Review World*, January 12, 1974, 10.
4. Ibid.
5. Carole Grau, "Listening Readiness: Taking Control of Yourself and Making It Possible to Concentrate," International Listening Association *Listening Post* (special issue), July 1990, 1.
6. Edward Colimore, "You're Getting Very Sleepy: Americans Suffering Deprivation of the Drowsiest Kind," Knight-Ridder News Service, *Dayton* (OH) *Daily News*, January 7, 1991, 1-C.
7. Ibid.
8. Ibid.
9. Jack C. Rang, "The Status of Radio as a Medium of the Future," Interview, July 20, 1991.
10. H. Lloyd Goodall, Jr., *Small–Group Communication in Organizations*, 2nd ed. (Dubuque, IA: Wm. C. Brown Publishers, 1990), 22, 331.
11. For additional study of small–group communication, see C. M. Moore, *Group Techniques for Idea Building* (Beverly Hills, CA: Sage Publishing Company, 1987); G. Phillips, J. T. Wood and D. T. Pedersen, *Group Discussion: A Practical Guide to Participation and Leadership* (New York: Harper & Row, 1986).
12. Ernest Parker Mills, *Listening: Key to Communication* (New York: Petrocelli Books, 1974), 36, 92.
13. Earl Koile, *Listening as a Way of Becoming* (Waco, TX: Word Books, 1977), 25.
14. Jacquelyn Wonder and Priscilla Donovan, *Whole Brain Thinking* (New York: William Morrow, 1984), 59–61.
15. Alan Garner, *Conversationally Speaking: Tested New Ways to Increase Your Personal and Social Effectiveness* (New York: McGraw Hill, 1985), 35.
16. Harry Lorayne and Jerry Lucas, *The Memory Book* (New York: Stein and Day, 1974), 9.
17. Ibid., 22, 76.
18. Chesley V. Young, *The Magic of a Mighty Memory* (West Nyack, NY: Parker Publishing, 1971), 147–52.
19. Lorayne and Lucas, 60, 76–77.
20. Carol Lacey, "Kids use daydreams to think creatively," Knight-Ridder News Service, *Dayton* (OH) *Daily News*, January 31, 1982, 8-H.
21. Ibid.
22. Emrika Padus and editors of *Prevention Magazine*, *The Healing Brain* (Emmaus, PA: Rodale Press, 1989), 28–32.

23. Research indicating positive effects of note taking on retention of aural messages includes: Jeanette Lynn Driskell and Edward L. Kelly, "A Guided Notetaking and Study Skills System for Use with University Freshmen Predicted to Fail," *Journal of Reading*, 24 (January 1980), 327–31; M. Maqsud, "Effects of Personal Lecture Notes and Teacher–Notes on Recall of University Students," *British Journal of Educational Psychology*, 50 (1980), 289–94; Andrea Weiland and Steven J. Kingsbury, "Immediate and Delayed Recall of Lecture Material as a Function of Note Taking," *Journal of Educational Research*, 72 (April 1979), 228–30; and Linda Annis, "The Effect of Encoding and an External Memory Device on Note Taking," *Journal of Experimental Education*, 44 (Winter 1975), 44–46.

24. Ralph G. Nichols, *Complete Course in Listening Conference Workbook: Manager Development Series* (New York: Dunn and Bradstreet, 1968), 39.

25. Charles E. Irwin, "An Analysis of Certain Aspects of Listening Training Conducted Among College Freshmen at Michigan State College," unpublished dissertation, Michigan State College, 1952 (Microfilm Publication 4039).

26. Gillis O. Einstein, Joy Morris and Susan Smith, "Note–Taking, Individual Differences, and Memory for Lecture Information," *Journal of Educational Psychology*, 77, 5 (1985), 522–32.

27. Sources used to prepare the sample speech on cigarette smoking include: Sandra Blakeslee, "Smoking, Why so many succumb to lure of nicotine," *Chicago Tribune*, January 27, 1985, 1, 5; Carroll Swart, "An Overlooked Cost of Employee Smoking," *Personnel*, Vol. 67 (August 1990), 326; K. A. Fackelman, "More evidence ties smoke to artery disease," *Science News* (May 26, 1990), 326; Lang Joel, "Up In Smoke, The death of an All-American habit," *Hartford Courant*, November 22, 1987, 10–16; Brian Moskal, "Hup 2-3-4! No smoking!" *Industry Week* (February 9, 1987), 24–25; Normal Sartorius, "Putting a higher value on health," *World Health* (June 1986), 2–14; Elizabeth Whelan, "Big Business vs. Public Health: The Cigarette Dilemma," *USA Today Magazine*, May 1984, 61–66.

28. Richard A. Kalish, *Making the Most of College; A Guide to Effective Study* (San Francisco, Wadsworth, 1959), 69–71.

29. Walter Pauk, *How to Study in College*, 4th ed. (Boston: Houghton Mifflin, 1989), 144–50.

30. Alton L. Raygor and David M. Wark, *Systems for Study*, 2nd ed. (New York: McGraw-Hill, 1980), 23.

31. J. DeWitt Fox, M.D., "It's More Fun to Be Healthy than 'Smoker Sick,'" Health Education Department, Hinsdale Sanitarium and Hospital, 128 N. Oak Street, Hinsdale, IL 60521.

32. Pauk, 212.

PART THREE

LISTENING
WELL

CHAPTER 7

OBJECTIVITY CAN BE ATTAINED:
MAINTAINING EMOTIONAL CONTROL

They have ears, but they hear not.
— *Psalms 115:6*

THESIS A careful and objective analysis of our reaction to speakers, the words they use, and the ideas they present, always pays dividends. We learn to exert some control over our emotional responses and to listen with a degree of objectivity.

CHAPTER OBJECTIVES

1. Identify feelings and emotions and assess their effect on listening competency.
2. Learn which people, subjects, or elements of language are most likely to short-circuit listening ability.
3. Know the effects of stress on listening ability.
4. Learn and put into practice a plan for achieving a degree of objectivity.

CHAPTER PREVIEW

- Impact of emotions on listening ability.
- Emotions as listening filters.
- Awareness of emotional filters.
- A plan to evaluate listening filters.
- Using the plan.

Most students of listening agree that uncontrolled emotional involvement creates the greatest single obstacle they experience in working toward listening improvement. Our listening behavior when we are emotionally involved is far different from that which we exhibit when we feel calm and objective. It is evident that we listeners must work to develop objectivity and thereby exert some control over the powerful impact of our emotions on listening. To begin this we must understand something about emotions and feelings.

CONCEPT 1. EMOTIONS: LISTENING ASSET OR LIABILITY?

Feelings and Emotions

Often we use the words emotion and feeling interchangeably. However, authorities make distinctions between them that we will consider. *Feelings* are mild levels of arousal, which, if positive, stir us and put us in a state of alertness for the task at hand and, if negative, can detract from this alertness. William Howell of the University of Minnesota defines feelings as "less intense than emotions. Feelings bring a heightening of sensitivity and sensation. . . . They result from personal involvement with people and events and their effects can be positive or negative, either enhancing performance or inhibiting it."[1]

We might illustrate how positive feelings enhance communication by recalling the exhilaration we feel after making a fine presentation, the enthusiasm we feel when given the opportunity to talk about a favorite subject, the enjoyment of matching wits with a worthy opponent or exchanging ideas with a creative thinker. These feelings help us concentrate so that we can ignore distractions and focus on the subject at hand. Negative feeling, as Howell describes it, might be the "vague feeling that things just aren't going the way they should or that 'something is wrong.'"[2] Negative feeling can distract us and shift our attention to worry.

Feelings, then, are important to communication and can enhance or limit listening performance. When they enhance listening, we feel "keyed up," alert, and able to listen well. We welcome this. When they are negative and distracting, we must control them. Because they are mild levels of arousal, by making use of STTD (Speech-Thought Time Differential), discussed in Chapter 4, Five Power Tools of Listening, we usually can concentrate on substituting appropriate feelings for the negative ones.

Emotions, on the other hand, are strong feelings accompanied by physiological changes that can affect our behavior drastically. Erica E. Goode calls them a "complex mix of perceptions, sensations, and judgments."[3] Psychologist James R. Averill believes "few other questions have proved as troublesome" as defining emotions. He calls emotions "socially constituted syndromes (transitory social roles) which include an individual's appraisal of the situation and which are interpreted as passions rather than actions."[4]

When we consider emotions in relation to listening, we look at the way the passion of emotion affects the action of listening. That very passion, we believe, prompts Howell to posit that "because emotions change people more than feelings do . . . emotions always deteriorate performance and the more intense the emotion, the greater the deterioration."[5]

That deterioration is most often identified by researchers who describe emotion as a condition in which the body reacts physiologically to a given situation. The physiological changes from an intense emotion vary. Rapid heartbeat and breathing, pupils of the eye dilating and flashing fire, dryness of the throat and mouth, hairs on the skin standing erect to cause goose flesh, butterflies or a sinking feeling in the stomach as blood rushes from the stomach and intestines to the brain and muscles, increased muscle tension, nervous perspiration or a cold sweat, trembling hands or feet, and the inability to concentrate, are all physiological manifestations of strong emotion. These symptoms come from activity of the sympathetic division of the autonomic nervous system as it pumps hormones into the body preparing it for emergency action. This is often called the "fight or flight" syndrome, a condition whereby the body becomes ready either to fight or run from an enemy.

The same hormones that prepare our bodies for emergency also make our minds race. Ordinarily, as noted in Chapter 4, Five Power Tools of Listening, we speak at a rate of about 150 words per minute and mentally process words at about 400 to 800 words per minute. When our minds race under emotional stress, we zoom along at maximum speed — 800 to 1,000 words per minute. No wonder we can lose the speaker's message completely.

The more intense emotions burn us up, put us out of control, and greatly hamper our ability to handle the same task that we perform efficiently while stirred by feelings.

Howell believes three conditions — shock, diffusion and transference — exist in emotions and contribute to burning us up. He identifies them:

1. An emotional person is in *shock* when reasoning processes don't operate effectively and thinking and problem solving are impaired.

2. *Diffusion* is excessive and uncontrolled physical activity. An angry person may shout, make faces, wave arms, and pace the floor.

3. *Transference* is sometimes termed "psychological spillover." The owner of the emotion treats everyone and everything as if they caused the emotion. Emotional persons lose objectivity . . . they perceive everything in relation to themselves. Such a self-centered orientation is particularly destructive.[6]

Positive and Negative Scenarios

Feelings, then, both positive and negative, often can enhance communication, specifically listening. However, we believe that emotion, whether positive or negative, is seldom useful in communication because emotionally controlled communicators lose objectivity.

Scientists question whether the very complexity of emotions can be a cause for this lack of control. They find that different hemispheres of the brain govern different emotions. Psychologists Richard Davison at the University of Chicago and Donald Tucker at the University of Oregon believe this is what happens:

1. The brain's right and left hemispheres may divide negative and positive emotions.

2. When subjects report feeling negative emotions such as fear and disgust, their right frontal lobes show increased electrical activity.

3. Sadness seems to diminish activity in the left frontal lobe as measured by an encephalogram (EEG).

4. Positive emotions such as happiness and amusement increase electrical activity in the left frontal lobe.[7]

Perhaps more research into the right-brain, left-brain concept of dominance in communication will shed more light on why emotions destroy concentration and how they create shock, diffusion, and transference.

Even a positive experience, if it results in emotional shock, diffusion, and transference, can affect listening. Most of us can remember when the powerful emotion of love or infatuation impaired our thinking, affected our physical actions and caused us to transfer this feeling to those around us. We may remember our inability to listen to any negative information about the object of our affection.

A friend reported that when she returned to the school and community she had left the year before, she felt overwhelmed with joy at visiting her closest friends. As she drove home after the visit, she realized that the intensely positive experience had impaired her listening. She said "I was so excited that I talked and talked; I wallowed in my experience. Later I couldn't remember anything that anyone else had said." Too intense an emotion, even a positive one, can hinder communication.

Intense negative emotions interfere with our pleasure, waste energy, and short-circuit communication by making us feel pressured, tense, on edge, or out of control. Most of us experience the emotional injuries of being hurt or treated unfairly. Most of us react to these emotions with various degrees of fear, anger, guilt, or frustration. If the original injury was traumatic, that same emotion or vestiges of it can be called back by the presence of the person who caused it, or by a similar situation, language, or environment.

Generally, emotional reaction builds over time, usually becoming stronger as time passes. Thus we have time to review our real or imagined hurt.

A listening trainee confided that he had once been humiliated by a first-grade teacher who spoke harshly and rapped him over the head with her knuckles. His intense emotion of fear and helpless anger remained and accompanied every day of first grade. It gradually became associated with all schoolrooms and all teachers. Many years later he attended an evening workshop where this same teacher was a member of the group. His old emotional responses came back in full force. "I didn't contribute to discussions because I had listened so poorly. I concentrated on that person and my old resentment for her."

The causes for emotional short circuits can be old indeed, but we can keep the emotion new. Negative emotions of anger, fear, loss, and guilt trigger all the physiological and mental responses described earlier. Whether it is the first experience or a similar one several years later, our minds and bodies can become so busy preparing for disaster that our ability to think rationally and to listen diminishes greatly.

Avoidance Conditioning

This recurrence of an earlier emotional reaction is part of avoidance conditioning to stress. We remember the experiments in which Pavlov trained dogs to salivate at the sound of a bell. Psychologists know that rats that have received an electrical shock in one area of a cage will learn to avoid the place where the punishment was administered. We humans do the same thing. If an event has been painful, we condition ourselves to try to avoid that stimulus in all circumstances.[8]

When John was five he was very fond of a toy snake that he carried around in his pocket. It was jointed, painted in lifelike colors, and wriggled convincingly when shaken. His sister, who had once been frightened by a snake, screamed and ran whenever she saw him take it from his pocket. He quickly realized that he could create a furor whenever he chose by slowly taking the snake from his pocket. If Nancy saw him move his hand toward the pocket, she leaped to her feet screaming. She became so conditioned to this emotional response of trying to avoid the snake that eventually John didn't even need it. He merely made a move toward his pocket to evoke a scream. Naturally, he did a lot of feinting toward his pocket when his sister irritated him.

Similarly, we make many responses to plastic snakes rather than to real threats. Thus, Nancy, who had once been frightened by a real snake, responded similarly to a toy snake and finally to John's movement toward his pocket. The listening trainee responded negatively to the actions of a teacher who had hurt him long ago and still conditioned himself to react to the presence of that person in the same room.

When an emotional injury threatens, we instinctively try to avoid it. If we cannot, we are forced to set up defenses to protect ourselves against further injury. Louise, a newly divorced parent, knows that telephone conversations with her former spouse may be necessary to arrange visits for the children, but she knows they hurt. They call to mind the original pain, anger, and hurt that accumulated as part of the divorce. She instinctively tries to avoid them. When she must speak, she limits her participation to brief answers and hangs up. This is the way she has devised to defend herself against emotional injury and to deal with her instinctive wish to avoid hurts similar to those from the past.

Whenever we call up an old emotional response, we re-experience the *shock* which impairs our reasoning process, the *diffusion* which impairs our physical activity, and the *transference* whereby we spread our emotion to others.

Unfortunately, unless we devise a plan for working toward objectivity, the avoidance defenses can continue to use up just as much energy and can call up physiological and mental responses similar to those caused by the original hurt. As we show later in this chapter, many of us diminish our listening efficiency by instinctively responding to emotions begun in the past rather than to real messages.

Retraining: Guidelines for Evaluating Emotion — a Listening Asset or a Liability?

1. During listening, use STTD listening time to identify symptoms of the "keyed-up" condition that accompanies feelings.

2. During listening, use STTD listening time to identify symptoms of the "burned-up" condition that accompanies emotions.

3. During evaluation of listening, recognize times when you indulge in avoidance conditioning.

4. Evaluate your listening performance by identifying stages of shock, diffusion, and transference in a listening event.

CONCEPT 2. THE PROBLEM: EMOTIONS CAN CREATE LISTENING FILTERS

In writing about listening, Jiddu Krishnamurti said:

> There is an art in listening. To be able to listen one must abandon or put aside all prejudices, pre-formulations, and daily activities. When you are in a receptive state of mind, things can be easily understood; you are listening when your real attention is given to something. But unfortunately we listen through a screen of resistance. We are screened with prejudices, whether religious or spiritual, psychological or scientific; or with our daily worries, desires, and fears. And with these as a screen, we listen. Therefore, we listen really only to our own noise, not to what is being said. It is extremely difficult to put aside our training, our prejudices, our inclinations, our resistance, and reaching beyond the verbal expression, to listen so that we understand instantaneously.[9]

Emotional Filters to Listening

The screen of resistance that Krishnamurti described damages our receptive state of mind and is detrimental to our ability to understand and respond to messages. The examples noted earlier in this chapter represent times when present and past emotions created screens of resistance or emotional filters through which a speaker's message attempted to pass. An emotional filter is similar to the filter we use in a coffee pot to prevent coffee grounds from entering our morning cup of coffee. Similarly, our emotional filter prevents some ideas from entering our mind.

When we show a model for listening in Chapter 2, Listening Power Generates Knowledge, we showed a straightforward passage of aural messages and feedback between speaker and listener. One could presume, from looking at it, that spoken messages move easily between speaker and listener. However, if we were to modify that design to include emotions that create listening filters, the added segment might look like Figure 7–1.

We each create our own emotional filters from old angers, fears, hurts, and stresses in our own lives. We can imagine the filter to be make up of a series of wires — each representing an emotional event that caused shock, diffusion, and transference. Imagine each wire to represent an old hurt — therefore, rusty, sometimes barbed, always dangerous. These become tangled into a kind of screen or filter through which messages must pass. Some messages hit an old emotion and are changed or partially deleted by our emotional response. Some are blocked completely by emotional filters. We do not listen to them at all.

Emotional filters function not only during the original injury, but can be recollected each time someone or something reminds us of the original hurt. We create avoidance responses that can be lasting.

FIGURE 7–1   Model of emotional filtering in listening

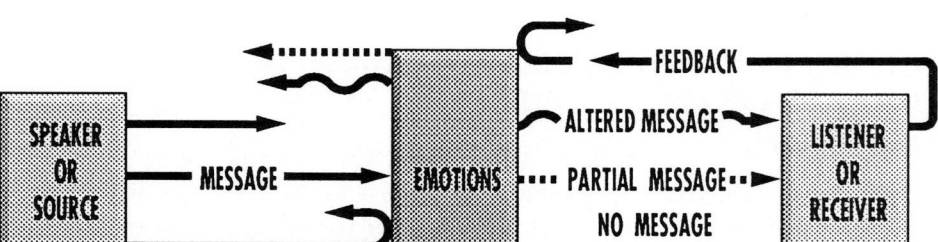

This retroactive quality of emotional filtering can be seen in the following example. While examining his listening habits, Joe confessed that he found it almost impossible to communicate with one of his supervisors. He recalled that several years before this supervisor had been instrumental in denying Joe a promotion for which he was qualified and which he thought he deserved. When Joe originally questioned the decision and requested a review of his qualifications, the supervisor turned away and remarked, "I know your qualifications." Joe considered the loss of position to be compounded by insult; he experienced blinding anger.

Joe doesn't remember whether the supervisor said anything else. The screen of resistance erected by his powerful emotions blocked out any further message. Thereafter, Joe found working with this man to be markedly stressful. When they communicated on any subject, his buried anger remained and the same filters operated between them. Even though the event happened years before, intense emotion remained. Joe had listened, not to what was being said, but to his own mind, his own thinking. Years later, his own humiliation was all that he could remember. His emotional reaction to listening filters had blocked out any valuable information Joe might have received from the supervisor. Joe had allowed this to cripple him as a listener.

The people in these examples are not hot-headed individuals who angrily search for irritating situations. They are conscientious listeners who, during and after training sessions, attempted to improve their listening objectivity. They discovered that they had been operating in a predictable pattern when faced with specific people and situations. Under most circumstances, these people are singularly even-tempered, but all of them experience times when their private emotions short-circuit messages.

The Role of Stress in Listening

Not only do single incidents such as the ones that these people experienced affect our ability to listen, but so do our inner mental states. Worry, regret, frustration, and preoccupation can permeate every aspect of our life, including our ability to listen. Worry can cause such distractions that no matter how much we want to listen we return to the source of our worry. (See Chapter 4, Five Power Tools of Listening, for a plan to control worry.) Students who don't have the money for their tuition payment find their in-class listening filled with distraction. Workers fretting about their health, their children leaving home, or a fight with their spouse may be so immersed in worry that they cannot listen to the messages of those around them.

Psychologists know that intense stress caused by preoccupation and worry can result in both mental and physical illness. While most of our worries do not disrupt our lives to that degree, all personal worries affect our listening efficiency. Dr. Hans Selye, a recognized authority on the subject of stress, warns that both positive and negative events produce stress. From the point of view of its stress-producing or stressor activity, it is immaterial whether the agent or situation we face is pleasant or unpleasant; all that counts is the intensity of the demand for readjustment or adaptation.[10]

In 1970, psychiatrists Thomas Holmes and Richard Rahe considered the role of both positive and negative stress in our lives. They ranked the degree to which several events in our lives cause emotional stress and set up emotional screens that intrude in our lifestyle. They worked out a point system to record the relative impact of each event in a person's life. Some of the points designated were: 100 for the death of a spouse, 73 for a divorce, 63 for the death of a close family member, 35 for a change in the number of arguments with a spouse, 29 for a son or daughter leaving home, 23 for trouble with the boss, 20 for a change in residence, 20 for a change in schools, 16 for a change in sleeping habits, and 12 for Christmas.[11] Holmes and Rahe suggest that amassing 300 stress points can predict a 90 percent chance of contracting a serious illness. Such is the powerful effect of positive and negative stress.

Most of us expect to experience high stress situations seldom, if at all. However, we all will face one or more — death of a spouse, divorce, marital separation, or death of a family member, for example. In addition, most of the least stressful and the positive events — Christmas, vacations, change in eating habits, change in social habits — will be part of everyone's life and occur often. If these situations can intrude so strongly that they affect our health, it is easy to see how they affect our listening ability.

Some events are so stressful that we are unable to summon the necessary energy to deal with day-to-day living. The stress of a marital break-up can cause people to forget to eat or to drive to and from work without remembering the trip. The stress of rape or other physical attack can cause complete communication blocks whereby victims are unaware of most events around them. In research on the role of stress and life-threatening diseases, Stephanie Simonton reports that cancer patients are relatively poor listeners. Under that kind of stress, "we comprehend and remember very little of what we hear. When faced with a life-threatening illness we are likely to miss important statements and misinterpret others."[12]

Students cramming for important exams forget to read newspapers or keep appointments. All of us occasionally find it impossible to keep worry about financial problems out of our minds. These and other preoccupations create severe listening impairments.

Our own cause for worry, stress, or preoccupation will be different from some-one else's. However, it is our own situation that is real and important to us. There-fore we must deal with those individual stresses and emotions in an individual manner. As we work to identify our emotions and attempt to separate them from the messages we receive, we will make strides toward listening objectivity.

Perception and Reality

Scientists know that our perception of what we believe exists can profoundly influ-ence our behavior.[13] When our emotions take over as we listen, we often respond, not to what happened, but to what we perceive to have happened. *Perception* means any insight, intuition, or knowledge we become aware of in our minds. *Reality* means that which exists objectively and in fact. The two may be quite different.

In our struggle with emotions and listening, we must learn to distinguish be-tween what we believe the situation to be (perception), and what the situation actually is (reality). We must strive to deal with the reality of a situation rather than our perception of it.

After considering the impact of emotions and stress on listening, we recognize that we will not be able to listen productively until we assess the strength of specific emotions in our own lives and devise specific steps to control them. Each of the people whose powerful emotional filters were described in this chapter discovered them while doing just that. All were able to make progress toward listening objec-tively because they analyzed the elements that cause emotional filtering and became aware of why they overreacted in each case. None of them achieved total objectivity, but each recognized those times when they dealt with perception rather than reality.

Retraining: Guidelines for Identifying Emotions that Create Listening Filters

1. Take time to recall messages which were distorted or short-circuited by listening filters.
2. Identify present stressful situations in your life. Estimate ways in which they could become listening filters in the future.
3. When listening, be aware of those stressful situations that can become listening filters and make use of STTD to remind yourself to listen.
4. Identify your perception of events which interfered with listening. What was the reality of each event?

CONCEPT 3. THE SOLUTION: BECOME AWARE OF EMOTIONAL FILTERS
Awareness: The Key to Listening Objectivity

Because we hear with the ears but listen with the mind, we interpret what we hear and then think back to what we perceive the message to mean in the light of an original hurt, anger, frustration, guilt, or pleasure. Unless we attempt to gain control over our reveries — pleasant or unpleasant — unless we become aware of what causes these reveries, we cannot make progress toward listening objectivity.

Although a dictionary would define *objectivity* as uninfluenced by emotion, surmise, or personal prejudice, there are times when our objectivity cannot reach the degree that makes us uninfluenced in communication.

Some events in our lives are too traumatic for us to deal with immediately. The death of a spouse or family member, divorce, abandonment, rape, or other physical attack precipitates a crushingly difficult emotional block. Before we can attempt to work toward objectivity, most of us need a *healing interval* (a period of time where we give much thought, and often formal study, to the problem or event in an attempt to *understand* it). While we may never reach objectivity in many of these areas, the healing interval can bring us to a level of understanding whereby we can communicate and listen on some level.

We can aim for the ability to recognize our emotions in order to exert some control over our patterns of response. We aim for some level of *listening objectivity* (recognizing the influence of our emotion and controlling our response to it). This definition suggests that we can learn what causes traumatic emotional involvement, its influence, and some strategies for communicating objectively even when we may not feel objective. As we search through our own listening patterns we can identify what perceptions make us respond. Communication consultant Lyman K. Steil and his co-authors believe that as we do this we will probably recall people, subjects, and language that trigger set patterns of emotional response.[14]

People Create Emotional Filters to Listening

It is not even necessary for the original person to be present for us to erect emotional screens. The speaker to whom we listen can merely remind us of someone who caused an original hurt. Several years ago, Ralph G. Nichols, while a professor at the University of Minnesota, identified a student who was failing several courses because he could not learn from lectures. Although he went to class with good intentions, the lecturers grated on his nerves and caused such irritation that he could not bear to listen. After approaching the problem from several angles, the student and Nichols hit upon what probably caused his inability to listen.

While talking about his home, the student revealed that he felt his mother constantly complained and nagged him. "I could never get in a word. Eventually, I learned simply not to listen. I guess I would sort of reach up to my brain and turn her off."[15] Whenever this student listened to sustained talk of any kind, the speaker reminded him of his mother's constant complaining. He became irritated and turned off his listening.

We listeners can resolve to become conscious of those times when we react emotionally to a person. We can make a mental or written note of the person who has inspired us to add a wire to our screen of listening filters. Has this person caused emotional trauma in the past? Does this person remind us of someone else who caused emotional trauma? Does the speaker look, sound, dress, or walk like someone to whom we have responded emotionally? Making a list of people who have caused emotional stress in the past can create awareness that a problem could arise and can prepare us for our attempt to avoid an old set pattern of emotional response.

Subjects Create Emotional Filters to Listening

We will also find that subjects as well as people trigger emotional trauma. Each of us will find different emotional subjects since specific events linked to the subject will cause our emotional reaction. The ideas that threaten our values create emotional listening filters to sift out or distort what we do not wish to hear. Attitudes and values are linked to emotion-producing subjects. *Attitudes* are learned sets of evaluations that predispose us to respond to a given stimulus in a certain way. For example, we might have a positive attitude toward learning to listen. *Values* are closely related to attitudes. They are those principles, standards, and qualities that we see as being good and having great importance in our lives. They are made up of several attitudes and come from our environment, our experience, or our frustrations.[16] Values affect all aspects of our lives and should result from our choosing freely from alternatives after considering the consequences, prizing the choice and affirming it to others, and acting upon this choice and repeating it in some pattern of life.

Whatever results from our values, they do direct our thinking, affect our behavior, and influence our emotions. For this reason, when a speaker touches on a subject or expands an idea that is contrary to our system of values, we often react with negative emotional filters. Conversely, the speaker who agrees with our values can stimulate us to positive emotions.

When we learn which subjects have the potential to destroy our objectivity, we are forewarned and forearmed. We cannot become perfectly objective; however, we will listen with caution. We will become listeners who know what subjects have the potential to hamper listening objectivity. We will attempt to move our attitudes and our same old patterns of response toward neutrality. The more neutral our attitudes, the more likely we are to achieve listening objectivity. Because our values are involved, our feelings will keep us keyed up to listen with awareness. We will struggle against allowing our emotions to burn us up, thus screening out what we do not want to hear. We can remind ourselves that we may not be able to change the existence of the subject, but we can change the intensity of our response to it.

Language Creates Emotional Filters

Just as specific people and subjects affect our emotional stability and our ability to listen, so can specific elements of language build emotional barriers. Our emotional response to words, accents, and usage is based on some event in the past just as it is for people and subjects.

A speaker's grammar and usage can affect our listening. If the speaker exhibits a regional accent that we do not like, we can respond negatively toward it and be tempted to distort the entire message. If the speaker's grammar is not up to our own standards, we can filter out an entire message. Jill, a college student, found one of the courses for her major presenting severe difficulties. She was puzzled about her inability to listen to the speaker until she analyzed the situation and discovered she responded negatively to several mistakes in grammar made by the lecturer. She had been turning off everything the speaker said because she considered it to be poorly stated. In her mind she equated poor grammar with poor intelligence.

After considering this problem, she decided, "I am a poor speller; I'd hate to have people discount everything I write on the basis of my spelling. I won't discount what he says because I don't like the way he says it." She still didn't like the lecturer's grammar, but she was able to view her problem with it more objectively. Her listening performance improved dramatically.

Listeners can respond emotionally to words themselves. Crudity and profanity can set up barriers to listening. The connotations of words, those nuances of association and meaning our minds ascribe to words because of experience, permeate our listening.

It would be a boon to listeners everywhere if we could list the words that are the most emotion producing, and are therefore the most detrimental to listening. However, the list would be different for everyone. We can see evidence of our unique responses in the following example. A petite young woman explained that she had become deaf to the message of a speaker during a city council meeting. She had asked a question and the responder prefaced the answer with, "Now see here, little girl. . . ." Whenever she had been criticized or disciplined as a child, her father had begun with, "Now, see here, little girl. . . ." These words activated her listening filters and blocked out the rest of any message.

Several trainees in listening objectivity discovered that the tone or quality of voice of the speaker held strong emotional connotations for them. They found themselves tuning out speakers whose voices reminded them of another to whom they had once responded negatively or being drawn positively toward a voice they liked.

On occasion, a speaker's accent will inspire an emotional reaction. Just as a person who reminds us of one who hurt us can cause negative emotional filters, so can the accent of a person we like trigger a positive emotional response. Many believe a British accent to be cultured or a southern accent to denote a relaxed attitude. Most expect radio and television announcers to have a midwestern accent, and some find any other accent creates an emotional filter.

We must take care to recognize and list those elements of language, accents, and voice quality which trigger emotional reactions. They can create filters which dramatically skew our response to people and subjects.

Retraining: Guidelines for Becoming Aware of Emotional Filters

1. Carry a small notebook in your pocket or purse. Whenever you become aware of a person who is a listening filter, write it down under a special heading, "People."

2. In the same notebook, under a separate heading, "Subjects," write each subject or topic of discussion that creates a listening filter for you.

3. Under the heading "Elements of Language, Accents, and Voice Quality," write specific words, accents, voice qualities that create emotional filters for you.

4. Make an effort to maintain awareness by examining and updating these lists regularly.

CONCEPT 4. A FIVE–STEP PLAN TO EVALUATE LISTENING FILTERS

There may be dozens of persons, scores of subjects, ideas, accents and elements of language, and hundreds of words that affect listening efficiency. We will not discover all of them at once, but our job now is to make an effort to begin noticing them. For each that you discover, add it to a specific list labeled: "People," "Subjects and Ideas," "Elements of Language and Voice Quality."

Once you have listed as many filters as possible—and you must work on this list regularly—you can, for each entry, discover the answers to these questions:

1. What happened originally? Search past communication encounters and your memory of them to discover when you first responded to this person, this subject, or this element of language.

2. How did I react originally? Recall your original emotional response. Was it anger, fear, joy, or a combination of emotions? Did you experience shock, diffusion, and transference?

3. Do I still react the same way? Claudell Stocker says, "Some emotional filters are so instantaneous and so traumatic that they can never be controlled. However, there are old set patterns that we are individually faced with."[17] If we find ourselves re–experiencing the same reactions in the same pattern, we must consider how many years of emotional strain and lost messages this has cost.

4. Is this still important? Some traumatic events in our lives are so hurtful and create such violent emotional response that they and the people connected with them continue to affect us many years later. However, most of the events that first cause us trauma and emotional reaction grow less important with years.

5. If the event is still important, can we devise a plan to manage it? By "manage" we mean personally exert control or authority over the event as it exists today. It has already happened, we cannot change that. We can, however, change the way we react to it.

One way to manage the emotion might be to join a self-help group, another might be to talk it over with the person involved or a trusted friend. Still another plan might be to decide to give it no more of your time. Lyman Steil suggests that we will not be able to manage our emotions until we answer this question, "Who controls your emotional triggers?" and warns us, "Anyone who is in a position to know more about your emotional triggers than you do is in a position to control you."[18] Naturally, we wish to exert control over our own emotional triggers or filters. Managing those that remain important is an important step in doing so.

The decision to say, "This is no longer important in my life; I will no longer give it control over my emotions," is the first step in gaining control over that which is no longer important.

When we have answered these five questions for each person, subject, or element of language on our list, we will be on our way to developing a degree of emotional objectivity. We will not have changed anything that has happened nor be able to predict what will happen, but we will have a plan for managing our emotional filters.

Emotional Filters Affect Every Kind of Listening

It is important to remember that our emotional responses to people, subjects, elements of language, and voices occur in every kind of listening, and our need for objectivity and emotional control exists in each.

The emotional filters encountered in discriminative listening are not always easy to recognize. However, they are evident when we react to the speaker, the subject of the message, or the language and vocal quality used. We can become aware of our reactions and analyze them.

In evaluative listening we often hear messages that are accidentally or deliberately aimed at our emotions. Both trained speakers and casual conversationalists use these devices. Listeners must be wary. To listen with power, we must recognize each emotional appeal and evaluate it objectively.

In appreciative listening, background noises, inconsiderate people in an audience, or a less-than-inspired performance can trigger anger or irritation that can destroy the therapeutic quality of appreciative listening. Analyze these causes and set up a plan to try to remove them.

In empathic listening we often hear messages that run counter to our own values. In these situations it is imperative that we keep our emotions under control and listen objectively to the message only. Excessive emotional response to what we perceive can inspire us to judge and to make critical observations. Judgmental remarks or even communicating judgment in facial expressions or body posture can dissipate the nonjudgmental acceptance necessary in an empathic listener.

In self–listening, it is easy to replay events and hurts and spend time in imagining clever ways to "cut down" the offending speaker or present our own ideas more articulately. It is possible to focus on old hurts and old emotional filters to the detriment of health and well-being and certainly to the detriment of perceptive self-listening. Evaluating each emotional filter by use of the five assessment questions can also help manage emotions in self–listening.

Our emotional involvement will always be there. Our old patterns of listening need not be there. We can assess our emotional filters in all the listening we do and strive toward developing new patterns of listening objectivity.

Retraining: Guidelines for Evaluating Listening Filters

1. Recall and describe the time and place of the original happening.
2. Recall and describe your original emotional response. Focus on the shock, diffusion, and transference involved.
3. Describe how you respond today. How is it similar to the original reaction?
4. Ask yourself how important the event involving this person, subject or element of language is today.
5. If the event is still important, devise and write out a plan to manage it. During emotional self-preparation to listen, plan for what you can say or do under various circumstances.
6. If the event is no longer important, drop it as an emotional filter.

CONCEPT 5: PUTTING THE FIVE-STEP PLAN TO WORK

Foresight and effort can help put the five–step plan into effect to increase listening objectivity. We can apply the following suggestions to use while and after we compile our lists, answer the questions in the five-step plan, and observe new listening filters.

Once we have completed the plan, the next step may be to talk it over, preferably with the one involved. Often the person who causes difficulty is part of our everyday life — a family member or a co-worker. The subjects which cause emotional filters may be topical issues which will surface often. Poet William Blake wrote:

> I was angry at my friend,
> I told my wrath, my wrath did end.
> I was angry at my foe,
> I told it not, my wrath did grow.

Blake gracefully describes the results of rationally talking about a problem. We believe that if we talk about it, the filter can disappear. If we harbor it, the filter can become more and more powerful.

Cancer counselor Stephanie Simonton believes open expression of feelings and emotions is vital to physical health and to mental and emotional well-being. "Talking your feelings over with someone allows you to feel them fully which helps release them."[19]

Anticipate Emotional Filters

When we cannot talk over the results of the plan, we can anticipate what emotional filters to watch for. We have already spent much time discussing how to identify people, subjects, language, or quality of voice which trigger emotional responses. We need to recall the old wires in our listening screen. We can review them regularly and analyze the reasons for their power over our listening. It takes time and determination to overcome them. Often it may seem that we cannot gain control over these emotional filters. However, we must exert the necessary mental effort to set aside our defensiveness little by little. In Chapter 6, Three Basic Concepts to Enhance Listening Comprehension, we discussed Barbara's emotional self-preparation for a discussion of her job assessment. As she planned her role in this discussion, she anticipated possible emotional filters — the subject of prejudicial attitudes toward women, for example — and ways to manage them. This was an example of anticipating emotional filters. Identifying them beforehand is the first step toward the awareness that is the key to listening objectivity.

Delay Final Evaluation

It is often wise to wait until we understand the entire message and weigh all the evidence before we make a final decision to agree, disagree, or make no change.

We do not suggest that listeners refrain from evaluating messages. We continually assess as we listen, and we should focus our energy on making sound assessments. Therefore, we carefully monitor the degree to which our emotional reaction to the speaker, the message, or the language affects our role as a perceptive listener. During the brief interval during which we listen to one message, we may make emotion-laden evaluations. However, during a post-message interval (a time designated for message review), we can reflect on that message.

New York University neuroscientist Joseph LeDoux believes the amygdala (the center, deep in the temporal lobe of the brain, which communicates with many other parts of the brain) stimulates us to make a kind of instantaneous reaction to a stimulus — the "fight or flight" reaction. This "quick assessment" is then refined by the neocortex and other brain regions.[20] This means that a listener, after the first instantaneous response, can recognize the stimulus as an emotional filter and either reject responding to it or set it aside for delayed evaluation with the five-step plan. At this time we can also sort out the degree to which the emotion should and did affect our final response.

Search for Negative Evidence

When we become emotionally stimulated as listeners, most of us mentally hunt for any positive evidence to support our pet belief and to prove our opponents wrong. We work hard to create an argument. We can reverse this and work toward listening objectivity by trying this experiment. We should deliberately instruct ourselves to search for evidence that counters our pet belief and supports the opposite. This is a very difficult move to make because it demands courage. It places us in the position of discovering and understanding another's point of view. We place ourselves in the position of understanding how life appears to another. We run the risk of being changed ourselves. Many of us refuse to take this risk. We do not wish to see from another's perspective, or to risk change. However, a listener who wishes to develop objectivity will take this step.

Hunt for Evidence of Inferior Feelings

When we detect in ourselves hostility or unwillingness to listen, we should hunt for evidence of our feeling inferior to the speaker. Apply this hunt to the speaker as well. It is possible, even likely, that speakers experience the same feelings of inferiority that listeners do. If they do, they often present messages in a hostile manner that in turn triggers our hostility. We can overcome both our own and sometimes the speaker's hostility and defensiveness by recognizing these all-too-common feelings of inferiority.

Make A Realistic Self-Analysis

Take time to evaluate each emotion-riddled communication process. Carefully consider the exact source of the emotional reaction, the familiarity of the emotion, and the degree of importance this holds. Analysis can make it less and less important until it no longer has power to destroy communication.

Plan to Create Habits of Listening Objectivity

Communication expert William S. Howell describes habits as "units of mental or physical activity that, once started, complete their simple or complex cycle automatically."[21] The *American Heritage Dictionary* defines habit as a "constant, often unconscious inclination to perform some act, acquired through its frequent repetition." If we accept these definitions, we know we can exert control over starting the response and turn the first steps into emotional objectivity by repeating them frequently. Deliberate repetition develops our unconscious inclination to put them into practice whenever we listen.

Be Alert to Emotional Filters

Whenever we recognize a person, subject, word, or voice that has caused listening filters in the past, we should strive for the habit of on-the-spot objective reaction.

After each communication encounter that has been defeated by emotional involvement, strive for the habit of objective introspection. We can review our step-by-step awareness of what caused emotional filtering. We then will be prepared to respond more objectively the next time this situation arises.

Rewards of Listening Objectivity

Objectivity gives us a broader intellectual base with which to process messages. Psychologist Edward C. Tolman discovered that rats, when faced with a problem, figure out a tentative mental map. He thought this map of routes and environmental relationships determined what responses a rat would make. He made distinctions between what he called a *strip map*, in which the animal had developed one rigid and undeviating path, and a *comprehensive map*, in which the animal had a generalized view of matters and might vary the procedure used or the path taken to solve each problem. Both maps provided solutions to particular problems. But Tolman pointed out that the comprehensive map with its several solutions seemed superior to the single, often useless, solution provided by the strip map. Tolman felt humans possess an obvious advantage if their own cognitive maps are comprehensive rather than strip maps. He thought that emotional strip maps could push us into blind, unintelligent rages and hates.[22] Developing listening objectivity helps us develop a comprehensive cognitive map.

Management Professor Michael LeBoeuf observed, "For someone to successfully utilize his ideas, he must have a strong enough self-image to believe in himself and be able to let his mind wander without losing control."[23] As we develop listening objectivity we often experience positive feelings about ourselves because we know our own emotional filters, know what affects us, and know what we can do about it. We know individual speakers have feelings and emotions similar to ours. We know that whether the action which caused emotions was deliberate or accidental, its effect develops the listener's own mind.

Psychologist David Viscott believes, "Life should be lived in the present, for it is only in the present that we're able to exert any control over our lives. We can't change the past, and the future is constantly formed in the present. We must learn to invest our energy in the present where it will do the most good."[24] In our attempt to achieve objectivity, we can consciously attempt to listen to each message in the present. We can try to set aside old hurts and ignore the possibility of new hurts in the future. We can invest our energy and our listening time where it will do the most good — in increasing listening objectivity.

Retraining: Guidelines for Putting the Five-Step Plan to Work

1. While listening, call upon your fantasy artist to draw the listening filter that you wish to avoid — PIM can remind us of known filters.

2. While listening, call upon your fantasy artist to draw or diagram PIM (Pictures In Mind) of whatever new filters you discover.

3. After listening, evaluate whatever new filters you have discovered by using the five-step plan for each.

4. As you examine each filter, ask yourself what arguments exist against your emotional position.

5. As you examine each filter, ask yourself what role your own defensiveness played in its establishment.

6. Deliberately put the five steps into practice until they become habit.

7. Regularly review your lists of people, subjects, and elements of language and evaluate your progress toward listening objectivity with each.

8. Before each planned listening event and during each impromptu listening encounter, review your plan for managing important filters and your decision to drop unimportant filters.

WRAPPING IT UP: A SUMMARY

Emotions are intense, complex feelings that are manifested in profound physiological changes. They affect all humans, but the sources of emotions are different for everyone.

Emotional reactions can stimulate our minds to erect powerful filters that distort, filter, or block out messages. It is imperative that we attempt to develop listening objectivity in order to hear and attend, interpret, and recreate, and retain and respond to messages as closely as possible to the way they are meant to be perceived. We can identify our own listening filters, determine their importance, and follow a step-by-step plan for increasing listening objectivity in our own lives.

If we attain listening objectivity, we enjoy listening power no matter how emotion-laden the message that comes to us. We are then headed toward becoming holistic perceptive listeners.

DISCUSSION AND STUDY GUIDES

1. Can you identify a time when positive feelings about an event or person enhanced your listening ability? Can you describe the condition of being "keyed up"?

2. Can you identify a time when positive or negative emotions interfered with listening? Describe the condition of being "burned up" by emotion.

3. Can you identify a time when emotional filters seriously interfered with listening? What was the cost in time, money, or relationships?

4. How often do emotional filters interfere with your own listening objectivity?

5. Can you identify a specific time when worry or preoccupation interfered with listening or kept you from listening?

6. What specific stress situations in your life have interfered with, or are interfering with, listening competency?

7. How have listening filters interfered with each kind of listening? Provide an example from your life: discriminative, evaluative, appreciative, empathic and self-listening.

8. Can you think of specific instances when you withheld evaluation and searched for negative evidence? Did it improve the communication encounter? How?

9. What was your most successful effort at using the five-step plan for emotional objectivity?

10. Can you think of specific steps, in addition to those in the five-step plan presented in this chapter, that would help you identify emotional filters and stressful situations and help you attain listening objectivity? Write them down and discuss each.

LISTENING EXERCISES THAT WORK

EXERCISE 1. (Identifying Emotions) Identify one event in your life that caused a strong emotional reaction. Describe:

a. The immediate condition of *shock*. (How was your thinking impaired?)

b. The *diffusion* of this shock. (What was your uncontrolled physical activity?)

c. Your *transference* of this shock. (What psychological spill–over did you transfer to other people?)

EXERCISE 2. (Examining Emotions) Re–examine the event you studied in Exercise 1.

a. What was your *perception* of the event? (What did you understand happened?)

b. What was the *reality* of the event? (What actually did occur?)

EXERCISE 3. (Discover Emotional Filters) In your pocket–sized notebook, list and categorize under "People," "Subjects and Ideas," and "Elements of Language" those events that cause or have caused strong emotional reaction.

EXERCISE 4. (Evaluating Listening Filters)

Under the following headings, list that which operates as an emotional filter to your listening.

PEOPLE	SUBJECTS	ELEMENTS OF LANGUAGE
		Words
		Accents
		Tone of Voice

Choose one entry from your list. Answer these questions about it:

A. What original incident triggered this emotional response?

B. How did I react originally?

C. Do I still respond by dredging up the old familiar emotion each time it comes up?

D. Is the original event still important in my life today?

E. If yes, can I devise a plan to handle it without resorting to the same old set pattern? If no, can I set it aside and stop wasting emotional energy on this filter?

EXERCISE 5. (On-the-Spot Listening Objectivity) The next time one of these listening filters triggers an emotional response, remind yourself: (a) This is an emotional filter with which I have already dealt. (b) A conditioned familiar response keeps me from listening. (c) I will put it aside while I am listening and work out a plan later.

EXERCISE 6. (Identifying the Cost of Emotional Filters) Can you answer yes to any of these questions?

_____   1. I tend to blow up when friends/spouse/parents/children bring up personal subjects.

_____   2. My spouse/friends/co-workers complain that when they talk about important things I clam up or walk away.

_____   3. There are certain subjects that cause me to see red; I just want to straighten out the speaker's thinking.

_____   4. There are certain people to whom I simply will not listen.

_____   5. I cannot listen if the language or tone of voice irritates me.

_____   6. I listen better when I like the subject or agree with the speaker.

_____   7. I listen better when I like the way the speaker sounds or if I feel comfortable with the way the speaker looks.

_____   8. I am so tense and worried when I go to my doctor that I can't concentrate on what is being said.

_____   9. When I have my car repaired I worry so about how much it will cost that I don't listen to what the mechanic says.

_____   10. When I go to the dentist I am so frightened and in such pain that it doesn't matter what the advice is; I just can't listen.

The ideal, of course, is to have answered no to each of these questions. However, if you have answered yes to one or more, you might want to rate your performance by using the scale below:

1–2:   You have achieved a high level of listening objectivity.

3–5:   You are able to maintain listening objectivity to a fair degree.

6–8:   Your listening performance is too often short circuited by emotions.

9–10: You are allowing your emotions to exact too high a cost in dollars, health, good will, and interpersonal relationships.

How can you control the emotional interference you have discovered?

EXERCISE 7. (The Effect of Trauma on Listening) Interview a professional who deals with emotional trauma. (This could be a police officer, paramedic, nurse, doctor, counselor, etc.) To evaluate the interview, consider these questions: (a) What are some other traumatic events that could cause similar emotional trauma? (b) What effect does severe emotional trauma have on listening? (c) Why is a healing interval necessary to handle trauma and, once more, listen with some efficiency?

EXERCISE 8. (Learning to Hold Our Fire) List below five subjects on which you consider yourself an authority, such as life in a small town, growing up in an ethnic neighborhood, being short, being tall, results of divorce in a family, rearing children, starting out in a new job, etc.

A.

B.

C.

D.

E.

Choose one of the subjects on your list. With a partner, or in a small group of three to five persons, discuss:

A. How do you react when a speaker offers an opinion you know is incorrect?

B. Would you describe the reaction as feeling or emotion?

C. Give specific examples of what happened to communication when you reacted in this manner.

D. Can you use STTD to remind yourself to control this feeling or emotion?

With your partner or your group, devise a plan for managing these communication situations in order to remain objective and to listen perceptively.

EXERCISE 9. (Listening and Positive Feelings) Describe a listening situation in which your positive feelings enhanced your listening experience. In small groups, discuss each member's findings.

EXERCISE 10. (Assessing the Results of Shock, Diffusion, and Transference) Frank Snowden Hopkins believes that in all communication, first we communicate emotion and then we communicate a concept.[25] In groups of three to five members, let each member relate an example from experience of a speaker whose first message to the listener was the emotion behind the message. As a group, consider, for each:

A. What was the evidence of shock to you as a listener?

B. What was the evidence of diffusion in you as a listener?

C. What was the evidence of transference in you as a listener?

D. What was the reality of the speaker's message? What intellectual message did the speaker send?

NOTES

1. William S. Howell, *The Empathic Communicator* (Belmont, CA: Wadsworth Publishing Co., 1982), 57–58.
2. Ibid., 58.
3. Erica E. Goode, "Scientists Study the Passions of Our Lives," *Minneapolis Star Tribune* (July 21, 1991) 4th Ed.
4. James R. Averill, *Anger and Aggression: An Essay on Emotions* (New York: Springer-Verlag, 1982) 6.
5. Howell, 56.
6. Ibid., 57.
7. Goode, op. cit.
8. Calvin S. Hall and Garner Lindzey, *Theories of Personality*, 2nd ed. (New York: Wiley, 1970), 425–89.

9. Jiddu Krishnamurti, *The First and Last Freedom* (New York: Harper & Row, 1975), 78.
10. Hans Selye, *Stress Without Distress* (Philadelphia: J. B. Lippincott, 1974), 28–29.
11. Kenneth R. Pelletier, *Mind as Healer, Mind as Slayer* (New York: Dell, 1977), iii.
12. Stephanie Matthews Simonton, *The Healing Family: The Simonton Approach For Families Facing Illness* (Toronto: Bantam Books, 1984), 36–37.
13. John Clement, "Students' Preconceptions in Introductory Mechanics," *American Journal of Physics* 50 (January 1982), 66.
14. Lyman K. Steil, Larry L. Barker and Kittie W. Watson, *Effective Listening: Key to Your Success* (Reading, MA: Addison-Wesley, 1983), 98.
15. Ralph G. Nichols and Leonard A. Stevens, *Are You Listening?* (New York: McGraw-Hill, 1957), 90.
16. Anita Taylor, Theresa Rosegrant, Arthur Meyer and Thomas B. Sample, *Communicating*, 2nd ed. (Englewood Cliffs, NJ: Prentice-Hall, 1980), 38–42.
17. Claudell Stocker, *Listening for the Visually Impaired* (Springfield, IL: Thomas, 1973), xx.
18. Steil, Barker, Watson, 96–97.
19. Simonton, 86, 133.
20. Goode, op. cit.
21. Howell, 52.
22. Hall and Lindzey, 250–51.
23. Michael LeBoeuf, *Imagineering: How to Profit From Your Creative Powers* (New York: McGraw-Hill, 1980), 16.
24. David Viscott, *The Language of Feelings: The Time and Money Shorthand of Psychotherapy* (New York: Arbor House, 1976), 149.
25. Frank Snowden Hopkins, "Communication: The Civilizing Force," *The Futurist* (April 1981), 39.

CHAPTER 8

ATTENTION, CONCENTRATION, AND MEMORY CAN BE IMPROVED

It is not enough to have a good mind. The main thing is to use it well.
— Descartes

THESIS Attention, concentration, and memory are crucial components in the process of listening. It makes little sense to retrain and become expedient, perceptive listeners of oral messages unless we can remember and use the information.

CHAPTER OBJECTIVES

1. Understand the importance of focused attention, sustained concentration, and retentive storage of messages during the listening process.
2. Be aware of the integrated processing of attention, concentration and storage in short-term memory (STM), short-term memory with rehearsal (STM-R) and long-term memory (LTM).
3. Begin to retrain by applying the special behavioral techniques to improve attention, concentration, and memory as a perceptive listener.

CHAPTER PREVIEW

- Techniques to help focus attention.
- Ways to refocus to improve concentration.
- Devices to boost memory power.

" ■ 'm sorry, I mistakenly mailed the contract to 606 Stewart Street; are you positive that you said 660 Seward Street?"
"I wasted my time attending that meeting; I wasn't interested in any of the reports."
"I feel terrible about missing that appointment; I forgot."
Apparently the first speaker had difficulty focusing full attention while listening to instructions for mailing the contract. The second speaker lacked the ability or

desire to sustain concentration during the entire meeting. The third speaker failed to properly store the appointment date in short-term memory (STM).

Let's examine the first major concept, the focus of attention.

CONCEPT 1: THE FOCUS OF ATTENTION

As we begin the discussion of attention and concentration, we need to be familiar with the terms, noted in Definition Box 5.[1]

DEFINITION BOX 5:   Terms of Attention and Concentration

focus: directing mental activity toward a stimulus or message

attending: selecting to focus on an aural stimulus or message

sensory stimulus: perceiving messages by sound, sight, smell, taste, touch, and observing movement

attention: focusing and directing mental activity toward a stimulus or message; also, to transfer from sensory storage to short-term memory (STM)

margin of attention: dimly perceiving a stimulus or message

shifting of attention: changing focus of mental activity

refocus: redirecting mental activity to a perceived stimulus or message

concentration: continual refocusing upon a perceived stimulus or message

---

Note that "focus" and "refocus" are the key words in defining attention and concentration. A wide array of sensory stimuli compete for our attention. Most of us occasionally have trouble focusing full attention on a speaker's message. And when we do, are we able to refocus and sustain intense concentration to interpret the speaker's intended meaning of that message?

Fortunately, we do have the ability to focus our attention on a limited number of sensory stimuli, the ones that we choose to attend. After selecting which of the countless aural messages to attend to during a busy day, we must focus attention and concentrate to listen to the message which we have selected to perceive.

Attention and concentration are crucial stages in the listening process just as they are in reading. To use our listening time wisely and expeditiously, we focus attention and concentrate on the aural and nonverbal stimuli generated by a speaker.

Focusing attention and sustaining concentration may well be the keystones of success in the perceptive listening process. Therefore, let us examine the theoretical base of each mental activity. What is attention? How do the characteristics of attention influence the level of intensity with which we concentrate to listen?

Attention Defined

Psychologist Neil R. Carlson uses a scenario to explain the concept of attention. The attention of an angler watching a large trout is completely focused on the behavior of the fish. The angler is poised, ready to respond if the fish takes the bait. Carlson defines attention as "a selective process that controls our awareness of events in the environment."[2] Like the angler, listeners need to focus attention and be poised to respond to speakers' messages.

Professor Anthony J. Clark, of the University of Florida, defines attention as "a condition of readiness to interact."[3] He claims that no perceptual process is possible without a prior and concurrent act of attention.

The focus of attention enables us to select certain verbal and nonverbal stimuli for processing while excluding others. Selective perception and attention are closely integrated in the process of listening. Without the ability to select, focus on, and direct our mental activity toward stimuli or oral messages, we could not listen.

Shifting of Attention

Attention divides our field of aural experience into a focus and a margin. Any change in the focus and margin of attending sensory stimuli causes a shifting of attention. We are able to focus attention on those messages and events that we perceive clearly. They are the ones that we attend to and draw out from the background. At the same time, we perceive dimly other stimuli in the margin of attention. Beyond the margin of attention are still other stimuli that exist outside our field of attention; we are unaware of these.

This shifting of attention means that sensory stimuli may receive the focus of attention one second, exist in the margin of attention the next second, and a bit later, may pass from conscious awareness. Although our attention shifts, we do it with a certain orderliness; otherwise we would be unable to carry out any extended activities. This pattern of orderliness enables us to listen to and retain a series of unique names and identities when being introduced to a group of people in spite of shifting attention from one person to another. We discipline ourselves to focus and shift attention upon the sound of different names and identities. This enables us to retain pertinent information relevant to the names of new acquaintances for immediate recall and future use, as discussed in Chapter 6, Three Basic Concepts to Enhance Listening Comprehension.

Dave Thomas, the founder of Wendy's International and its spokesman, was not a success when he started appearing in commercials for the fast-food chain. "He was just another dull CEO talking about how great his company is."[4] Then Thomas changed; listeners liked his straightforward talk and dry humor.

In one commercial, an uncomfortable Thomas is shown hobnobbing with guests at a trendy cocktail party. When the hostess trills that he just has to try the crab puffs, Thomas replies in his typically deadpan way, "Man, I can hardly wait!" A recent study of attention–attracting commercials ranked Wendy's spots within the top fifteen — the highest since the company stopped using Clara Peller asking

"Where's the beef?"[5] A speaker's use of language and style of delivery can affect a listener's shifting of attention.

Certain characteristics of sound influence the way we focus and shift our attention. These factors determine which external and internal stimuli we will perceive most clearly, perceive faintly, or not perceive at all.

Focusing Attention on Aural Stimuli

Duplication of sound attracts more attention than an isolated or infrequent sound. We are apt to focus attention more readily on a series of gunshots than on a single shot, on the exciting sound of winning a slot machine jackpot than on the clanking of two or three winning coins, and on the steady dripping of water from a faulty faucet than on an occasional drip. This pattern of immediate reinforcement or repetition of aural messages invariably captures our focus of attention.

On the other hand, prolonged or frequent repetition of sound may cause us to become conditioned and indifferent to it. How many airline passengers are attentive to messages from the pilot or attendants? One airline tried an experiment. After take-off the pilot gave his name, the co-pilot's name, flight time, altitude, and speed. Shortly afterward, the flight attendant announced an in–flight contest with a prize for the person who could remember the most information from the pilot's announcement. Nobody remembered, because nobody was listening. Experiencing frequent and familiar events often gives us a sense of security and we stop listening. However, we never know what will happen when we pay attention and listen.[6]

Researchers J. Bryant and D. Zillmann studied the effects of both humor and audiovisual "fireworks" in children's television (e.g., fast-moving, colorful objects accompanied by unusual noises, exploding stars, etc.) on increased vigilance and learning. Interspersing stimuli with high potential to attract attention facilitated learning by the five- to eight-year–old subjects. The results indicated that audiovisual fireworks may work as well as humorous stimuli in recapturing the attention of an audience whose alertness is fading.[7]

The *attention span*, or how long we can be attentive to sensory stimuli, differs for each of us according to age, intelligence, health, past experience, and motivation. Author Robert Bostrom reaffirms earlier research findings about the duration of attention span. Fifteen-second attention spans are common for adults and may be followed by rehearsal or a renewed effort to focus and maintain attention on the stimulus.[8] However, the novelty of aural stimuli is apt to extend and reinforce our focus of attention.

Manufacturers rely on novel advertising to sell their products. Novel messages in commercial slogans set to music entice many listeners. We become drinkers of Diet Pepsi (You've got the right one, Baby, uh-huh, uh-huh) or Coke (to get the "real thing"). The novelty of combining catchy tunes and simplistic messages directs attention to radio and television commercials.

Novel sounds are incorporated into alarm systems to attract attention. We give high-priority attention to the piercing sound of electronic sirens warning of approaching police cars, fire trucks, or ambulances. We listen and heed the warning whether driving or walking.

The movement of sound also attracts attention. We listen attentively to the whining sound of a speeding motorboat, to the stirring cadence of a marching band, to the explosions of fireworks at July Fourth celebrations, and to the rumble of thunder during an electrical storm.

What effect does this movement of sound have on the focus of attention in relation to speaking and listening? Author James Maclachlan poses an even more specific question: "If people want what they say to be remembered, should they speak slowly, at a moderate pace, or rapidly?"[9] His study reveals that in platform or one-way communication (when one person does all the talking), faster talkers are generally more persuasive and more favorably regarded by the listeners.

We are not implying that everyone who speaks faster automatically transmits worthwhile, articulate, and well-received messages similar to those prepared for experimental research. Obviously, such is not the case. Of a lawyer he didn't like, Lincoln once said, "He can compress the most words into the smallest ideas better than any man I ever met."[10] Our point is that the rapid speaker has a much broader range for variations of rate or tempo than does the slow speaker. To accelerate tempo and speak articulately may be difficult or even impossible for the slow speaker. A broader tempo variation permits the rapid speaker to select intentional changes of pace to intensify interest, emphasis, clarity, interpretation, and expression of emotion. Such speakers become much clearer communicators because they hold the listeners' attention.

The word *intensity* means an exceptionally great concentration of sound. Intense sound commands our attention. We respond to the loud sound of a bursting balloon, to the ring of an alarm clock, to the roar of a jet-powered plane, to an unexpected clash of thunder, or to a terrifying scream.

However, intense sounds may adversely affect our hearing mechanisms. Levels above 85 decibels, or units of sound, particularly in high-frequency or high-pitched tones, can cause permanent hearing loss. Consequently, workers are required to wear ear protectors while operating high-noise level machines or directing the landing of jet-powered planes. This offsets the approximately 130 decibels of sound typical of these acoustical environments. As noted in Chapter 2, Listening Power Generates Knowledge, this same level of sound intensity has become a popular way to listen to music at concerts, night clubs, dances, parties, and at home with stereos blaring at deafening volumes. Many young persons already have suffered varying degrees of irreparable hearing loss that can handicap them in the workplace and throughout life.

Listening Techniques for Focusing Attention

Occasionally we find ourselves in frustrating listening situations. We are expected to be attentive and listen to a professor, administrator, parent, or friend when actually we prefer to be elsewhere and involved in other activities. However, once we recognize that such messages may help us achieve either short- or long-term goals, the need to be an attentive listener becomes apparent.

Understanding and practicing the following listening techniques may be helpful in directing and strengthening our focus of attention.

Vocalized Listening Technique

Both the speaker and the listener can use the vocalized listening technique. It requires a sharp, persistent focusing of attention on aural and nonverbal messages.

As we strive to become more effectual speakers we may need to apply this specialized technique in order to monitor our vocalized messages. What the speaker does is to focus attention to listen from within. Then the speaker repeats and assesses the major parts of the vocal message word for word via verbal thought or silent speech. At this point the speaker is involved in *self-listening*.

Authors Charles Brown and Paul Keller refer to the self-listening speaker:

> But we also hear, as we talk silently or aloud, our own speech, and so listening is also a response to ourselves. . . . Indeed, all that we call well-organized speech . . . is the product of hearing our speech as we speak, assessing — saying to ourselves, "And what does that mean?" — matching what we said with our purpose, and then proceeding.[11]

Competent listeners apply the vocalized listening technique while decoding the aural and nonverbal messages generated by the speaker. Because thought speed is at least two to four times that of speech, we have adequate time to apply the technique. What we do is repeat whole or major parts of the speaker's oral message via silent speech. As messages flow from the speaker's mouth, the silent-speaking listener analyzes, questions, and refocuses attention for longer retention of the message in short-term memory.

However, short-term memory has an extremely limited capacity, as we have mentioned in Chapter 2, Listening Power Generates Knowledge. It can retain data for only a few seconds. Author James McConnell at the University of Michigan explains that from the moment the brain inserts an item into short-term memory the data remains strong and clear for immediate recall. By the time the brain has processed five or six items, the original item has lost most of its strength and has begun to fade away. Once the data drop out of temporary storage, they may be lost forever.[12] The silent-speaking listener can prevent this from happening.

We have observed that successfully applying the vocalized listening technique has a considerable effect on our efforts as self-listening speakers and silent-speaking listeners. We make this effort to refocus attention on aural and nonverbal messages. Specifically, how can we apply this technique?

Retraining: Guidelines for Applying Vocalized Listening Technique

1. As a speaker, use the vocalized listening technique reservedly and only as needed to enhance speaking in unique communication settings.

2. Practice listening to yourself as you speak. Focus attention on listening to what you say in vocal messages to detect how you sound to others. Do the words you select convey your intended meaning accurately? Monitor the volume, pitch level, tempo, and quality of your voice. Is your voice appropriate for the message, the listeners, and the situation? If not, adjust it. Be articulate without sacrificing naturalness and empathy.

3. As competent listeners we need to practice silent speech for refocusing attention on aural messages to reinforce retention of data in short-term memory. If we do that, we are able to hold data in short-term memory long enough to thoughtfully interpret both aural and nonverbal cues of a speaker's message.

4. As a silent-speaking listener, refocus attention on the speaker and message and become more actively involved as a competent listener in the circular process of communication. Thus we gain keener understanding of human interaction.

Dichotic Listening Technique

Have you ever wondered how in a crowded room at a cocktail party we are able to communicate effectively in spite of the overbearing, babbling sound of mixed conversations? The answer is that we apply the dichotic listening technique. Author Gregory Kimble et al. define *dichotic listening* as a "technique for studying attention and information processing in which simultaneous but differing messages are presented to each ear via earphones."[13] Daniel Kahneman relates research studies in which adults were instructed to be attentive to and shadow or repeat all words of a particular message. The shadowed message was directed to one ear. It was called the *intended-ear message*. Meanwhile, the researchers directed a second message to the other ear called the unshadowed or *unattended-ear message*. They manipulated the unattended message by switching from one language to another, by interchanging male and female voice, and by changing from a prose message to a listing of words. As instructed, the participants directed greater attention and energy toward the intended-ear message and less toward the unattended-ear message.[14]

Researchers draw interesting conclusions from dichotic listening studies. The subjects were aware of two manipulations in the unattended ear: (1) a distinctive change in the speaker's voice, and (2) the use of their names in the messages. In a 1981 study, subjects immediately noticed and remembered a third manipulation of the unattended message: sexually explicit words.[15]

Throughout the day many of us are forced or choose to use dichotic listening in both formal and informal communication. During a public address, auditory distractions are seldom intense enough to compete with the featured speaker's message. Occasionally, however, inconsiderate members of the audience may converse among themselves loudly enough to force us to resort to dichotic listening. If so, we follow the speaker's message word for word in hopes of blocking out the distractors' unattended messages. But we are apt to apply the dichotic listening technique more during interpersonal communication at social or other gatherings. Competent listeners focus attention in one direction (within the group of friends); this reduces the energy we direct elsewhere (toward surrounding groups). Intermittently, we may be able to listen to bits of information from the unattended messages of the surrounding groups. Possibly dichotic listening may be one reason why we wander from group to group at social gatherings. In messages emerging from surrounding groups, we may have heard our names mentioned, the sound of an unusual or familiar voice, or a comment about a topic that interests us. Consequently, we dichotic listeners politely excuse ourselves to join and converse with others.

Intense sounds preclude any possibility of applying dichotic listening. When engulfed by excessively loud sounds from a lawn mower, chain saw, jackhammer, or rock music, we are unaware of other aural stimuli competing for our attention. Totally unattended messages cannot be perceived. However, those who wear earplugs on the job are able to listen dichotically. Earplugs weaken the reception of intense sound. Thus listeners are able to direct reduced energy to other aural messages: a colleague's warning, the sound of a shrill whistle, or the drone of industrial machines.

Dichotic listening may be beneficial or harmful to the listener. Feeling obligated to converse briefly before asking to be excused, we may try to literally extend the second ear to decode bits of data of a more relevant message. For example, while being warmly greeted by the host, we may be able to decode bits of an unattended message revealing that our friend's missing car keys are locked in the car. It is comforting to learn that the missing keys are discovered. It is discomforting to suspect that we may have nonverbally communicated lack of attention to the host's graciousness as we listened dichotically.

Most importantly, how can we apply the beneficial and avoid or adapt to the harmful effects of dichotic listening?

Retraining: Guidelines for Applying Dichotic Listening Technique

1. Clearly understand that dichotic listening is not an ideal, desirable, or effective kind of listening. It is only a supplementary or alternate tool for effective listening. Use it sparingly.

2. Occasionally practice dichotic listening even when there is no immediate need to do so. For example, converse with a friend while standing in a crowded area such as a main entrance gate at a stadium before a tournament game. Plan to attend and shadow part of your friend's comments. Then listen dichotically and decode bits of unattended messages from the crowd without losing the major thrust of your friend's attended message. Be careful. Do not overpractice the dichotic listening technique. It could cause you to lower your level of listening competency by becoming an easily distracted listener.

3. Do not allow yourself to apply dichotic listening at lectures or other events because of inconsiderate and boisterous members of the audience. Whenever you can benefit from applying dichotic listening, do so, but only until you can reposition yourself to attend the aural message you wish to hear.

4. Finally, realize that in practicing dichotic listening we can apply the vocalized listening technique. For example, we can refocus attention on the attended message word for word as a silent-speaking listener. In a moment, we can do the same to decode an unattended message. Remember to integrate nonverbal cues when decoding both messages.

We have discussed vocalized listening and dichotic listening. Both techniques can be applied in developing and practicing the scopic listening technique.

Scopic Listening Technique

Scopic listeners are inquisitive listeners. They are eager to attend and respond to the aural stimuli. They seek to broaden the base of knowledge, extend the range of experience, and enrich the overall frame of reference. Applying the scopic listening technique enables us to direct the focus of attention over a wide spectrum of speakers, messages, and situations.

Naturally, we attend to and perceive most readily those messages that, directly or indirectly, satisfy our basic and personal needs. We listen primarily to achieve specific goals. But there are negative side effects when we limit our listening experiences exclusively to kinds of messages that affect only ourselves.

When we purposely restrict ourselves to limited kinds of listening experiences we are *nonscopic listeners*. Nonscopic listeners are easy to detect. They are interested only in a limited scope of speakers and topics.

Retraining: Guidelines for Applying Scopic Listening Technique

1. Frequently attend a lecture on a topic that is unfamiliar to you. Make every effort to listen to learn the new information. Take appropriate and meaningful notes.

2. Each day approach at least one person whom you know only by sight. Encourage these persons to talk freely. Manifest genuine interest and listen to them empathically. Store significant parts of their messages in long-term memory as a base for future interaction.

3. Broaden your listening experience to include your personal and others' personal kinds of messages. Include the selfish approach to listening to answer your needs. Use the extended approach to listen to others who want to share their experiences or personal problems with you.

4. Get involved in organizations. Challenge yourself to practice scopic listening both informally during social events and formally during specialized public presentations. Assess the ways you have benefited and have grown as a scopic listener.

5. Periodically review what you know about practicing and developing this technique. Consider the rewards you can gather through diligent application of the technique.

We have defined attention, clarified the factors influencing the focus of attention, and discussed three techniques to increase, direct, and reinforce attention on aural stimuli. Once we have learned to focus our attention, we are at the threshold of concentration.

CONCEPT 2: THE REFOCUS OF CONCENTRATION

Concentration is a continuous mental activity to refocus upon, process and interpret a perceived stimulus or message. Our attention span or the ability to focus on a stimulus ranges from about 15 seconds to a maximum of 60 seconds, including time for rehearsal or repetition. At that point, the focus of attention and perception of the stimulus or message would be lost if we, as perceptive listeners, did not discipline ourselves to refocus on the message continuously every 15 to 60 seconds until the message is completed. In Chapter 4, Five Power Tools of Listening, we learned how the listener's self-concept influences the ability to concentrate and decode messages and "hear the speaker out." Without the ability and desire to concentrate or refocus on the message, we could not listen.

Curiosity: The Key to Concentration

How do we focus our mental powers? The key to concentration is curiosity. If we keep curious about things — how things work, how they are made, how things function — there is no limit to the heights to which we could climb. The most precious attribute that we possess is intellectual curiosity. Unfortunately, it is not for sale. And unfortunately many of us methodically and painstakingly stifle the curiosity we were born with.

Every newborn infant is a bundle of curiosity. Little arms and legs fly in every direction. Tiny hands instinctively grasp and try to put any object into the mouth. Youngsters learn fast in the first three or four years of life. But somehow, as the years pass great portions of curiosity are driven out of us. We may be left with none at all by the time we are 15 or 16 years old.

Nichols describes three ways to kill curiosity.[16] The first is through intemperance. If we eat too much, drink too much, or nightly watch the late-late movie, we are going to lose some curiosity.

A second way to kill curiosity is by failing. Suppose a third-grade school teacher says at some point, "Walter, will you read the third sentence on the page, please?" Walter tries, but stumbles and fumbles, mispronouncing words, reading and rereading each phrase. The teacher finally breaks in. "For heaven's sake, Walter. Why don't you prepare your lessons? Mary, will you read the third sentence on the page?" Mary stands and reads it smooth as silk. The teacher praises her for effort with "Well done, Mary, very well done." Mary has experienced success. Poor Walter has failed, and everyone knows it.

A third way to kill curiosity is to join a crowd that is methodically killing it. All of us are influenced by our close associates. If those close to us are intellectually growing, we will grow. If those near us are only vegetating, we probably will vegetate along with them.

Though curiosity is the key to concentration, mind control unlocks the door to deep and sustained powers of concentration.

Concentration and Mind Control

The electroencephalograph is a machine that graphically records the pattern of brain waves. *Alpha rhythm* in the brain is caused by small, fast electric waves of 10–12 cycles per second. *Delta rhythm* is caused by large, slow electric waves of 1–3 cycles per second. Experts claim that Albert Einstein and Thomas Edison used their alpha waves when concentrating on inventions and solving difficult problems.

Concentrating to listen requires a swift, purposeful movement of our mental faculty to sustain the focus of attention on one stimulus. If we could examine the processing of thought in the brain of an efficient listener for a single instant, we would find that the impact of only one aural message has a clear focus at any given moment. We must exert strenuous effort to extend and reinforce the focus of attention by refocusing repeatedly to concentrate on the chosen message. We do this to resist other competing stimuli floating on the surface of our thought stream. Concentrating to listen demands self-discipline. It is a form of mental exercise and individual mind control.

Hypnosis, a form of mind control, induces a sleeplike trance. It requires deep concentration to create the necessary physiological change from delta to alpha brain waves. Listening and the ability to concentrate are key factors for successful hypnosis. To induce a hypnotic trance, author Margaret Hyde explains, the subject is persuaded "to relax and focus attention on the hypnotist's directions while the hypnotist repeats certain phrases or sentences along with suggestions and encouragement."[17] *Yoga*, a Hindu form of mind control, requires deep concentration by the participant, who, through sustained meditation, assumes the identity of an object. Recent studies show that when master yogis are in a deep state of meditation, they show much more alpha brain–wave activity than the average person.[18]

We do not suggest hypnosis or yoga as forms of mind control to improve the power of concentration among listeners. However, we do know that deep concentration causes physiological changes resulting in greater alpha wave activity in the brain. Therefore, we suggest deeper and more sustained concentration when listening to activate the alpha waves of the brain. We need more practice in concentrating to listen.

In his book, *Listening Made Easy*, Robert Montgomery explains that total and honest listening requires concentration. He advises us to avoid distractions and maintain order. "Keep meetings private. No phones ringing, no knocks on the door. Keep your desk, briefcase, and even your pockets from being overloaded. Order and organization foster concentration. It's a matter of self-control that improves with practice."[19]

Disrupted Concentration and Listening

As we learned in Chapter 3, Ten Axioms About Listening, listening and reading are the two receptive communication skills. Disrupted concentration on written messages produces poor readers. These readers frequently glance back to reread sentences or paragraphs to clarify the meaning of the writer's message. Interfering with the stream of concentration while reading jeopardizes performance and efficiency. Consequently, poor readers develop poor reading techniques and skills.

Unlike the reader, who has direct recourse to the writer's message, listeners have no way of retrieving the speaker's original message. Oral communication is unrepeatable. Even if we request the speaker to repeat the message, the nonverbal (bodily movement) and paralinguistic (changes in voice and diction) cues, and the situational conditions (changes in time and the physical environment) interwoven with the verbal message cannot be duplicated. In fact, repeated messages become original second messages. Authors Bobby Patton and Kim Giffin point out: "The words of a teacher, even when faithfully repeated, do not produce the same effect, but may lead to a new insight, increased tension, or complete boredom."[20] Therefore, if our concentration on the speaker's original message has been disrupted we never can receive the full, original, intended message. That message is lost forever.

Regardless of age, the pattern of concentration can easily be disrupted. The thought patterns of the older brain occasionally may meander in the cluttered traces of thought. The younger listener's brain can trace a comparatively straight channel of thought. However, this is not always true when concentrating to listen. Disrupted concentration plagues many young listeners. These pretending listeners, instead of concentrating to listen, daydream, analyze problems, or try to catch up on missing sleep. No matter what our age, we must try to avoid disruptions in our pattern of concentrating to listen. Therefore, as we listen to patients, students, supervisors, friends, loved ones, or anyone who reaches out for us to listen throughout the day, it is crucial that we sustain concentration. We can do so by applying certain techniques for increasing concentration to listen.

Techniques for Increasing Concentration

During formal and informal communication we can apply several techniques to increase our power of concentration and level of listening competency.

The Self-Discipline and Concentration Technique

Exercising self-discipline to sustain the refocus of attention is difficult and requires persistent application.

We need a great deal of discipline to control the direction of thought as we listen. One of your authors can recall the comment of a university professor who, during the first class period, explained that one half of life is luck and the other half is discipline — "and that's the important half, for without discipline you wouldn't know what to do with your luck." If we listen efficiently, we practice self-discipline to control the direction of our thoughts during more than half of each day's waking hours. Efficient listeners grow and benefit from the knowledge they acquired by practicing self-discipline to concentrate.

Lack of self-discipline plays havoc with all who should be listening but do not concentrate on it. Nearly three out of every ten college freshmen flunk at the end of the first term or semester for not achieving academic standards. In most cases they have not exercised enough self-discipline to concentrate to listen and learn in the classroom and use their time wisely.

The following suggestions may be helpful for improving self-discipline to concentrate.

1. Preview your daily schedule of expected listening events. Daily schedules revolve around the time we awaken, eat, go to classes or work, and enjoy recreation. Visualize the persons with whom you communicate in such events (spouse, roommate, family, close friends, and other students or colleagues). Realize that we often fail to discipline ourselves to concentrate to listen to those most involved in our daily lives.

2. Make a list of persons who invariably distract you from concentrating to listen. Regardless of the kind of listening you may be expected to do, silently talk yourself into being an empathic listener. Try feeling for the speakers rather than feeling for yourself. Also, by directing yourself to convert negative emotional response into positive emotional response, you can expend more energy on concentrating to listen.

3. Remind yourself that the mind is as limitless as the universe. Be firm with yourself to concentrate and use this remarkable power. Review and preview the message. Weigh the evidence presented. Direct your fantasy artist to draw mental pictures of messages. Monitor, repeat, question, and analyze the speaker's verbal and nonverbal messages.

4. Use self-talk as a monitoring process to sustain the refocus of concentration.

Stop-and-Go Listening Technique

To use this technique successfully, we need to remember the operation of the one-process brain and the STTD (Speech Thought Time Differential) listening time, discussed in Chapter 4, Five Power Tools of Listening. We know that the brain can focus and sustain the refocus of concentration on only one stimulus or message at a time. Incorporating these concepts with the stop–and–go listening technique determines how effectively we handle interruptions. Short interruptions of the listening process may be planned or unplanned.

In Chapter 6, Three Basic Concepts to Enhance Listening Comprehension, we stressed taking minimal notes in using any of the seven note–taking systems. To jot down a short note during STTD listening time means we stop listening. After the notation, we go back to listening. Only small segments of listening time should be used for taking notes.

Listeners can plan and control interruptions while listening to audio books. Clip your tape player on your belt and go to work. Merely turn off the recorder to handle an interruption.

Books on tape can be "read" while listeners are driving, walking, gardening or performing any activity where the "hands are busy and the mind is free." Books are taped by professional readers or by the author. Most public libraries offer audio books free on loan.[21]

It may be more difficult to handle unplanned interruptions in listening. In the following examples, we need to use the STTD (Speech Thought Time Differential) segment of listening time to advantage.

- Responding to an urgent request: While on the telephone you notice a concerned colleague, and you stop listening for a split second to convey the message, "Not now — later." Then you go back to listening.
- Car radios in the workplace: Surrounded by a constant barrage of car radio messages, police officers listen intently to colleagues' explanations or citizens' complaints. After decoding a message, they either rush to investigate a crime or return to a former task. These professionals use the stop–and–go listening technique frequently on the job.
- Viewing a startling TV report: You are engrossed in viewing the tragic plight of "sewer children" when your roommate excitedly enters the room to share important news. Should you use the stop–and–go listening technique and try to receive the most information from both sources? Research indicates that mature television viewers are able to be involved in secondary or even tertiary activities. But the auditory mode plays a more important role in processing content information.[22] However, one cannot receive the complete content of either message and adequately respond.

Retraining: Guidelines for Using the Stop–and–Go Listening Technique

1. Use the stop–and–go listening technique only as needed. Overuse of the technique may become habitual and downgrade the level of listening competency.
2. While using the technique remind yourself that listening interruptions need to be short to fit the STTD listening time slots.
3. When the technique must be applied consistently on the job, be on guard against using the technique when not required — at home, in social encounters, and other listening events.
4. Do not interrupt the listening process on a mere whim. Learn to assess the need to use the stop–and–go listening technique. Use it wisely.

We have discussed two of three major concepts included in this chapter: the focus of attention and the refocus of concentration. The third concept, memory power, is a crucial element of the listening process.

CONCEPT 3: MEMORY POWER

We need to study and understand a series of terms relating to retraining to improve memory, noted in Definition Box 6.[23]

DEFINITION BOX 6:   Terms Relating to Improving Memory

memory: mental storage and retrieval involving sensory, short-term and long-term memory

storage: the memory system consisting of short-term memory (STM), short-term memory with rehearsal (STM-R), and long-term memory (LTM)

sensory memory: represents the original stimulus and all or most of the information perceived; lasts a second or less

visual sensory memory: a brief sighting for transfer into short-term memory

auditory sensory memory: holds initial sounds until words are completed and transferred into short-term memory

short-term memory (STM): immediate memory of perceived stimuli with storage limit of seven to nine items for maximum of 15 seconds; called primary or working memory

rehearsal buffer: a "special rehearsal" storage in short-term memory (STM-R); can last about 60 seconds, if opportunity exists to repeat or rehearse the data silently or orally

long-term memory: permanent storage; not activated until at least 60 seconds after presenting the stimulus or message; contains mixtures of new and old information tied together with a thread creating continuity; called secondary memory

episodic memory: long-term memory about specific things we have done, seen, heard, smelled, and tasted at certain events

semantic memory: long-term memory of academic type of knowledge

explicit memory: long-term memory of which we are aware; we know we have learned something

implicit memory: long-term unconscious memory; cannot talk directly about its content; i.e., skills in riding a bicycle

short-term listening (STL): brief listening events in dyadic (two persons) and small–group interactions; informal greetings

short-term listening with rehearsal (STL-R): intermediate-length listening events with time for repetition to store ten items or more; informal and recreational encounters

long-term listening (LTL): lengthy or prolonged listening tasks; a lecture or an extended report

memorizing: ability to recall, recognize, and remember exact data for future reference; used for hard-to-learn information

mnemonics: memory aids; using formulas, rhymes, charts, and other devices to train the mind and improve memory

retrieval: a process of regaining, restoring, recalling, and remembering

acronym: a series of initial letter cues to recall specific data (AMA, American Medical Association; NBA, National Basketball Association; IRS, Internal Revenue Service; AA, Alcoholics Anonymous)

acrostics: word or sentence cues for easy recall of specific data (the word HOMES to name the Great Lakes: *H*uron, *O*ntario, *M*ichigan, *E*rie and *S*uperior; FACE to name spaces on the treble clef music staff; the sentence, *Every good boy does fine*, for the lines on the treble clef: *E, G, B, D, F*)

rhyme: similar speech sounds (an effective diction exercise is to repeat *how now, brown cow*); use extreme LOMM (large open moving mouth).

We have stressed the importance of the attention and concentration processes involved in listening. It makes little sense to enhance these processes as we hear and attend, interpret and re-create, retain and respond to verbal and nonverbal stimuli unless we remember or use the information transmitted. We suspect that each of the three major components of memory (short-term, rehearsal, and long-term) is involved in listening behavior in different ways with different listeners.[25]

To expedite storage and retrieval of oral messages, we need to learn to apply mnemonics, memory-aid devices taught and used in ancient times.

Mnemonics

The astounding results of mnemonics training continues to amaze contemporary scholars. It is recorded that ancient Hindus chanted detailed hymns recounting the history of civilization.[26] These chants provided listeners with more detailed data than could have been recorded on stone or papyrus scrolls; and there are other recorded alleged feats of memory:

- Hortensius, a celebrated Roman orator, could recite in order the names of buyers, the articles purchased, and prices paid after attending a day-long public sale.
- Seneca, a Roman philosopher, could recite 2,000 names after hearing them once.
- ibn-Sina (Avicenna), a tenth–century Arab philosopher, could recite the Koran at the age of ten and the works of Aristotle at age fourteen.
- Themistocles, an Athenian scholar, knew each one of the 30,000 citizens of Athens by name.
- Scipio Asiaticus, a Roman scribe, could address each one of the 243,704 arms-bearing Romans by name.
- Michelangelo and Leonardo da Vinci, as youths, could accurately draw detailed portraits of people after one encounter.
- Napoleon knew the names of every military officer and thousands of details of the maps of Europe.

....

New Patient: "Doctor, I don't know what to do. You've got to help me; I just can't remember a thing. I hear something one minute, and the next minute I forget it. What should I do?"
Doctor: "Pay in advance!"[24]

Later, scholars became dependent on the written word; there appeared little need to commit teachings to memory. It was not until the early nineteenth century that scholars rediscovered mnemonics as effective systems to develop highly trained memory.

Your memory is the "bank" of your mind. Life experiences, the facts and ideas you accumulate, and the teachings you master are all stored in the "vaults" of your memory bank.[27]

Storage and Sensory Modalities

Memory expert Alan S. Brown states that we process information into memory via the visual, auditory, and motion modalities. While most people use all three sensory modalities, the effectiveness of the modes differs from person to person. Most of us use a combination of two modes.[28]

Visual Modality
You are a visual person if you respond well to written communication — memos, letters, reports and outlines; you prefer to send written memos to colleagues or friends. You rely on your fantasy artist and PIM (Pictures in Mind) to decode and store messages. While listening to a new telephone number (436-3924), a graphic pattern flashes in the mind: make a dot for the 4; go down one dot to 3; up three dots to 6; see the dash; down three dots to 3; up six dots to 9; down seven dots to 2; up two dots to 4. With the help of the fantasy artist, a visual person creates images in the mind effortlessly while listening.

Auditory Modality
You are an auditory-oriented person if you easily remember phone messages; quickly grasp catchy slogans, commercials and songs; and prefer informal discussions and phone calls to receive information. Often you listen to self-talk conversations about your experiences.

Motion Modality
You are a motion-oriented person if you are keenly aware of your own actions and those of objects and people around you. You like to demonstrate by touching and holding objects and walking through a process. You tend to touch those with whom you talk or walk to enhance communication. Pacing back and forth stimulates ideas. You remember others' movements, body postures, and gestures.[29]

Identifying the modality or combinations we use most frequently as we listen to learn and store data can direct us to retrain to improve memory. (To identify your natural modality pattern, turn to the end of this chapter and complete exercises 7 and 8 to assess your natural modality patterns.)

....

You can remember any new piece of information if it is associated with something you already know or remember in some ridiculous way.[31]

Memory can be improved despite a common belief that a good memory is inherited. Granted, some are born with superior memories. However, each of us can significantly strengthen and improve our memory by applying the same methods for improving listening behavior. It requires a knowledge of various techniques, the discovery of a method that works for you, and practice.[30]

In Chapter 6, Three Basic Concepts to Enhance Listening Comprehension, we discussed the concept of PIM. To train the mind and improve memory, the ability to direct our fantasy artists to create PIM increases the effectiveness of memory management. While listening we can more easily decode, retain, store, and retrieve data during short-term memory with rehearsal (STM-R) to maximum capacity (ten items). After listening, we can store an infinite amount of data in long-term memory (LTM).

Let's examine several mnemonic techniques which are basic to retraining to improve memory power.

PIM—(Pictures in Mind) Link Mnemonic Technique
Begin listening to a list of twelve objects (clock, flag, goblet, ruler, scissors, spool, hat, piggy bank, necklace, baseball, book, bowl). While applying the PIM link technique with rehearsal of data during the STTD (Speech-Thought-Time Differential) listening time, chunk or cluster the first four words: clock, flag, goblet, ruler.

You see a clock, mounted on a flag that is waving to a goblet of wine being stirred by a ruler. (The data is processed by the *vision and motion modalities*). Rehearse the data. Chunk the next group of words: scissors, spool, hat, piggy bank.

You hear scissors cutting thread causing the spool to roll by a hat being trampled upon by a squealing piggy bank. Rehearse. (The data is processed by the *motion modality*.) Chunk the last four words: necklace, baseball, book, bowl.

You hear the jangle of a gold chain necklace around a baseball speeding toward an audio book reciting to a fine crystal bowl. Rehearse. (The data is processed by the *auditory modality*.)

By applying PIM—link technique and rehearsing data, we have stored in STM-R three chunks of data (12 items) that later can be stored in LTM (long-term memory).

A new bank president did his memory homework. While listening to an associate read a list of major bank clients during the first staff meeting, he applied the PIM—link technique as follows:

MAJOR CLIENTS	PIM LINKS BY FANTASY ARTIST
Hamil Feedlot	A huge pig is gorging at a trough in Princess Di's oil field. She sprinkles heavenly spices onto rows of corn houses built in western style. Women's skirts flare out around the furniture.
Royal Petroleum	
Celestial Seasonings	
Corn Construction	
Wild West Disco	
Fairmont Furniture	

The new president was able to store and use seven of 15 clients' names during the meeting. Shortly after the meeting, he had memorized all 15 clients' names using the PIM-link mnemonic technique.[32] (Students can use this device to learn and remember the ten axioms of listening discussed in Chapter 3.)

PIM *Loci* Technique

This device involves pairing images of places with images of objects in precise location *(loci)*. For example, we can remember who attended a recent meeting by directing our fantasy artists to draw each attendee at successive locations: Morlan, Harwood and Blatt climbing the steps; Heilson and Gross, entering via the front door; the Brown brothers conversing in the foyer; Wadell and Gautherie, checking the food in the kitchen, etc. Rehearse the data by mentally reentering and walking through the house while applying the PIM-*Loci* Technique.

This technique expedites listening and learning in various environments. The same location for another familiar location can be used repeatedly to implement the technique.

Students can benefit from using the PIM–*loci* technique to learn and store concepts. For example, the title of this chapter is "Attention, Concentration and Memory Can Be Improved." See yourself staring at words on a huge sign (attention = focus) hanging above your front door. You enter the living room and see hundreds of friends refocusing their cameras to take your picture while repeating, "Concentration = refocus"; blocking your bedroom door is a gigantic box labeled *memory* with two side holes marked *storage* and *retrieval* (memory = storage and retrieval). You have learned and stored in memory three important concepts.

The effectiveness of the PIM-*loci* technique to improve recall has been demonstrated by psychologist Gordon Bower and others in laboratory settings.[33] Anthropologists describe a similar technique used by the Arunta of Australia, who repeated long folk tales with amazing accuracy. The Arunta associated various parts and details of the landscape and countryside with tribal myths. Telling a story was a matter of taking a PIM-*loci* walk through the countryside.[34] Using the PIM-*loci* technique to increase memory power can be as successful in the twentieth century as it was 2,500 years ago.

By using the PIM–link and PIM–*loci* mnemonic systems, we can recall a series of words, names, and activities; but, we cannot instantly identify the *order* of the data in the series. Using the peg-word system enables us to do so.

Peg–Word System

The peg–word system helps listeners remember abstractions that are more difficult to remember than concrete items. The PIM technique, an intricate part of the system, facilitates remembering the sequential order of items and other data.

This is how the system works. Use PIM to see the peg word for each phonetic sound and its rhyming associated number. We list ten such pairs adapted from the peg–word system of memory experts Wonder and Donovan to illustrate the concept.[35]

1. gun	6. sticks
2. shoe	7. heaven
3. tree	8. gate
4. door	9. wine
5. hive	10. hen

Practice reciting these peg words forward and backward until they are a part of you. Let's use the peg words to memorize the names of the ten Canadian provinces.

1. gun   Nova Scotia: Nova Scotians armed with guns lie in

2. shoe   New Brunswick: new bronze shoes

3. tree   Newfoundland: hanging from new-found trees on Prince

4. door   Prince Albert Island: Albert's four island doors.

5. hive   Saskatchewan: Sassy bees from sticky hives carry

6. sticks   Manitoba: sticks in shiny marching band bass tubas

7. heaven Ontario: onward and upward to heaven where

8. gate   Alberta: Alberta greets them at the gate

9. wine   Quebec: with a queenly wine toast to the tenth

10. hen   British Columbia: province, British Columbia.

We know how difficult it is to listen to and learn numbers. The phonetic system can simplify the process.

Phonetic System
The phonetic system changes numbers, which are difficult to remember to letters and uses them as words or codes for easier recall. The phonetic alphabet consists of ten pairs of one or more consonant sounds assigned to each digit.[36]

1 — t (has *one* downward stroke)

2 — n (*two* downward strokes)

3 — m (*three* downward strokes)

4 — r (the word *four* ends in *r*)

5 — l (five extended fingers of your hand make an *L*)

6 — j, sh or ch and soft g (letter *j* turned around resembles a *6*)

7 — k or hard co (*k* is two *7*'s back to back)

8 — f, g, j (the three letters are formed with loops like an *8*)

9 — p, b, d (have loops like a *9*)

0 — z, s (first sound in the word *zero* is *z*)

Once listeners memorize the code, numbers can be converted into phrases or sentences by adding vowels between them, for example, the number <u>9894</u>: <u>D</u>ow

Jones Prices Rampage; or an automobile license # ZG 7299 as K N B B or Ziggy (ZG) has knobby knees.

$$\begin{matrix} K & N & B & B \\ 7 & 2 & 9 & 9 \end{matrix}$$

The phonetic system can be applied to remember codes for pricing, inventory, invoices, account numbers, phone numbers, addresses, etc. It requires left- and right-brain operations to associate and formulate unique words, phrases and sentences. Many persons find the phonetic system difficult to apply; others love to use it.

Other mnemonic techniques to expedite listening and increase memory power are acronyms, acrostics, and rhymes. Definitions and examples of these mnemonic devices are noted in Definition Box 2.

Acronyms and acrostics are closely related. Acronyms are initial *letter cues* to signal and identify names: AIDS (Acquired Immune Deficiency Syndrome) and AAA (American Automobile Association). Acrostics are *word and sentence cues* used to recall specific data. We used the word *SMART* as an acrostic for goal setting and evaluating listening (see Chapter 1, Listening to Succeed).

We easily remember sentences that rhyme, like "Thirty days has September, April, June and November. . . ."

Retraining: Guidelines for Improving Memory Power

1. Begin retraining to improve listener memory power by selecting several mnemonic techniques to apply on a daily basis in the home, workplace, and other settings.

2. During listening events, remind yourself to direct the focus of attention and refocus of concentration to implement PIM (Pictures In Mind) with rehearsal time to retain, store, and retrieve information.

3. Initially, memorizing codes of the peg-word and phonetic systems may seem difficult to learn. However, goal-oriented listeners who envision themselves as "sophisticated beginners with perseverance" can progress to an advanced level of memory–power retraining.

4. Retraining to improve and increase memory power works hand in hand with developing a balanced pattern of left- and right-brain thinking. Integrating creative, emotional, and nonverbal information processed by the right brain with factual and analytical information processed by the left brain to store in memory enables us to become holistic perceptive listeners.

5. Regardless of which mnemonic devices you decide to use in your memory retraining program, don't become discouraged. As you apply the concepts and techniques described in this chapter, you will notice a dramatic change in your ability to listen and remember.

6. Peruse books written by memory specialists. A number of memory systems, strategies, and tactics are included in the books documented at the end of this chapter in the Notes section.

WRAPPING IT UP: A SUMMARY

In this chapter, we discuss three interrelated concepts crucial to the process of listening: attention, concentration, and memory.

The focus and shifting of attention are affected by repetition, change and contrast, novelty, movement, and intensity of sound. Certain listening techniques can strengthen and sustain the focus of attention: vocalized, dichotic, and scopic listening techniques.

The refocus of concentration is positively or negatively affected by the degree of intellectual curiosity and mind control. Two techniques related to sustaining concentration are: the self-discipline and stop-and-go listening-techniques.

To improve and increase memory power, there are seven memory aids or mnemonic techniques: the PIM-link, PIM-*loci*, peg-word system, phonetic system, acronyms, acrostics, and rhymes. The basic rule to be observed for successful application of mnemonic techniques is: You can remember any new piece of information if it is associated in some ridiculous way with something you already know.

DISCUSSION AND STUDY GUIDES

1. Briefly describe and give an example for each of five characteristics of sound. Which ones attract your immediate focus of attention? Why?

2. Explain the difference between focus of attention and refocus of concentration. What bearing does accelerated speech have on attention, concentration, and listening competency?

3. List and briefly define ten terms related to improving memory. Which of the terms listed in Definition Box 9 do you consider most likely to help you improve and increase your memory power?

4. Of the seven mnemonic techniques, which ones have you been using in short-term memory while listening? Which ones have you not been using? Specifically, what are your goals and plans to improve storage and retrieval of information during listening events?

5. Using the three concepts presented in this chapter (attention, concentration, and memory), assess your listening behavior in each category. Specifically, what are your plans to retrain as a holistic perceptive listener?

LISTENING EXERCISES THAT WORK

EXERCISE 1. (Spatial Focus of Attention on Aural Stimuli) In the Listener Log, make four columns with the headings: Exterior-Building Sounds, Exterior-Room Sounds, Inside-Room Sounds, and Intrapersonal Sounds. In a quiet room and with your eyes closed, focus attention and concentrate for 15 seconds on sounds that come exclusively from outside the building. Then focus attention for an additional five seconds on only one of the exterior-building sounds. In the appropriate column in the Log, list the exterior-building sounds to which you listened; underscore the isolated sound. Repeat this procedure as you focus attention and concentrate on exterior-room sounds, inside-room sounds, and intrapersonal sounds. Record the results in the Log. Share the recorded data with other students or trainees.

EXERCISE 2. (Analysis of Attention Focus of Aural Stimuli) Form small groups for discussion of the following questions relating to Exercise 1: (a) In each category of the four sound areas, what percent of the total number of sounds identified by others in the class did you perceive? (b) After classifying each sound as common or uncommon, which sounds in each category would you identify as the most common and uncommon? (c) Which of the characteristics influencing attention to sound, discussed in this chapter, directed your attention to sounds in the different areas? (d) What have you learned about disciplining yourself to be an attentive listener and your ability to concentrate?

EXERCISE 3. (Concentrating to Listen and Retain) Form small groups. Each person is to prepare a five-item list of: (a) numbers, (b) foods, (c) popular songs, and (d) prominent personalities. Each group listens attentively as members take turns reading a list, pausing two seconds after each item. Each speaker, after reading the complete list, will ask three questions, such as which was the third number listed or which was the largest number or which was the fifth number? Members keep score of their responses to the different lists. After the four rounds of exercises are completed, identify the group winners with the highest cumulative scores in the respective groups.

EXERCISE 4. (Assessing Attention and Concentration While Listening) How proficient are you in focusing attention and concentrating to listen? Carefully assess your listening behavior in respect to the following 12 listening traits. After each one, place a check in the most appropriate of the assessment columns.

WHILE LISTENING I:	ALMOST ALWAYS	USUALLY	SOME-TIMES	SELDOM	ALMOST NEVER	SCORE
1. Focus attention despite many distractions	___	___	___	___	___	___
2. Focus attention on difficult material	___	___	___	___	___	___
3. Prefer to sustain rather than shift attention	___	___	___	___	___	___
4. Apply dichotic listening when necessary	___	___	___	___	___	___
5. Do not expect to be rewarded for being attentive	___	___	___	___	___	___
6. Discipline myself to concentrate when listening	___	___	___	___	___	___

	ALMOST ALWAYS	USUALLY	SOME-TIMES	SELDOM	ALMOST NEVER	SCORE
7. Concentrate on speaker's verbal/ nonverbal messages	_____	_____	_____	_____	_____	_____
8. Use the Speech-Thought-Time differential to advantage	_____	_____	_____	_____	_____	_____
9. Concentrate to listen and care about others	_____	_____	_____	_____	_____	_____
10. Concentrate intently in the role of an empathic listener	_____	_____	_____	_____	_____	_____
11. Concentrate and ask probing questions later	_____	_____	_____	_____	_____	_____
12. Am satisfied with my power of concentration to listen	_____	_____	_____	_____	_____	_____

YOUR TOTAL LISTENING COMPETENCY SCORE _____

EXERCISE 5. (Interpreting Your Attention/Concentration Score) Using the sixth column of the assessment chart, tally your score as follows:

For every Almost Always checked, give yourself a score of 10.
For every Usually checked, give yourself a score of 8.
For every Sometimes checked, give yourself a score of 6.
For every Seldom checked, give yourself a score of 4.
For every Almost Never checked, give yourself a score of 2.

Interpret your total score as follows:

High: 110 and above = You are an extraordinarily attentive and concentrating listener.

Medium: 90-110 = You focus attention and concentrate well to listen.

Retrain: Below 90 = You need to retrain yourself to be more attentive and to listen with more concentration.

EXERCISE 6. (Analyzing Your Power of Concentration while Listening) On which of the 12 traits, noted in Exercise 4, have you scored extremely high and extremely low? Do you think your behavior affects your level of listening competency? Are your scores on the remaining traits basically clustered in a high or low range? In your Log, write a one-page personal evaluation on retraining to improve attention and concentration. Analyze and discuss your scores with other students or trainees.

EXERCISE 7. (A Self-Assessment Modality Scale)[37] For each statement, check one of the three choices that most closely suits your preference or behavior, not what you think is the *right* answer — there aren't any *right* answers.

1. I get the most out of information when it is presented in:
   - _____ c. trial-run actions
   - _____ a. graphs
   - _____ b. conferences

2. If I have a problem to solve, my first impulse is to:
   - _____ b. gather advice from others
   - _____ c. conduct an on-site investigation
   - _____ a. read current information about the problem

3. When saying good-bye to a friend, I am most likely to say:
   - _____ b. "Talk to you later."
   - _____ c. "I'll be in touch."
   - _____ a. "See you soon."

4. I can most easily tell when people are nervous by:
   - _____ b. listening to their voice
   - _____ c. noting their body posture and movements
   - _____ a. watching their facial expressions

5. To get feedback from someone about an idea, I am apt to say:
   - _____ b. "How does this sound?"
   - _____ a. "Can you picture this?"
   - _____ c. "Let me run this by you."

6. I derive the most enjoyment and learning of a new topic by:
   - _____ a. reading a description of the topic
   - _____ c. having it demonstrated
   - _____ b. hearing someone explain it

7. I am most likely to be kept awake at night by:
   - _____ c. an uncomfortable bed
   - _____ b. a dripping faucet
   - _____ a. a light in the room

8. In analyzing a new procedure, I find it most helpful to:
   - _____ a. draw a diagram
   - _____ c. review the steps
   - _____ b. talk about it

9. I am most easily distracted by:

_____ a. objects that are disordered or out of place

_____ b. loud or unusual noises

_____ c. sudden or erratic movements around me

10. Complex data are most easily summarized in:

_____ c. a working model

_____ a. a table

_____ b. a descriptive report or narrative

EXERCISE 8. (Identifying Your Modality Pattern) Below, check the modality that you believe is your strongest mode of sensory perception and memory.

_____ visual   _____ auditory   _____ motion

Now refer back to Exercise 7 (A Self-Assessment Modality Scale). Total the number of a's, b's, and c's. In the scoring, *a = visual; b = auditory and c = motion*. The highest number should represent your strongest mode and the lowest your weakest mode. How does your personal assessment of memory style in Exercise 8 compare with the results of the self-assessment scoring in Exercise 7? How can you use this information in retraining to improve your memory?

EXERCISE 9. (Popular Mnemonics to Improve Memory) Form into triads. Write the headings of three columns: acronyms, acrostics and rhymes. Allow ten minutes for group members to list three examples they have used in each device. After sharing each other's data, answer the following: Which mnemonic device seems easier to use to improve memory? Which examples do you use frequently and infrequently? Explain how you can use mnemonic devices to improve memory in classes or on the job.

EXERCISE 10. (Listening to the News with PIM) Using your fantasy artist, listen intently to a newscast for fifteen minutes using the PIM-link technique. Go to a quiet place. Visualize the PIM links used during the newscast and write minimum notes of what you remember. Repeat this exercise using the PIM-*loci* technique. Are you listening more perceptively when applying mnemonic devices? Which technique enables you to store and retrieve information more effectively? Do you plan to use mnemonic devices in daily listening events? Explain. In your Log, write a summary of what you learned from this exercise or discuss it with your colleagues.

NOTES

1. Definitions are adapted from: Robert N. Bostrom, *Listening Behavior* (New York: Guilford Press, 1990), 10–11, Marie T. Harris, *How to Be Successful in Reading, Studying, Taking Exams, and Writing in College* (Warminster, PA: Surrey Press, 1983), 106.
2. Neil R. Carlson, *Psychology: The Science of Behavior*, 3rd ed. (Boston: Allyn and Bacon, 1990), 369.
3. Anthony J. Clark, "Sub-Threshold Auditory Stimuli in Listening," *Journal of the International Listening Association*, 4 (1990), 88.
4. Kim Foltz, "Folksy ads put folks in stores, says Dave," *Dayton (OH) Daily News*, September 3, 1990, 6.
5. Ibid.
6. John R. Ward, "Now Hear This: Without Listening, There Is No Communication," International Association of Business Communicators, *Communication World* (July 1990), 21.
7. J. Bryant, D. Zillmann and D. Brown, "Entertainment features in children's educational television: Effects on attention and information acquisition" in J. Bryant & D. R. Anderson (eds.), *Children's Understanding of Television* (New York: Academic Press, 1983), 235; cited in Bostrom, *Listening Behavior*, 189.
8. Robert N. Bostrom and Carrol L. Bryant, "Factors in the Retention of Information Presented Orally: The Role of Short-Term Listening," *Western Journal of Speech Communication*, 44 (Spring 1980), 137–45.
9. James Maclachlan, "What People Really Think of Fast Talkers," *Psychology Today* (November 1979), 113–17.
10. DeWitte T. Holland (ed.), a quotation noted in Religious Speech Communication Association, *Religious Communication Today* 2 (1980), 26.
11. Charles T. Brown and Paul W. Keller, *Monologue to Dialogue: An Exploration of Interpersonal Communication*, 2nd ed. (Englewood Cliffs, NJ: Prentice–Hall, 1979), 65.
12. James V. McConnell, *Understanding Human Behavior: An Introduction to Psychology*, 3rd ed. (New York: Holt, Rinehart and Winston, 1980), 522.
13. Gregory A. Kimble, Norman Garmezy and Edward Zigler, *Principles of General Psychology*, 5th ed. (New York: Wiley, 1980), 516.
14. Daniel Kahneman, *Attention and Effort* (Englewood Cliffs, NJ: Prentice-Hall, 1973), 113–15.
15. L. L. Nielsen and I. G. Sarason, "Emotions, personality and selected attention," *Journal of Personality and Social Psychology* 41 (1981), 945–60; cited in Carlson, *Psychology: The Science of Behavior*, 370.
16. Ralph G. Nichols, "Curiosity—The Key to Concentration," *Management of Personnel Quarterly*, 2 (Spring 1963), 23–26.
17. Margaret O. Hyde, *Brainwashing and Other Forms of Control* (New York: McGraw-Hill, 1977), 84.
18. R. K. Wallace and H. Benson, "The Physiology of Meditation," *Scientific American*, 226 (1972), 85–90.
19. Robert L. Montgomery, *Listening Made Easy: How to Improve Listening at Home, On the Job and in the Community* (American Management Association, Communication Division, 1981), 99.
20. Bobby R. Patton and Kim Giffin, *Interpersonal Communication in Action: Basic Text and Readings*, 2nd ed. (New York: Harper & Row, 1977), 35.
21. Laura Dempsey, "Stick it in your ears: Rest your eyes while listening to a good book," *Dayton (OH) Daily News*, Magazine Section, March 29, 1991, 16.
22. D. R. Anderson and E. P. Lorch, "Looking at television: Action or reaction?" in J. Bryant and D. R. Anderson (eds.), *Children's Understanding of Television*, cited in Bostrom, *Listening Behavior*, 183.
23. Carlson, 253–88; also Joan E. Grusec, Robert S. Lockhart and Gary C. Walter, *Foundations of Psychology* (Toronto: Copp Clark Pitman, 1990), 307–18.
24. Jacquelyn Wonder and Priscilla Donovan, *Whole Brain Thinking: Working from Both Sides of the Brain* (New York: William Morrow, 1984), 200.
25. Bostrom, 11.
26. William D. Hersey, *How to Cash In on Your Hidden Memory Power* (Englewood, NJ: Prentice–Hall, 1963), 2.
27. Ibid., 3.
28. Alan S. Brown, *Maximizing Memory Power: Using Recall in Business* (New York: John Wiley & Sons, 1987), 18–21.
29. Ibid.
30. Wonder and Donovan, 201.
31. Harry Lorayne and Jerry Lucas, *The Memory Book*, (New York: Stein and Day, 1974), 15.

32. Wonder and Donovan, 201.
33. Gordon Bower, "Analysis of a Mnemonic Device," *American Scientist*, 58 (1970), 496–516; cited in Robert Sommer, *The Mind's Eye: Imagery in Everyday Life*, New York: Dell Publishing Company, 1978, 123.
34. Sommer, 112.
35. Wonder and Donovan, 201–02.
36. Ibid., 216–17.
37. Exercises 7 and 8 are adapted from Alan S. Brown, *Maximizing Memory Power: Using Recall in Business*, 15–17, 22.

CHAPTER 9

LISTENING TO NONVERBAL MESSAGES

It is essential that we learn to read the silent communications as easily as the printed or spoken ones.
— *Edward T. Hall*

THESIS The unspoken *cues* sent from people and from our environment are an important part of communication. Listeners must look upon these as *clues* to the sender's meaning. We must learn to expend energy in recognizing, receiving, and evaluating these clues to become ever more skilled and accurate holistic and perceptive listeners.

CHAPTER OBJECTIVES

1. Understand the concept of sender cues and receiver clues in nonverbal listening.
2. Be aware of cues sent by the person.
3. Be aware of cues sent by the communication environment.
4. Recognize the importance of nonverbal elements in the process of listening.
5. Recognize possible pitfalls that can be encountered by perceptive nonverbal listeners.
6. Determine to retrain and correct listening behavior to include nonverbal listening skills.

CHAPTER PREVIEW

- Elements of nonverbal communication.
- Interpreting gaze, gesture, and paralanguage.
- Impact of space, time, and physical setting on listening.

When Julia stopped at her favorite coffee shop for breakfast she headed straight for "her" booth. The waiter looked up and asked, "The usual?" At Julia's nod, he smiled, filled a cup with coffee, and placed it before her, along with a muffin on a plate and a pitcher of cream. She smiled, nodded, and began to read her newspaper. When she wanted a second cup of coffee, Julia raised her cup slightly and glanced toward the waiter, who brought more coffee.

As Julia drank the second cup, Ted, who had just graduated from college, walked in. Noticing Ted's frown and slow walk, Julia waved to him to join her. Julia commented on Ted's appearance — suit, tie, fresh haircut, and shoeshine. Ted responded, "I had an interview at the XYZ company this morning." He toyed with the napkin dispenser and continued, "I'm really nervous, though; I think I made a poor impression." As the waiter approached, Ted stopped, gestured toward Julia's cup and plate and said, "The same." He continued explaining in a quiet voice that the interviewer had kept him waiting ten minutes beyond the interview time, had leafed through his résumé while Ted talked, and had made very little eye contact.

"I just don't feel very hopeful about the job," he concluded. "I don't think she liked me." As the waiter approached with the coffeepot, Ted put his hand over his cup, indicating "no more." Julia held up her hand and asked for both checks. She glanced at her watch and, as she turned to leave, gripped Ted's arm firmly and said, "Good luck on the job hunt."

In this scene, Ted, Julia, and the waiter were, at times, all senders of nonverbal cues and receivers of nonverbal clues that added to meaning and feeling. In all listening, we must learn to interpret "nonword" messages (clues) and to focus on sending "nonword" feedback (cues).

SENDER CUES AND RECEIVER CLUES

Actors use face, eyes, walk, voice, and costume to present an image. We accept this as part of the way we understand a character. This use of face, eyes, walk, voice, and dress is also one of the ways message senders and receivers understand each other. We call it nonverbal communication.

Communication expert Mark L. Knapp defines nonverbal communication as "all human communication events which transcend spoken or written words."[1] Albert Mehrabian, also an expert in the field, calls it "the many implicit ways in which humans communicate . . . the contribution of our actions and ways of saying things, rather than our words."[2] Judee Burgoon and Thomas Saine's definition points to action by both sender and receiver as "those attributes or actions of humans other than the use of words themselves which have social and shared meaning, are intentionally sent or interpreted as intentional, and are consciously received and have potential for feedback from the receiver."[3]

Burgoon and Saine's definition focuses on key phrases referring to the action of both sender and receiver. The phrase, "attributes or actions of humans" and "intentionally sent" alert us to the role of a message sender who transmits cues to listeners. The phrases "interpreted as intentional" and "consciously received" explain that a listener must be present and attentive to receive and evaluate cues.

This attention to nonverbal communication does not suggest that we have two (verbal and nonverbal) communication systems operating independently of each other. Actually, both operate as we send and receive messages. Nonverbal listening is being aware of and interpreting nonverbal messages that come singly or accompany words.

Listening Cues and Clues

Most of us believe "actions speak louder than words." Actually, actions—nonverbal cues—are so important to communication that researchers have found that they carry as much as ninety percent of every message. That is, when we receive a message, we interpret ninety percent of it from *nonword cues*. Often the message sender is not even aware of transmitting some of them.

In addition, Mehrabian reports that "when actions contradict words, people rely more heavily on actions to infer another's feelings. In other words, less controllable behaviors are generally assigned greater weight."[4] This means that message senders must work to be aware of all nonverbal messages sent. Message receivers (listeners) must be conscious of all nonverbal cues sent and be able to accurately attend, interpret, and re–create every nonverbal clue received.

Communication pioneer Edward Hall tells us that we learn our unspoken language just as we learn our spoken language. We observe and imitate the people around us.[5] Loretta Malandro and Larry Barker believe, however, that we are born with basic nonverbal instincts. They believe this can be seen by watching tourists in a foreign country. "Initially, tourists eagerly attempt to look up words and phrases in a dictionary. Eventually, however, many revert to nonverbal symbols to find food, restrooms, and motels."[6]

Your authors believe that while we are born with innate skills needed to signal basic needs, we very quickly learn a nonverbal language from those around us. As we learn that language, we learn how to transmit sender *cues* and how to unravel receiver *clues*.

Sender Nonverbal Cues

Sender *nonverbal cues*, decoded by the listener, are all the actions, expressions, and surroundings which add to or comprise a message. In our example, Julia's nod to the waiter, taking the same booth, and gripping Ted's arm were cues to the waiter and to Ted of her wishes and feelings.

In theater, a cue is a word or bit of stage business which signals another action or speech. It can also be a hint, a reminder, or a prompting. A cue is always something sent out or transmitted by a sender. The nonverbal elements of any message are sent to cue (hint or remind) listeners to understand the meaning or the feelings behind a message.

When senders use and transmit nonverbal cues, they do so for several reasons:

- To supplement words: We say, "Turn left," and point in that direction.
- To regulate the flow of interaction: We lean back to signal we have finished talking.
- To take the place of words: An umpire jerks his thumb upward to signal, "You're out."

These cues may actually repeat, contradict, complement, accent, regulate, or substitute for the speaker's message. Thus perceptive listeners should be able to define and interpret commonly used nonverbal signals.

Listener Nonverbal Clues

When Ted, in our example, said he didn't think he had done well in his interview, he based the remark on his interpretation of clues that he had deduced from the interviewer. *Clues* are anything that guide or direct us in the solution of a problem or mystery. Just as Sherlock Holmes and television's Columbo look for clues to direct them to the solution of a mystery, so do listeners look for nonverbal clues from message senders. A nonverbal clue always refers to that which has been received or taken in by a listener.

Ted took in several clues. He interpreted these clues — late interviewer, little eye contact, leafing through résumé — to mean that the interviewer didn't like him. Ted may have been correct, but deciphering and analyzing nonverbal clues can be very difficult. Communication specialist Baxter Geeting addressed this difficulty by comparing the listener to a television or radio receiver. "A good receiving set, accurately tuned, is just as important as a good broadcasting station."[7]

Suggestions for Nonverbal Listeners

Fine tuning the listener's receiving set involves considering these cautions:

1. Consider the context in which a message is sent. This means the particular flow of events in which an episode occurs can change its meaning. If Bob's doctor gives very little eye contact when they unexpectedly meet in a restaurant, he can presume she is distracted, tired, or didn't see him. If, however, she gives very little eye contact when explaining the results of a biopsy, Bob may panic because he presumes she brings bad news. The lack of eye contact by the same person came in two different contexts.

2. Remember that messages occur in several channels simultaneously. If the doctor delivered bad news, she could have signaled it through a verbal channel (words) or several nonverbal channels. She could have looked down (gaze), spoken slowly (paralanguage), or leafed through Bob's records (gesture). If most channels appear to send the same message, we usually can guess we have read the clues accurately. When messages occur on several channels, however, we must attempt to observe as many channels as possible to interpret the sender's intended message.

3. Study nonverbal communication. The listener who makes the best judgments about nonverbal clues is the listener who knows the most about them. When the television character Jessica Fletcher, in the mystery series *Murder, She Wrote*, sees a clue, for example, slightly blue fingernails on a corpse, she knows the victim died of arsenic poisoning. Why is Jessica so perceptive? Because, as a mystery writer, she has studied various forms of murder. Perceptive listeners to nonverbal clues must follow this lead by studying the ways in which people and environments offer clues to meanings of messages.

4. Ask questions. Listeners cannot expect to evaluate complex emotions on the basis of one or two cues. Nor should our entire judgment of a person be based on nonverbal messages alone. If you are aware that a sender's nonverbal cues are the only thing influencing your reaction, ask some questions. This questioning

is called *perception checking* (a verbal statement that reflects your understanding of another's nonverbal cues plus a question checking its accuracy). There is no way to judge the accuracy of our evaluation of listener clues without putting them to the test.

Retraining: Guidelines to Sender Cues and Receiver Clues

1. Determine to focus on nonword messages in order to gather as many sender cues as possible.
2. Remind yourself to consider the context of all nonverbal messages when attempting to turn them into clues.
3. Determine to learn all you can about nonverbal communication.
4. Whenever it appears that verbal and nonverbal messages do not agree, perception check by stating your understanding of the message and asking if you are correct.

Once perceptive listeners have learned to recognize sender cues and their own listener clues, they must turn to learning what kinds of nonverbal cues are sent by the person.

NONVERBAL CUES FROM THE PERSON

Can the way people walk and talk influence what we think of them? Can a judge's tone of voice or behavior influence a jury in a criminal trial? Peter D. Blank reports that it can. "Even when a judge does not say anything prejudicial, his or her behavior can signal a point of view to jurors."[8] What is it in the judge's behavior that sends that signal or cue? What should listeners examine as clues to that point of view?

Nonverbal Cues From The Face

Shakespeare's lines, "Your face, my thane, is a book where men may read strange matters," in Act I of *Macbeth*, suggest what many people believe: Facial expressions reveal what the person actually feels. Most experts agree that the face is the most important source of emotional information. Some believe it is second only to words as a source of information.

As we listeners search for information in sender cues from the face, we can keep the following two points in mind.

1. Facial displays can show many emotions. Researchers Paul Eckman and W. V. Friesen discovered that facial muscles clearly reflect six basic emotions: fear, anger, disgust, surprise, happiness, and sadness.[9] It is also possible to identify more complex "blends" of emotions, but the more familiar listeners are with the sender's face, the more likely they are to identify correctly the emotion it sends. Good listeners watch facial cues with care.

2. The face can send multiple messages. Not only does the face send cues about the sender's emotional state, but it can also be a conversation regulator. When senders turn the face toward us, they signal interest and a wish to continue communication. When they turn the face away, they can signal disinterest.

Nonverbal Cues From The Eyes

Many sayings in our language reflect our long–held preoccupation with the power of eye contact, also called *gaze*. "The eyes are the windows of the soul," "his eyes shot daggers," "she has a gleam in her eye," and "he has shifty eyes" are just a few expressions which reflect this preoccupation. Actually listeners can learn much about senders' messages by observing both gaze and pupillary response.

In addition to transmitting emotion, communicators use eye contact for other reasons. They may use it to regulate the flow of communication. "Catching one's eye" is an accepted way of signaling that communication channels are open. When message senders avoid eye contact, they can avoid beginning or responding to messages. Senders also use gaze to signal turn taking. When speakers look toward the listener, they often signal the listener's turn to speak.

Eye contact can also be used to monitor feedback. When senders seek feedback, they look toward listeners. When listeners return eye contact, speakers know they are listening. Both speakers and listeners, however, tend to look away when attempting to process difficult or complex ideas. This eye shift can be an important clue to a nonverbal listener. It signals an emotion-filled message.

Eye contact can also communicate the nature of relationships. Increased eye contact suggests increased positive or negative attitude toward the other person. Generally, we look more and longer at people we like and for shorter duration at those we dislike. It is, however, possible to use hostile extended staring to intimidate another.

Most of us know that the pupils of our eyes become smaller in bright light and larger in dim light. However, in the 1960s Eckhard Hess, at the University of Chicago, discovered that constriction and dilation of the pupil could be an index of attitude. He discovered that our pupils dilate when we are pleased with an image, noting, for example, how Chinese jade merchants scrutinized the eyes of prospective buyers to detect what piece of jade they really wanted.

Hess also learned that our pupils constrict when we are displeased or repelled by an image. Poker players of old, for example, wore green eye shades to hide the pupillary constriction or dilation which could signal the player's hand.

Hess further determined that viewers are attracted to large pupils. When people were shown photographs in which the eyes had been air–brushed to show large or small pupils on the same face, most viewers considered the face with large pupils to be the most attractive.[10]

Face and Eye Elements of Listener Behavior Formula

In Chapter 4, Five Power Tools of Listening, you were introduced to Power Tool 5, Listener Behavior Formula. You already have learned and put into practice

DDOT (Don't Do Other Tasks), DMP (Don't Make Plans) and DD (Don't Day-dream). Here, we present two additional elements of the listener behavior formula: LSEF (Look into Speaker's Eyes and Face) and UMF (Use My Face). They help us create the habit of making use of what we have learned about nonverbal messages from the eyes and face.

1. LSEF (Look into Speaker's Eyes and Face): We use our eyes to initiate interaction. By maintaining contact with the speaker, listeners signal their level of interest and involvement. Listeners who do not capitalize on facial expressions of speakers are unable to receive the full impact of the message. The next time you interact with someone who makes you feel liked, notice what the person does with the eyes. Chances are you received frequent and longer eye contact.

2. UMF (Use My Face): We have discussed the importance of eye and face contact to monitor the speaker's nonverbal cues. Possibly even more important is the listener's nonverbal feedback, the primary mode of response to the speaker. Feedback to the speaker transmits the listener's ongoing response to the speaker and the message. This valuable component of the listening process creates a positive effect on the speaker's self-image.

As we use the two elements of the listener behavior formula, LSEF and UMF, we can use the directives below to help upgrade our nonverbal listening competency.

Listener Eye-Face Contact Technique

Maintain steady eye contact for three to ten seconds or as long as both parties appear comfortable during the interaction.

Leave the speaker's eyes and slowly gaze around the circumference of the speaker's face. After several face rotations, return to the eyes. Again, maintain eye contact and repeat the technique.

Do not turn from the speaker's eyes and face to glance at distant objects. If these objects are unrelated to the message, that kind of "eye travel" nonverbally signals the speaker that the message is no longer the listener's center of attention.

Remember: The head is important. It is what you speak and listen to, and it is what speaks and listens back to you.

Nonverbal Cues from Body Motion

Body motion, called *kinesics*, was first described by Ray Birdwhistell, the most prominent specialist in that field.[11] He believes that every movement has meaning. Assuredly, facial expression and eye contact are bodily movement. But, in this section, we focus on the larger movements of body orientation, posture and gesture.

Body orientation refers to the way we position our body, feet, and head during communication. An example of sending messages through body orientation can be seen in the individual positioning of the arm, hand, and thumb as well as the position of the torso and head that signals one is hitchhiking and is not signaling "thumbs up."

Books on body orientation abound. Experts in body language interpretation advise public figures, from attorneys selecting juries to presidential candidates, on how to send the best cues and understand body orientation clues.

Posture is often seen as an extension of body orientation. The way message senders sit, stand, or walk communicates their relation to and like or dislike of others. Like (positive orientation) is distinguished from dislike (negative orientation) by forward lean, closer proximity, more gaze, more openness of arms and body, more turning toward, more touching, and a more relaxed posture. People of higher status usually exhibit a relaxed posture, and those of lower status appear more upright and tense. Imagine the contrast in the posture of judge and defendant or military sergeant and recruit.

Gestures are the movements of the head, hands, arms, and fingers that we use to describe or emphasize. When message senders say "about this big," or instruct one to "put it there," they usually accompany it with gestures. Basketball players who give "high fives" (slapping hands with all five fingers extended) use gestures without words.

Body Motion Elements of Listener Behavior Formula

We suggest that listeners adopt the LF (Lean Forward) elements of the listener behavior formula in making use of information gathered while studying signals of body orientation, posture, and gesture.

By leaning forward and toward the speaker in a sitting or standing position, listeners send positive feedback. Nonverbally, we say, "I'm interested in you and your message"; "I'm willing to listen"; "You are worthy of my time and attention."

Compare the leaning–forward position with that of a person slouching over papers piled on a desk or stretching back in a chair with hands behind the head. Speakers may decode the nonverbal messages to mean: "With all this paper work I'm too busy to listen" or "I'm beat, I'll rest and listen."

Misinterpretation of listeners' nonverbal cues may cause filtering or distortion of intended messages. This restricts the transactional process of meaningful interactions. Leaning forward and toward the speaker clearly communicates that the listener is willing and prepared to receive the message.

You may wish to memorize this part of the formula. From this point on, apply and reinforce it each time you listen, both during planned listening events (meetings or classes) and unplanned listening events (unexpected encounters with colleagues, friends, or family).

Nonverbal Cues from Touch

Touch has the special power of sending messages of union and communion. It can be both part of a sender's cues and can be examined as a listener clue or be a feedback cue. The event described below illustrates one of the dynamic results of tactile behavior:

In May, 1985, Brigitte Gerney was trapped for six hours beneath a 35–ton, collapsed construction crane in New York City. Throughout her ordeal, she held the hand of rescue officer Paul Ragonese who stayed by her side as heavy machinery moved the tons of twisted steel from her crushed legs. A stranger's touch gave her hope and the will to live.[12]

Touch can be a gesture of warmth and concern. Politicians know that touch can sway strangers; therefore, they walk through crowds shaking hands. This is also the kind of touch we give a suffering friend (a touch on the arm or an arm around the shoulder).

Touch can signal power. Generally, the person with power may touch the person with less power. In fact, listeners can infer status clues by watching who touches whom. We usually believe the toucher to be more assertive, more powerful, and of higher status.

Touch can show camaraderie. Sports is one place where we may observe touch as universally accepted. Teammates encourage, applaud, and console each other with hugs, slaps, and other physical touches. This tactile communication plays a large part in establishing closeness.

Touch can communicate inclusion. Medical experts report that simply touching or holding a patient's hand can contribute to calming patients of any age. Physician Bernie Siegel says that medical persons who touch heal even if they cannot cure. He quotes a dying young woman who wrote, "Don't run away . . . wait . . . all I want to know is that there is someone to hold my hand when I need it."[13]

As listeners we receive and send feedback almost continuously. We can unintentionally send nonverbal cues. Using STTD we can monitor each touch cue we send and each touch clue we receive and ask ourselves what that touch probably communicates.

Nonverbal Cues from Paralanguage

In contrast to kinesic behavior (movement, posture, gesture, and touch) which we can see, *paralanguage* or vocalics refers to sounds we hear. Paralanguage concerns how something is said rather than what is said.

Listeners must become aware of four major characteristics of the voice: pitch (the highness or lowness of tone), rate (speed), volume (loudness), and quality (the individual sound of the voice).

Each of these characteristics, by itself or with one of the others, completes, adds to, or contradicts the meaning sent by words. For example, the deep pitch of television news anchors Tom Brokaw's or Dan Rather's voice adds to the credibility of the messages they send. A loud voice may complete an angry message or a high pitch may contradict words chosen to communicate control.

Each of us has our own vocal quality which cannot easily be changed, but each of us can attempt to exert control over volume, rate, and pitch when sending cues as speaker or as sender of feedback.

In addition to pitch, rate, volume, and quality, many speakers exhibit interrupters or interferences in their messages. The most common are: "uh," "er," "um," "right," and "you know." Even the best speakers, while thinking on their feet, occasionally use "um" or "you know." Most of us find these interferences to be irritating clues, and we have difficulty maintaining perceptive listening skills at these times.

We must, both as receivers of paralinguistic sender cues and as senders of para-linguistic feedback, observe and monitor both vocal characteristics and vocal inter-ferences. We can remind ourselves to choose our volume and to monitor our pitch and rate as carefully as we monitor our words.

Nonverbal Cues from Appearance and Clothing

Although Knapp tells us that "the exact role of appearance and dress in the total system of nonverbal communication is still unknown,"[14] we do know that physical attractiveness has a bearing on whether we are sought out and are able to persuade others.

Several researchers have concluded that of the three body types — endomorph (soft, round, fat); mesomorph (bony, muscular, athletic); and ectomorph (tall, thin, fragile) — most of us prefer the mesomorph. Most people consider this body type to represent an energetic, enterprising, assertive, competitive person.

What does this preferred body type tell nonverbal listeners? Just this: Many senders struggle to achieve the attractive body type by diet, exercise, and adornment. As message senders, they attempt to persuade listeners that they are all the things that make that type attractive to most others. They know that sending those cues means they will enjoy a higher credibility rating, are likely to be judged less harshly and be accepted as more socially desirable.

During the past several years, hundreds of articles have been published describ-ing how to send the most convincing message through clothing. Several consultants wrote books documenting steps one could take to "dress for success."[15] While many of the ideas in these books have become quickly outdated, their popularity explains how much control we senders and receivers of cues believe clothing can exert.

Uniforms send messages. Those who understand the rules know a great deal about a person by glancing at the uniform worn. Uniforms worn by military personnel or by waiters and service people make it easy to know how to respond to the message sent.

Uniforms sometimes can present listener difficulties. When Susan had surgery in a large teaching hospital, she quickly learned to identify doctors by their green "scrubs" (pajama-like uniforms with caps and booties worn in the operating rooms). Identifying nurses was more difficult. The nurses Susan remembered from her childhood were women who wore white dresses, white shoes, white hose, and white caps. Today nurses are both men and women and, in this hospital, wore white trousers and brightly colored shirts. Only by wearing her reading glasses to scruti-nize name tags could Susan tell who were nurses and who were other floor workers.

Interestingly, the multitude of "dress for success" books grew out of a wish to understand the uniforms worn by management. Those who call themselves image consultants tell corporate members how to wear and project the correct uniform image.

Artifacts and accessories send messages. When we examine cues from a sender's clothing we can look for accessories such as purses, wallets, eyeglasses, and articles in pockets and purses and consider what messages they send. Equipment—briefcases, tool belts of construction workers, guns of police officers—tells about occupation. Appearance—grooming of the hands, fingernails, skin, and hair—can send cues about occupation, and even health.

It is evident to perceptive listeners that appearance, clothing, and personal artifacts can send multiple messages. We must monitor cautiously our response to these cues lest we allow attractive presentation to blur the true message. Clothing cues are often carefully and intentionally planned, thus listeners should become familiar with generally accepted clothing messages and keep them in mind as they listen.

Retraining: Guidelines to Nonverbal Cues from the Person

1. During each communication encounter, immediately remind yourself that each message sender transmits unspoken cues that listeners must observe, analyze, and use as clues to interpret and re-create the message.

2. Make use of STTD (Speech-Thought-Time Differential) to note each nonverbal element to be observed and analyzed.

3. Resolve to make use of the listener behavior formula segments: LF (Lean Forward), LSEF (Look into Speaker's Eyes and Face), and UMF (Use My Face).

4. As you listen, observe the message sender's pattern of nonverbal message sending. Watch face, eyes, bodily movement, touch, and clothing, and listen for paralanguage cues.

5. Remind yourself of the importance of nonverbal cues and clues in learning how to function as a perceptive listener.

Once we have considered the importance of nonverbal cues sent from the person, it is necessary to look at ways the communication environment sends cues.

CUES FROM THE ENVIRONMENT

Nonverbal communication involves more than the nonverbal signals emanating directly from the person who sends them. The way senders use the environment in which communication occurs is also a nonverbal cue. That is, the way senders use space, time, and physical setting sends cues to which listeners must be alert.

Nonverbal Cues from Space

Edward Hall introduced us to the fact that space is an element of communication. He showed us that we not only use space to communicate, but we use it in three ways: territorial space, bubble of space, and space patterns.[16]

Territoriality means we identify certain areas as our own and protect them from others. Professors know that very soon in a term, students will have chosen the same seat for each lecture. When someone else sits there, the "owner" of the seat will show irritation. Regular churchgoers may sit in the same place each Sunday and feel irritation toward another worshiper who encroaches on this territory. Sports fans often refer to their team's having a "home court advantage," that is, playing better in their own territory — the gym or field where they practice.

When others encroach on our territory, we respond by prevention or reaction. Prevention stakes out territory (signs saying "Keep Out"). Reaction refers to actual physiological symptoms (increased heartbeat, clenched fists).

Hall believes that each of us carries around us an invisible bubble of space which becomes smaller or larger depending on our emotional state or the activity we're performing.

When we are angry or under stress, our bubble expands and we require more space; when we are happy, our bubble shrinks and we are pleased to have people near. We can understand this by noting how athletic teams react after a game. The winners' bubbles are small. They hug each other and carry the coach or star player on their shoulders. The losers' bubbles of space are large. They avoid eye contact, shake off the consoling hand, and walk quietly and far apart to the locker room.

Proxemics is the study of how people and animals use patterns of space. Listeners sometimes can tell how people feel toward each other by observing the distance between them. Hall defined four distances we use in our personal and business lives: intimate, personal, social, and public. Each distance has a near and far phase and is accompanied by changes in volume of the voice.

1. Intimate space is used between those on very close terms. This space varies from direct physical contact to 6 to 18 inches and is used for the most private communications in the most intimate relationships. The voice is very soft.

2. Personal space is used between friends. The close phase is 18 inches to 2½ feet. This is the space spouses might stand from each other in public. The far phase — 2½ to 4 feet — is used most commonly in conversation between friends. This distance keeps others "at arm's length" and, at this distance, message senders use a soft voice.

3. Social space is used for casual exchanges. It is an impersonal distance used for communication with service persons. People who work together or who interact at social gatherings use the close phase of 4 to 7 feet. The far phase — 7 to 12 feet — is the distance in business transactions. Often the desk in an office and the counters in a shop create this distance and force use of a fairly loud voice.

4. Public distance is used in formal exchange. Its close phase of 12 to 15 feet is used by professors in classrooms, speakers at public gatherings, and ministers delivering sermons. They use a loud voice to be heard by all. The farthest phase of public distance — over 25 feet — is used for important public figures. Only a very loud voice or a mechanically amplified voice can be used at this distance.

Nonverbal Cues from Time

The clichés of our language that refer to time — "Don't waste time," "This will save time," and "Invest your time wisely" — signal our vision of time as a commodity to be used, saved, and invested. When we communicate with time, we focus on several cues.

Listeners can observe that sender verbal cues, such as "I'll be there in ten minutes" or "This job will take two weeks," signal duration, which means we find time to be measurable. When a class is scheduled for fifty minutes, we expect it to take that amount of time but no more. Punctuality means arriving on the point of the hour prescribed — on time. Listeners recognize that in business, in the classroom, at the professional meeting, arriving even five minutes late requires an apology. For social occasions, listeners must learn the informal punctuality cues of the persons involved. Some people's social time is quite flexible.

Another aspect of time is urgency. The time of day we perform an action can signal this. Most of us would not make a telephone call before 8 a.m. or after 10 p.m. except in an emergency. Persons receiving calls at such times would expect a level of urgency and might respond, "What's wrong?"

Another sender cue that listeners must be alert for is *monochronism*. This refers to our expectation that most people will do only one thing at a time and will listen when we talk. If another person reads the paper or chops vegetables while we speak, we are offended. The interviewer who leafed through Ted's résumé offended him because Ted interpreted this to be a clue to the interviewer's indifference.

Nonverbal Cues from Physical Setting

Listeners may have begun to think that everything in their environment sends nonverbal messages. Everything manipulated, chosen, or designed by human communicators does appear to send cues that listeners can observe. We can look at the attractiveness of surroundings — color, temperature, lighting, and furniture arrangement — and decide what clues each might provide.

Several years ago researchers studied the impact of "ugly," "average," and "beautiful" rooms on the emotional response of participants. The "ugly" room looked like a janitor's storage closet, the "average" room like a professor's office, and the "beautiful" room like a decorator showroom. One result of this study showed that attractive surroundings send strong nonverbal cues. Subjects in the ugly room experienced fatigue, headaches, and hostility while those in the beautiful room reported comfort, enjoyment, and the desire to continue activity. Nonverbal listeners will consider surroundings to be part of a message.

We also use clichés in our language to illustrate our understanding of color symbolism and the cues it sends. We talk about blue Mondays, being in the pink of condition, seeing red, having a yellow streak, being green with envy. Most experts suggest that the most appealing colors are blue, green, red, and yellow. Red is thought to be arousing, followed by orange, yellow, violet, blue, and green.[17]

Listeners who observe color cues in restaurants or business offices, for example, may use this information to examine the mood the message sender wishes to create.

Temperature is an additional element of physical setting that can send cues. We know that a hot environment can lead to hot tempers. Cool temperatures are thought to produce efficient work and calm interactions. A business manager, preparing to leave for a workshop in Florida, mentioned that he had to pack several sweaters. Why? The workshop presenters set air conditioning at a level that kept the rooms very cool to keep attendees alert and productive. Listeners can use this information to consider the mood message senders wish to create with temperature cues.

Lighting and Furniture Arrangement Send Cues

When we dine in an elegant restaurant we can observe what we mean when we say lighting communicates. Low lighting creates a relaxed, intimate environment where people want to linger. Bright lights, such as one finds in fast–food places, stimulate us to act quickly and move on. Generally, dim lighting is conducive to social conversation and intense lighting to task–oriented communication. Nonverbal listeners can gather cues about the nature of communication by observing lighting cues.

Message senders can arrange furniture in such a way that they dictate the kind of space communicators will use. With chairs placed at right angles, people can move into each other's personal space. When a desk is placed between two people, the space shifts from personal to social. "As a result of furniture arrangement . . . people often become more distant — in both senses of the word."[18]

When message senders want people to converse, they place chairs or couches facing each other or at right angles. If they want them to remain quiet (in classrooms, theaters, or churches) they arrange seats side by side, often with barriers (armrests) between them.

Many nonverbal message senders and receivers believe power emanates from where they sit at a table. Often, even at a round table, the place where the most powerful person sits is judged to be the head, and people nearest that seat are judged to be close to power. Square tables suggest equality — one person on each equal side. The rectangular boardroom table's two long and two short sides suggest one short side can be signaled as head of the table.

Retraining: Guidelines to Cues from the Environment

1. During each communication experience, immediately remind yourself that nonverbal cues from the communication environment must be observed, analyzed and used as clues to complete meaning.

2. Use STTD (Speech-Thought-Time Differential) to note the nonverbal messages generated by the use of space and time.

3. As a listener, take note of a message sender's cues sent by furniture placement to indicate the kind of interaction the sender intends.

NONVERBAL LISTENING CAN BE LEARNED

In 1989 a test that measured nonverbal skills in children showed that "unpopularity, poor grades, and a host of other problems that afflict children may derive from the inability to read nonverbal messages of teachers and peers."[19] Because so many of the emotional messages between people are communicated nonverbally, the inability to understand (or listen to) nonverbal clues or to send nonverbal cues can be a major social handicap.

Stephen Nowicki, of Emery University in Atlanta, who developed the test, states:

> Because they are unaware of the messages they are sending, or misinterpret how other children are feeling, unpopular children may not even realize they are initiating many of the negative reactions they receive from their peers. . . . They get rebuffed and don't know why. . . . Such children develop a sense that they have little or no control over how people treat them. By extension, they feel they lack control over their fate in general.[20]

The positive element of these findings is that children—or nonverbal listeners of any age—can be taught to send nonverbal cues and interpret nonverbal clues. Readers of this Chapter 9, Listening to Nonverbal Messages, already have begun to improve their listening to nonverbal clues and sending nonverbal feedback cues.

WRAPPING IT UP: A SUMMARY

In this chapter we learned that holistic perceptive listening means recognizing and responding to nonverbal cues as well as to verbal cues.

Nonverbal cues are signals from the sender; nonverbal clues are the signals that listeners select, interpret and re-create, retain and respond to.

Nonverbal messages can come directly from the person communicating or from the environment which the sender uses. Messages from the person come from: the face; the eyes; bodily movement (body orientation, posture, and gesture); paralanguage (the sound—not the words—of the human voice); touch; body type; and clothing.

Messages from the communication environment are sent through the sender's use of space, time, and physical setting: attractiveness, light, color, temperature, and furniture arrangement.

DISCUSSION AND STUDY GUIDES

1. Recall times in the past when you did not reap the rewards of perceptive listening because you did not observe sender nonverbal cues and therefore were not able to use them as clues to complete meaning. Did you listen differently?

2. Which kinds of nonverbal cues are hardest for you to recognize—those from the person or those from the environment? Why do you think so?

3. Recall your own use of space as a communicator. Recall examples where the

effect of misuse of space in communication short circuited communication. What did you do and how did you handle it?

4. Are you consciously aware of nonverbal cues and your evaluating them? How do you perception check when you are puzzled as you try to turn cues into clues?

5. What kind of clues do you gather from chemical adornments, such as hair dye, shaving lotion, perfume, or cosmetics? How would you classify these as nonverbal cues — personal or environmental?

LISTENING EXERCISES THAT WORK

EXERCISE 1. (Identifying and Profiting from Recognizing Nonverbal Cues) For each statement below that identifies you as a listener, answer "yes." Answer "no" for each that does not.

_____ 1. I am careful to look for patterns of nonverbal cues that send the same message.

_____ 2. I am careful not to jump to a conclusion based on one nonverbal cue.

_____ 3. I observe time rules by arriving for a job interview a few minutes early.

_____ 4. I signal my level of interest by looking into the speaker's eyes and face.

_____ 5. I send nonverbal feedback by using my face.

_____ 6. I lean forward to signal by posture that I am interested in a subject.

_____ 7. I take note of furniture arrangement and use it to develop clues about the kind of message it sends.

_____ 8. I am careful about use of distance in interpersonal communication. I take clues from the other person's cues and feedback and I adjust the space if necessary.

_____ 9. I proceed with care when I believe touch would be good feedback. I check other nonverbal cues to determine whether this person would welcome touch.

_____ 10. In telephone conversations I focus on paralinguistic cues and attempt to make judgments based on similarity of several clues.

Total your "yes" and your "no" answers. The ideal is to have answered "yes" to each of the statements. Count your "yes" answers and rate your performance by using this scale:

10–9: You have achieved a high level of nonverbal listening competency.

8–6: You are a competent nonverbal listener.

5–3: You often have difficulty as a nonverbal listener.

2–0: You need to work at learning nonverbal cues and using them as clues to meaning.

EXERCISE 2. (Observing Message from Person) Choose a television drama and turn down the sound. What messages do you gather from: facial expressions, eye contact, body orientation, posture or gestures. In your Listener Log, summarize what you determine to be nonverbal cues from this exercise based on what you learned in this chapter.

EXERCISE 3. (Observing Message from Environment) Using the same television drama, turn up the sound and consider what messages come from the use of: paralanguage, color, and arrangement of furniture. Summarize what you learned from examining these cues. Identify the cues and what you believe each meant based on what you learned in this chapter.

EXERCISE 4. (Observing Person and Environment Cues) Walk through a shopping mall. Observe the outside of shops and decide what elements of space, color, or arrangement have been used to attract you as a customer.

Enter a shop and observe how clerks use space, eye contact, facial expression, body orientation, gestures, clothing, or paralanguage to communicate pleasantness (or unpleasantness). Write a summary of this exercise. Explain how you think deliberate planning of decor and training (or no training) of personnel accomplished the message you received.

NOTES

1. Mark L. Knapp, *Nonverbal Communication in Human Interaction* (New York: Holt, Rinehart and Winston, 1978), 38.
2. Albert Mehrabian, *Silent Messages: Implicit Communication of Emotions and Attitudes*, 2nd ed. (Belmont, CA: Wadsworth Publishing Co., 1981), 2.
3. Judee Burgoon and Thomas Saine, *The Unspoken Dialogue* (Boston: Houghton-Mifflin, 1978), 9.
4. Mehrabian, 87.
5. Edward T. Hall, *The Silent Language* (Garden City, NY: Doubleday, 1959).
6. Loretta A. Malandro and Larry L. Barker, *Nonverbal Communication* (Reading, MA: Addison-Wesley, 1983), 8.
7. Baxter Geeting, "Speaking of Listening," *International Listening Association Listening Post* 25 (April 1988), 6.
8. Peter D. Blank, "Guilty Looks," *Scientific American* 254 (June 1986), 72.
9. Dale G. Leathers, *Successful Nonverbal Communication: Principles and Applications* (New York: Macmillan, 1986), 23.
10. Eckhard Hess and J. M. Polt, "Pupil Size as Related to Interest Value of Visual Stimuli," *Science* 132 (1960), 349–350.
11. Ray Birdwhistell, *Kinesics and Context* (Philadelphia: University of Pennsylvania Press, 1970).
12. Stephen Thayer, "Close Encounters," *Psychology Today* (March 1988), 31.
13. Bernie Siegel, *Peace, Love and Healing* (New York: Harper & Row, 1989), 229.
14. Knapp, 186.
15. See, for example, John T. Molloy, *Dress for Success* (New York: P. H. (Wyden, 1975), *Women's Dress for Success* (Wyden, 1978), *The New Dress for Success* (Wyden, 1988), and Lois Fenton, *Dress for Excellence* (New York: Rawson Association, 1986).
16. Hall, 105–09.
17. Albert Mehrabian, *Public Places and Private Spaces* (Belmont, CA: Wadsworth Publishing Co., 1976).
18. "Reading Nonverbal Cues Can Make or Break a Kid," *St. Paul* (MN) *Pioneer Press Dispatch* (October 10, 1989), 11 A.
19. Ibid.
20. Ibid.

CHAPTER 10

TEN LISTENING RETRAINING TECHNIQUES

Every time we retrain to listen, we enhance
our potential to learn, grow, and prosper.
— *Wolff and Marsnik*

THESIS The amount of listening we do is no guarantee of quality listening unless we retrain to correct substandard listening behavior. Focusing on ten listening retraining techniques enables us to achieve greater competency as holistic, perceptive listeners.

CHAPTER OBJECTIVES

1. Develop a greater awareness of the impact that habits or patterns of behavior have on accomplishments in life.
2. Detect how faulty habits of listening behavior prevent one from listening, learning, growing, and prospering.
3. Generate feelings of motivation and self-confidence and learn to apply the ten listening retraining techniques.
4. Realize the need to persevere in listening retraining.

CHAPTER PREVIEW

- Retraining our habits of listening.
- Ten retaining techniques to expedite listening behavior change.
- Seven rules of the listener behavior formula.
- Final tips for retraining to listen.

- "My parents always seem too busy to listen."
- "But I thought the conference was to start at 11:00 a.m., not 8:00 a.m."
- "Man, I have it worked out real cool. I sit in the back and get my calculus assignment done in speech class."
- "You repeated the motor number twice. How could I have it wrong on the purchase order?"

- "Since we're married we don't listen to each other as we did before."

How often have we heard or uttered comments similar to these? Such remarks often result from our strongly entrenched, careless listening habits. Such habits create formidable barriers to efficient listening behavior.

Again we ask the question, "Do you and I listen?" Truthfully, the answer is, "Not very well." In fact, most of us have had to learn how to listen on our own by mimicking or picking up the habits of too many uninstructed listeners around us. Most already had acquired incorrect and incompetent listening habits from other uninstructed listeners. Bad listening habits have grown and spread like a cancer. They cause most of us to receive and retain a mere one-fourth of the substance of aural messages.

Changing Our Habits of Listening

Habits determine the way we live. They exert a forcible influence on our lives. Psychologists explain that *habits* are strong and persistent inclinations that cause us to behave in predictable ways in certain situations.[1] We develop habits or learned responses and repeat them so often that we become habituated to respond in a specific way. We establish and regularly strengthen habits for the way we eat, clean our teeth, park the car, arrive at the office, study for an exam, and assume the role of listener. An insignificant pattern of overt behavior (the way we seal an envelope) and a significant pattern of covert behavior (the way we feel about capital punishment) often reflect habituated and ritualistic behavior.

The usefulness of habits depends on whether they exert a positive or negative effect on our lives. When we improve our listening ability by retraining we can acquire the power to prosper (a positive effect). Conversely, if we do not improve our listening ability and continue to reinforce wrong habits we will not acquire the power to prosper in relation to our potential (a negative effect).

By modifying or reinforcing certain sets of habits, we can develop either satisfactory or unsatisfactory techniques and skills. *Techniques* are methods or style of behavior, while *skills* are specialized, trained abilities resulting from applied techniques. The technique we apply to select and shift gears while biking affects our ability to ride up and down hills more easily and safely. Likewise, the techniques we apply to develop effective listening skills determine our high or low level of listening competency. The competent listener learns to avoid inept habits, the common barriers to productive listening.

We can decide to retrain ourselves to listen productively by changing our habits of listening. However, we must realize that a large number of careless listening habits, techniques, and skills have become deeply ingrained patterns of behavior from early childhood through adulthood. Retraining or modification of listening behavior therefore requires determination and consistent effort each time we listen.

....

The measure of our success is usually the measure of our habits. — *Montaigne*

1. LISTEN WITH AN OPEN MIND

True open-mindedness means being willing to consider all sides of an issue. In making value statements, use a "flexible I." When a person claims, "That movie was great," you might be tempted to respond, "Everybody else said it was terrible." Instead say, "*I* have heard mixed reactions about it; some liked it and others didn't." This response allows the other person enjoyment of the movie and feelings of self-worth. Open-minded listeners use the "flexible I" concept in covert and overt responses to speakers.

Open-mindedness reduces defensiveness that hinders effective communication. If a friend says, "I believe this plan is the best," your response, "That's the most stupid plan suggested," might cause the speaker to react defensively and end the conversation. A better response would be, "I am not sure that the plan will resolve the problem; give us more details." Open-minded responses of listeners and speakers enable both parties of the interaction to retain positive feelings of self-image, self-confidence, and self-worth.

The proper application of listening concepts and tools requires listeners with open minds.

The Open-Minded Scopic Listener Versus the Closed-Minded Nonscopic Listener

An open-minded person is receptive to new ideas or to reason and is free from prejudice or bias. As noted in Chapter 8, scopic listeners are open-minded, inquisitive, thirsty for knowledge, and eager to learn about and understand the needs and experiences of others. Scopic listeners broaden their base of knowledge and enrich their sense of humanity.

Nonscopic listeners lack curiosity and appear to be indifferent to the needs and experiences of others. They lack empathy to feel for others and tend to resist new ideas and change in attitude and behavior. Authors Ronald and Karen Lee use the term "dogmatic slumber" (lack of intellectual curiosity) as the major trait of closed-minded persons.[2] Unless closed-minded, nonscopic listeners retrain as open-minded, scopic listeners, they may serve a life sentence in a prison of indifference, prejudice, bias, and ignorance.

The closed-minded, nonscopic or "dogmatic slumber" type of listener can easily be detected. The family senses Marie's negative emotional stance on married women working outside the home. Helen's friends have been told that her religious preference is the only true faith. Professionals recognize closed-minded listeners immediately: Nonverbally they communicate their decision *not to listen*. The opposite of "dogmatic slumber" is intellectual curiosity, which, often equated with "escape from superstition," is the driving force of open-mindedness.[3] The same urgent need to know is typical of the open-minded, scopic listener. These intellectually curious listeners seek answers to various kinds of questions and problems. They investigate

Make good habits and they will make you. — *Parks Cousins*

explanations by probing for answers. However, philosopher Henry Johnstone, Jr. explains that an open-minded person takes the risk of having existing beliefs or behavior altered.[4] One thoughtful second–grader said to his father, "Dad, I don't want to learn in school because when I come home — I'll be different."

It is prudent to be intellectually curious and risk becoming different. It is imprudent and even devastating to remain closed-minded and refuse to expand one's knowledge base.

Scenario: The Closed-Minded Nonscopic Listener

(Ron, a college student, is standing at a bus stop. He pleasantly greets an elderly man also waiting for the downtown bus.)

RON: Hi. It's a great day, isn't it?

MAN: Yeah. (Pointing toward the university:) You go to that school?

RON: Yes, I'm majoring in —

MAN: So, you're one of those loud-mouthed, partying-around, spoiled-rotten kids wasting your old man's money!

RON: I'm a serious stu —

MAN: You're all alike — a generation of bums. You'll never hold a decent job or keep your nose to the grind like we did. This country's going to pot!

(The bus arrives. Both board and sit at opposite ends of the bus.)

This scenario portrays the pointlessness of communicating or arguing with the closed-minded man who exhibits nonscopic listener behavior. It exemplifies the man's state of "dogmatic slumber" as he climbs aboard the bus and deeper into his prison of prejudice, bias and ignorance.

The frustration and helplessness of trying to communicate with and listen to closed-minded people reminds us to apply the concepts, tools, and guidelines that will help us retrain to listen, learn, and grow with an open mind.

Retraining: Guidelines to Listen with an Open Mind

1. Realize that the listening process is jeopardized as we try to listen with a closed and cluttered mind while decoding and responding to verbal and nonverbal messages.

2. Recognize when the brain is overly occupied with complex tasks or serious problems. Firmly set aside these chores or concerns in preparation to listen with an open mind.

Ignorance doesn't kill you but it can make you sweat a lot. — *Haitian proverb*

3. Identify those persons, situations, or messages that tempt you to become a closed-minded, nonscopic listener, and analyze why these tend to dissuade you from listening with an open mind.

4. Reflect on others whom you suspect are closed-minded, nonscopic listeners. Listen to their verbal and nonverbal messages. Gain insight into understanding their reluctance to speak and listen with an open mind.

5. Frequently review the concepts and tools in this text that can help you listen with an open mind, and remind yourself to use them prior to each listening event.

6. Remember, the most powerful retraining technique is to listen with an open mind.

2. LISTEN TO GENERATE INTEREST IN AND CONCENTRATE ON THE SPEAKER'S TOPIC

Generating interest in a topic is a dual responsibility of the speaker and the listener. The speaker must feel and convey interest and even excitement in a chosen topic. Authors Michael Hanna and James Gibson suggest dressing up ordinary topics with novel ideas and delivery to entice listeners' interest: Make the ordinary into the extraordinary.

G. K. Chesterton, an English essayist and critic, said there is no such thing as an uninteresting topic; there are only uninterested people. If we accept Chesterton's claim, we understand that the interested listener, rather than the speaker, causes communication finally to occur. Effective listening is closely related to personal success and cultural growth. We should attempt to make every effort to generate inquisitive interest in topics presented in formal speeches and discussed during informal conversations. By so doing, we have little to lose and much to learn.

Both veteran and novice speakers exert great effort to select a topic. But human behavior is complex. It is difficult to understand each other's needs, motives, and past experiences. Therefore a topic that the speaker believes would captivate the audience actually may do just the opposite to certain persons. For example, a speech entitled, "Nuclear Waste—Don't Dump on Us," would immediately capture the attention of those in the audience who believe that nuclear power is neither a safe nor a realistic solution for America's energy crisis. A speech highlighting the uncertainties and ramifications of nuclear waste disposal would reaffirm such antinuclear attitudes. On the other hand, the pro-nuclear power members of the audience may not listen to such a message. They may reject valuable knowledge as being irrelevant, uninteresting, and undeserving of their attention.

Authors Lawrence Rosenfeld and Roy Berko remind us that the same topic can be developed with different angles.[6] Including a purpose statement, or declaration of the speaker's goal and how it will be accomplished, can attract a listener's focus of attention and refocus, or sustaining, of concentration throughout the message.

A basic maxim of economics is to receive the most in exchange for the least amount of money. This can be applied to listening.

Efficient listeners should be self-centered bargain hunters. Except for the amount of time and effort expended during the actual process of listening, they receive valuable knowledge at a sale price. The quantity and quality of knowledge that we receive and retain determine our power to learn, to grow, and to prosper now and in the future. In the previous example, regardless of their stand on the production of nuclear power, proficient listeners would have sought to add to their knowledge about the disposal of nuclear waste.

The habits we form toward generating interest in speakers' topics either open or close doors to enlightening life experiences. Few of us have had the opportunity to experience this type of retraining. However, by focusing our attention over a broader scope of topics we can modify this faulty listening habit. We can discover a source of limitless opportunities to learn, grow, and prosper throughout life.

Retraining: Guidelines to Generate Interest In and to Concentrate on the Speaker's Topic

1. Refuse to judge spontaneously the speaker's topic as uninteresting. Remember, most topics seem uninteresting to uninterested people.

2. Reserve more time for listening to challenging speakers, for viewing educational presentations, and for extended reading of scholarly works.

3. Be determined to acquire new knowledge and insights for your future needs and enjoyment.

4. When possible, prepare in advance for difficult topics by reading or inquiring about the topic before listening to a formal speech or lecture.

5. Control personal prejudices and biases that might influence you to turn off the topic. Be attentive and listen to others discuss topics contrary to your beliefs.

6. Practice self-discipline. Control your open mind to attend and concentrate on the speaker's topic rather than wander through patterns of irrelevant thoughts.

7. Develop a positive attitude of wanting to listen to and learn about a broad spectrum of knowledge and topics.

In addition to focusing on the speaker's topic, listeners must learn to adapt to three personal attributes of the speaker.

3. LISTEN AND ADAPT TO THE SPEAKER'S APPEARANCE, PERSONALITY, AND DELIVERY

We tend to react differently to each speaker's appearance, personality, and delivery, due to our attitudes. Psychologist Lefrancois states that "attitudes are positive or negative tendencies to react in a given way."[7] Unfortunately, we listeners may be guilty of reacting in a highly positive or negative manner toward a speaker's appearance, personality, and delivery. Some speakers attract us, others do not. It is important to understand the impact of such attitudes on listening behavior.

Adjusting to the Speaker's Appearance

Because of our deeply entrenched attitudes, we often mistakenly interpret certain aspects of a speaker's appearance (attire, hair style, physical features, stance) as denoting indifference, egotism, or other undesirable character traits. Concentrating on the speaker's appearance may cause us to stereotype or to apply erroneous judgments based on our past experiences. If we stereotype the speaker's appearance into a critical mental slot, it can prevent our listening objectively to the message.

Criticizing the speaker's appearance, particularly by negative stereotyping, affects our first and lasting impression of a person. For example, this incident occurred during the process of selecting a jury for a murder trial. A prospective juror stated to the judge, "I couldn't serve as a juror, your honor. One look at that man convinces me he is guilty!" "Quiet," the judge ordered, "that man is the district attorney!"

Adjusting to the Speaker's Personality

Psychologists define personality as those characteristics that are constantly evident in an individual, including physical appearance, behavior, intellect, and emotions. Personality is based not only on consistency of traits, but also on distinctiveness, the ways in which we differ from those around us.[8]

Adjusting to the Speaker's Delivery

Not only are speakers unique in appearance, but also in expressing verbal and nonverbal messages, commonly referred to as the speaker's delivery. Frequently we become more preoccupied with the speaker's delivery than with the actual content of the message.

Naturally, some speakers are more handicapped than others. Because of distracting eccentricities in the speaker's delivery, we may have difficulty sustaining attention during the complex process of listening. Certainly, most of us have strained to listen to the following types of speakers:

- The *slovenly speaker*, whose careless phonetic patterns include "didja" (did you), "gonna" (going to), and "givit tim" (give it to him), among other inarticulate speech patterns.
- The *unprepared speaker*, who is unable to maintain eye contact with the audience because of excessive referral to notes.
- The *tense speaker*, who fidgets and moves meaninglessly by pacing, rocking, swaying, and rubbing and moving the hands.
- The *additive speaker*, who pollutes pauses with such verbal mannerisms as *uh*, *er*, *you know*, and *right*.
- The *listless speaker*, who appears disinterested in the message.
- The *underprojected speaker*, who seems to be involved more with the self-communication process than with transmitting the message loudly enough to reach the ears of the listeners.

Listeners need to learn how to sift through dramatic and stylistic types of delivery in order to recognize and decode the speaker's basic message.

In October 1991, melodrama and stylistic delivery of testimony hindered an objective search and confirmation of a Supreme Court Justice.

The Melodramatic Hearing of Judge Clarence Thomas

Millions of listeners watched the confirmation hearing of Appellate Judge Clarence Thomas, a nominee for the lifelong position of one of nine Supreme Court Justices.

Dr. Anita Hill, Professor at the University of Oklahoma School of Law, accused Thomas of sexual harassment. The harassment, Hill said, occurred during the time she worked for Thomas, ten years earlier. She had served as Legal Advisor in the Department of Education and the EEOC (Equal Employment Opportunity Commission), both directed by Thomas. Being forced to testify in public due to a leak by a Senate Judiciary Committee staffer, Hill was a reluctant witness.

Thomas claimed the charges of Anita Hill were "unequivocally, categorically" wrong and that the hearing was a national disgrace. He added, "Unless you kowtow to an old order . . . you will be lynched, destroyed, caricatured by a committee of the Senate rather than hung from a tree."[9] It was clear he was fighting mad.

In a professional and dignified manner, Hill gave the most lurid description of any man's sexually harassing behavior ever witnessed on network TV. She claimed that because of the harassment she was hospitalized for stress on the job. Although the results were inadmissible as testimony, she submitted to and passed a lie detector test.

Style and drama restricted perceptive listening to objective testimony. Republican senators and supporters of Thomas interrogated Hill caustically in an attempt to degrade her character. Democratic senators and supporters of Hill attempted to assault Thomas's character while being careful not to antagonize black constituencies.[10] The nation listened to arguments among committee members regarding the hearing process, evasive responses to questions, and conflicting testimony of numerous corroborative witnesses.

The Thomas hearing exemplifies a melodramatic, stylistic event of partisan confusion. After four days of intense listening, followed by Senate confirmation of Judge Thomas, many Americans wonder which of the two credible witnesses spoke the truth regarding the sexual harassment allegation. They wonder, too, whether the hearing process exposed adequate testimony germane to what was best for the Supreme Court.

We need guidelines to help us adapt to the appearance, delivery, and personality of various types of speakers.

Retraining: Guidelines to Listen and Adapt to the Speaker's Appearance, Personality, and Delivery

To avoid being tempted to criticize the speaker's appearance, personality, and delivery, we can follow these procedures.

1. Be prepared psychologically to encounter and respond to different types of speakers. Make the effort to adapt to speakers' unique appearances, personalities, and styles of delivery in personal and media message events.

2. Resist the temptation to stereotype the speaker on the basis of appearance, personality, and delivery. We simply cannot risk distorted perception and interpretation of aural messages because we hastily stereotype the speaker.

3. Do not presume to determine the value of a message solely on your assessment of the speaker's appearance, personality, and delivery. Remember the wrappings of a present do not always reflect the value of the gift.

4. Be selfish. Plan a mental scavenger hunt to encode and retain a maximum amount of information to expand the apperceptive mass of the brain. (The *apperceptive mass* is the sum total of all thoughts, feelings, emotions, experiences, facts, and ideas that we have acquired.) Learning takes place when this mass is modified, refined, rearranged, or expanded.

5. Do not be misled by a speaker's near-perfect appearance, personality, and delivery. These factors are no guarantee that the speaker will present valuable and authentic information.

6. Wait until the speaker has completed the message before judging.

4. LISTEN FOR CONCEPTS AND CENTRAL IDEAS INSTEAD OF FACTS

Do you listen primarily for the facts in a message rather than for the central ideas? If so, learning to identify valuable clues like central ideas and topical sentences can improve your listening behavior.

Identifying Central and Subcentral Ideas and Supportive Facts

When listening to an informative speech or informal message it is important to identify the central idea or topic sentence. Ella Erway defines the *central idea* as the "significant point of a message." She advises, "Until you know what the message is all about, you should focus all your energy on finding that meaning. The details should confirm that your interpretation is correct."[11]

Frequently speakers include the purpose to communicate as part of the central idea or theme of the messages. For example, the speaker may say, "I will explain the university's recent policy change in registration." Thus we know the speaker's purpose is to inform us about changes in registration. However, central ideas may not include the speaker's purpose. For example, the same speaker may say, "The university will implement major policy changes in the registration process."

In a persuasive message, the topical sentence is stated as a proposition or claim. Author Charles Larson defines a claim as a proposition or statement that the persuader hopes will be believed, adopted or followed, and points out that claims need to be supported by evidence or data.[12] Central ideas are characteristic of informative messages, while propositions form the core of persuasive and actuative messages. If the university administrator in our example wants to convince an audience to agree with proposed changes in registration, the speaker may state, "We need to revise registration procedures." Central ideas and propositions are invaluable cues for decoding messages.

Detecting subcentral ideas is helpful in decoding messages. These are sentences that are of secondary importance to the central idea. As we listen to understand the changes in the registration policy example, we may detect a subcentral idea: the registration policy change will affect only juniors and seniors this term.

Supportive facts explain, expand on, or verify the central idea or proposition of a message. In both examples numerous facts or bits of information would be presented by the speaker. New locations for registration, different registration forms to be processed, and changes in schedules are examples of supportive data explaining the change in registration policy.

Competent listeners are able to sort out, associate, and retain the central and subcentral ideas of a message, plus several supporting facts. However, to retain most of a message for future reference, listeners can use an expedient note–taking system to take minimal notes during the STTD (Speech-Thought-Time Differential) listening time (see Chapter 6, Three Basic Concepts to Enhance Listening Comprehension). It is important to learn to detect the central idea or theme and then listen to the supportive facts clarifying the message.

Retraining: Guidelines to Listen for Concepts and Central Ideas Instead of Facts

1. Keep an open and analytical mind to grasp the central idea of the speaker's message.
2. Maintain a correct assessment of the differences between the central idea, the subcentral idea, and the supportive facts in the speaker's message.
3. Make every attempt to concentrate on the speaker's message while hearing, attending, interpreting, re-creating, and retaining the data in order to detect the major and minor ideas and the clarifying, supportive facts.
4. Do not dwell on one or two facts at the risk of becoming distracted from recognizing the central and subcentral themes of the message.
5. Even though the speaker may not specifically state the central idea, listen attentively to the overall message to grasp the major idea in relation to the supportive facts.
6. Refrain from trying to memorize the speaker's words at the risk of not hearing the complete message.
7. Be determined to change your listening behavior — to become a concept listener instead of a fact-finding listener.

5. LISTEN TO CURB AND OVERCOME DISTRACTIONS

Unsuspectingly, many of us yield to and tolerate a host of physical, mental, and semantic distractions. We should be able to overcome, or at least minimize, most of them.

Internal and External Distractions to Perceptive Listening

Countless physical internal stimuli (pain, pressure, and movement) can affect the quality of listening. While we listen intently to an interesting conversation or a formal speech, we might suddenly feel a severe digestive pain, an intolerable pressure on a toe from a pair of new shoes, or a sensation of dizziness from an attacking virus.

Stressful internal conditions can distract us from even the most enticing conversation or worthwhile speech. Think back. Recall the times when hunger pangs distracted your listening to the speaker's final comments at a lecture or business conference scheduled from 10:00 A.M. to 12:00 noon. Also, recall the times your listening competency dropped to an alarmingly low level. This can occur during an important social or business engagement. Possibly the discomfort of an ill-fitting shirt collar or undergarment became intolerable. Undoubtedly, pain and other stressful internal conditions of the body adversely affect our ability to listen proficiently.

Responsible listeners know that noise pollution and other external environmental distractions need to be curbed and overcome. These range from noisy members of an audience to poor lighting conditions and overheated and improperly ventilated rooms or auditoriums.

Mental Distractions to Perceptive Listening

Many developmental psychologists believe that basically the mind is an information-processing machine similar to a computer. Since we are born with innate reflexes or inborn computer programs, we are prewired to process information from the moment of birth. The kind and amount of information we select to process determines whether or not we yield to mental distractions during brief or extended listening episodes.

Perceptive listeners hear and attend, interpret and re-create, retain and respond to information transmitted by the speaker. We do not reprocess bits of information already stored in the apperceptive mass of the brain. However, many auditors do. They cease listening to the speaker and begin communicating intrapersonally. They might dwell on a personal problem ("Am I an alcoholic?"), a family problem ("Is divorce the answer for my parents?"), or a job-related problem ("Should I apply the Increase Production Formula in my division?"). Competent listeners know how to keep such concerns in proper perspective. They exert the needed willpower to concentrate on the speaker's message. They realize that such problems can be resolved at a more appropriate time. Careless listeners, however, nurture mental distractions by blocking out the speaker's words. These auditors process only the daydreams and fantasies that take over. They ignore the speaker's message until they decide to resume listening, if indeed they do. Yielding to mental distractions seriously hampers our ability to receive and decode verbal and nonverbal messages.

Semantic Distractions to Perceptive Listening

Semantic refers to the *meaning of words*. Words do not have meanings in themselves. They are but convenient symbols for us to use. Difficulties arise when a symbol has different meanings for the sender and the receiver. The story goes that Abraham Lincoln once accepted a neighbor's offer to trade horses sight unseen. When they met to complete the swap, the neighbor appeared with a sorry old nag, swaybacked and lame, with every bone showing under its ancient hide. Lincoln's horse was a carpenter's sawhorse that he carried over his shoulder. For each horse trader the word had a different meaning. In an unabridged dictionary, there is a full column of definitions for *horse* — equine to the slang phrase *to horse around* — rough play.

Frequently we yield to *semantic distractions* or distorted variations of word meanings. Because of the complexity and diversity of our experiences and our individual perceptions of the world, different words have different meanings to different people. If differences in word meanings are too great, semantic distractions add to the difficulty of understanding the speaker's message. For example, a person accustomed to using colloquial Pennsylvania Dutch speech might shock a Beaumont, Texas drugstore clerk by saying, "Please give me a poke." What the customer needs is a paper bag (called a *poke*, a Pennsylvania Dutch colloquialism) to carry small articles. The spontaneous reaction of the perplexed Texan might be to ignore the request, to ask for an explanation, or to accommodate the customer with a quick jab to the jaw. Needless to say, the alert clerk would listen carefully for an additional clue to clarify the customer's meaning. Active listening can minimize embarrassment caused by semantic distractions.

Travelers in foreign countries who do not speak or understand the native languages invariably notice familiar ads for American products, such as, Coca-Cola and the Big Mac (called a "Big Ming" in China). We see what we have learned to see. Furthermore, we prefer listening to songs, poetry, and scripture verses we have heard before rather than to unfamiliar selections. We give more attention to the political candidate whom we support than one we do not support. John Condon, Jr., a semanticist, explains that the effect of memory and expectations based on past experiences causes us to see things that are not really there and to not see things that are there.[13] Can you verify this concept? *Quickly* read the messages in the three triangles below.

Did you note errors in the triangles? If not, read the messages again.

This "see and not see" phenomenon operates similarly to the "listen and not listen" type of behavior. For example some parents fail to see their grown children as adults. They refuse to listen to and seriously consider their offspring's suggestions. Our unique experiences and our strongly entrenched biases may generate numerous semantic distractions to accurately processing aural stimuli.

Retraining: Guidelines to Listen to Curb and Overcome Distractions

1. Realize that distractions should not be tolerated at the expense of the interested and involved auditors who want to listen.

2. Whenever possible, take the initiative to remedy any distractions such as inadequate lighting, poor ventilation, and unnecessary noise.

3. Offset any possibility of internal distractions by anticipating your own physical needs and planning for peak listening conditions.

4. Become more aware of and informed about noise-control technology. Become more assertive about regulation of noise pollution in the community to safeguard the quality of listening and human interaction.

5. Plan well for lengthy periods of listening.

6. Assume the role of a perceptive listener.

6. LISTEN WITHOUT FAKING ATTENTION AND PRETENDING TO LISTEN

When we display little or no interest in or curiosity about the speaker's topic; when we criticize the speaker's appearance, personality, and delivery; and when we react to physical, mental, and semantic distractions, we often resort to faking attention. We often find ourselves in situations in which we are unprepared physically, intellectually, and emotionally to function as bona fide and attentive listeners. And we feel trapped. Too embarrassed to walk out during a classroom lecture, a board meeting, a business conference, or a social gathering, we withdraw mentally and pretend to listen. We fake attention and interest in the message primarily to deceive the speaker.

Speaker-Listener Feedback

Feedback is a continuous series of listener cues to inform the speaker on how the message is being received. The speaker can adjust the message in response to the listener's feedback. Our overt response to the speaker may be positive or negative nonverbal cues in sign language (a nod, shrug, smile, or frown). This kind of feedback signals that we are involved in the communication. The speaker transmits an adjusted overt response in the form of positive or negative verbal response, paralinguistic cues (change in volume, pitch, tempo, or quality of voice), and bodily movement, as discussed in Chapter 9, Listening to Nonverbal Messages. Most speakers of informal and formal messages, after only a short period of time, can readily detect false or dishonest feedback. Therefore, nonlisteners who play at faking attention initiate a breakdown in the circular process of communication.

Deceiving the Speaker as Pretending Listeners

Those who resort to faking attention as they tune out the speaker usually operate in a well-defined pattern of behavior easily detected by alert and experienced speakers. Rather than conveying relevant feedback, pretending listeners maintain one set of cues as an overall pattern of feedback. They may lean forward intently or slouch comfortably in a chair with the chin cupped in a hand.

They may focus starry eyes on the speaker, or keep a fixed smile or frown on the face. Such fixed, continuous reaction or feedback becomes distracting and frustrating to the speaker. This false-attention syndrome is usually a cover-up for inattentiveness, lack of interest, and lack of valid feedback to the message. Therefore, the speaker realizes that little, if any, of the intended message is being received and decoded. Actually, while not responding to the speaker's intended message, the pretending listener communicates a set of unique messages to the speaker that say, "I'm not listening. I'm taking a 'mental stroll.' My thoughts are more interesting and valuable to me than your message." At the same time, these irresponsible listeners limit themselves, because they might have benefited from listening to the speaker's message.

The never-changing smile, frown, or blank expression becomes the nonlisteners' first line of defense. They retreat and feel secure behind a façade of false attention. They quickly succumb to any number of mental distractions. Most habitual nonlisteners are determined not to listen. They are armed with invalid prejudgments about the topic, the speaker, the delivery, and the occasion. They grasp at any rationale to reinforce their decision to assume the role of a pretending listener. They change the circular process of oral–aural communication into a one-way, speaker/message transaction.

When we fake attention we cannot listen and learn. When we are content to fake attention rather than to participate as competent listeners, we fail to experience the magical quality of human communication. By encouraging the message sender, the receiver can make listening easier.

One way to prevent fake listening is to be sure the time and place are appropriate before you start your message. Any communication has a better chance to succeed when the time and place are right.

Scenario: Wrong Time and Place = Fake Listening

(Carl sees Ben hurrying down the hall.)

Carl: Hi, Ben. I've been looking for you.

Ben: Hi, yourself. Can't talk now — I'm in a rush. I'll check back with you later.

Carl: This will only take a minute. Need your help on project A. Will you prepare an outline management proposal on it for me by tomorrow afternoon?

(As Ben scurries down the hall, he responds over his shoulder.)

Ben: Sure, sure, Joe. See you tomorrow.

Ben didn't hear a word Carl said; he faked listening. He was late to an important meeting. His mind was focused on reviewing key points he planned to present at the meeting. Two days later Carl is upset. Ben never showed up with the proposal, and now project A is behind schedule. Result: Carl angrily calls Ben to his office; you can fill in the rest. The same scenario occurs when students wish to discuss grades or other important matters with professors who are hurrying to class.

Retraining: Guidelines to Listen without Faking Attention and Pretending to Listen

1. Remember that speakers usually can discern the nonlistener's fake-attention act.
2. Realize that the pretending listener loses the most valuable commodity of oral–aural communication—the opportunity to learn.
3. Remember that the messages we deliberately tune out can never be recalled in our frame of reference as rewarding learning experiences.
4. Understand that the longer we practice the faulty habit of faking attention, the more difficult it becomes for us to function as perceptive listeners.
5. Consider the vast amount of valuable knowledge we have discarded in the past and may reject in the future by faking attention. Work persistently to develop the necessary techniques and skills to change this wasteful pattern of behavior.
6. Avoid any listening situations in which we plan to function as a pretending listener by faking attention.
7. Set a personal goal to refrain from faking attention and to interact with the speaker.

7. LISTEN TO THE ENTIRE MESSAGE WITHOUT JUDGING AND REFUTING

Judgment is an evaluation of the rightness and wrongness of a concept. *Refutation* is presenting evidence to prove a statement wrong. Like listening, judgment and refutation are distinctive mental activities requiring separate processing of complicated data. Obviously, we are trying to perform three different mental processes (listening, judging, and refuting) simultaneously in this faulty pattern of listening behavior.

Attempting to Listen and Judge and Refute the Message

Although we can decode messages at a rapid rate, our one–process brain (discussed in Chapter 4, Five Power Tools of Listening) can process only one mental activity at a time. Trying to listen, comprehend, judge, and refute the message simultaneously is an impossible task. We can severely filter or completely block the complicated process of listening. In other words, at the very instant we begin to judge the message, our minds shift gears from listening to judging. At that point, although the speaker continues to transmit the message we become listeners *in absentia* who have assumed the role of judge.

Attempting to Listen and Refute the Message

Just as it is impossible to listen competently and judge a message at the same time, it is also impossible to listen competently and mentally search for facts to refute or disprove the speaker's message. Careless listeners tend to debate instead of listen. They become defensive when their pet theories are threatened. Perhaps many of us are reluctant to reveal ourselves honestly and openly enough to absorb and balance the speaker's thoughts with our own. We find it difficult to listen openly. We prefer to evaluate and prepare a rebuttal to state our side of an issue. Undoubtedly the greatest demand placed on listeners is to weigh the merit of the speaker's complete message before judging and refuting.

Obstacles to Nonjudgmental Listening

The type of speaker and selection of words can create obstacles that deter nonjudgmental listening.

- The ego speaker: This obstacle involves a spontaneous decision to stop listening and abruptly assume the role of speaker. The ego speaker decides that the interruption message is more important than the speaker's message and must be stated now. Discourteous interruptions startle and irritate the speaker and other auditors. The listening and learning by other auditors abruptly ends and the remaining unspoken message is lost.

- Red–flag words: Nonjudgmental listening stops when we permit certain red–flag words to evoke strong negative reactions that interfere with the desire and ability to listen. Different words affect listeners differently. For some, red–flag words like "death row" or "mandatory testing" trigger emotional reactions that prevent perceptive listening.

- Green–light words: Green–light words involve language that provokes strong positive reactions interfering with the desire and ability to listen. Green–light words for college students might include "spring break," "party," and "graduation." Green–light words used in the work force are "bonus," "flex time," and "superior assessment." A green–light person for students might be a special friend or parents; for employees, spouse or leader-manager.

Your authors use the term assumptive decision to classify the judgments made by listeners to ignore parts of messages. Such listeners *assume* that they know the exact content of the whole message. Most of us remember the times we stopped listening midway through messages to prepare responses to use after the speaker stopped talking. Unfortunately, we learned that such responses to partial messages often were irrelevant, illogical, and even embarrassing.

As listeners we err by permitting any obstacle or aspect of the listening event to interfere with our ability to listen without judging and refuting the speaker and message. We need to retrain if we are to change this unproductive listening behavior.

Retraining: Guidelines to Listen to the Entire Message without Judging and Refuting

1. Exercise self-discipline to permit both the formal and informal speaker to complete the entire message before judging or refuting the speaker and message.

2. Frequently check your motive to listen: Are you listening for complete understanding of the message? Have you stopped listening in order to plan how to respond when the speaker stops? Have you stopped listening to make a judgment and assemble facts to refute the message?

3. Remember that only one mental process can be accommodated by the brain at any given time. The intricate mental process of listening comprehensively to a message cannot be combined with any other mental process, including the difficult processes of judgment and refutation. If we judge and refute, we do not listen.

4. During your comprehensive listening to the message, apply the best techniques and skills to listen efficiently so that you will retain substantive information for later assessing and refuting the message, if necessary.

5. When tempted to judge and refute the speaker's message prematurely, remember that listening is an act of caring. In listening we give ourselves to another's word. We make ourselves accessible and vulnerable to that word.

6. Remember that responding prematurely to an incomplete message can be embarrassing. We become like the man who ran frantically to the pier to catch a ferryboat. He leaped across a strip of water, and landed with a resounding crash on the deck of the ferryboat. "Made it," he shouted with satisfaction as he picked himself up off the deck. "Very good, sir!" said an admiring deckhand. "But what's your hurry? We're just coming in." What is our hurry to stop listening and miss the message?

7. Be alert and recognize language that triggers our red judgmental flags and green lights. Exercise self-control to overcome these obstacles to holistic, perceptive listening.

8. LISTEN TO UNFAMILIAR AND DIFFICULT MATERIAL

The poorest listeners are the inexperienced listeners—inexperienced, that is, in listening to unfamiliar and difficult messages. There are several reasons why listeners cannot process challenging, informative messages: (1) As students we deliberately chose not to listen to complicated expository messages; (2) Our teachers failed to present graduated levels of difficult, informative messages, and (3) Our home environment offered little encouragement for us to be interested in listening to challenging messages. Many times our home life, our schooling, or our experiences do not teach us to assume the responsibility of listening to complex messages.

The Sesame-Street Listener Syndrome

Richard Weaver, II, explains that, like the young child who anticipates fun and entertainment in learning during the popular television program, *Sesame Street*, many adults expect entertainment with learning or they won't listen.[14] Therefore they may tune out the unembellished classroom, community, or television speaker with an unfamiliar or difficult message.

Researchers R. Tamborini and D. Zillmann tested two opposing theories concerning educational programming for children. One view holds that children can acquire information from rapid-paced formats, such as *Sesame Street*. The other view condemns this type of format for having several undesirable effects. The fast pace and complex form, it is claimed, fail to leave children time to reflect or rehearse information vital to relearning. Children, so goes the argument, learn and benefit more from other types of television programs, such as *Mr. Rogers' Neighborhood*, which leave time for children to reflect on material presented, ask questions of young viewers, and use more personalized communication—maintaining eye contact with the camera and addressing the audience as "you," etc.[15]

Although children do learn quickly from entertaining shows like *Sesame Street*, they may learn from several other styles as well. Psychologist John Rosemond claims that children come to school expecting to be entertained. When the reality of learning unfamiliar and difficult material unfolds, they often complain that school is boring. They have been led to equate entertainment with education from watching programs in which letters of the alphabet turn into dancing animals, math problems are presented in song, and the screen constantly flashes image after image after image.[16]

Difficult Messages and Listener Response

Difficult messages require an intense listener response. Let's examine several types of unfamiliar and difficult messages to understand the responsibility assumed by the listener.

Listening to Criticism

Criticism is one of the realities of life, but messages of criticism become difficult when listeners have trouble making a separation between criticism of their work and of themselves. They mistakenly think that if their work is unacceptable, then they are unacceptable. Also, these listeners feel intimidated when unable to respect or trust the motives of the critic.

The following suggestions can help the listener accept criticism as a constructive and more acceptable message:

- Clearly understand the problem. Ask questions; do not assume that you and your critic are on the same wave length.
- Listen with an open mind to criticism. Weight each point on its own merit and from the perspective of the critic.

- Develop ways to enhance your listener self, discussed in Chapter 4, Five Power Tools of Listening, so that criticism can be interpreted constructively, not destructively. As we become less dependent on others to meet our needs and to make us feel good, we are able to accept criticism in a positive manner.

Bilingual Speakers' Messages

Those able to communicate in two or more languages may have difficulty speaking clear, articulate messages. If the bilingual speaker's primary language is foreign and the second language is American English, accents and patterns of the foreign language often become interspersed in the English language. It is difficult and requires concentration to listen to this type of bilingual speaker.

Equivocal Language Messages

The unintentional or intentional use of words with two or more equally plausible meanings is called equivocal language.[17] For example, "I'll meet you out front" could mean the front of a restaurant, a theater, or an apartment. This *unintentional* use of equivocal language could result in a disappointing evening, depending on the listener's interpretation of "out front." When a friend asks for your opinion of an unattractive outfit, you might say, "It's really unusual—one of a kind." This *intentional* use of equivocal language is an attempt to spare embarrassment. During a job interview, you might say, "I had a B average last semester," or "I received a superior rating from my supervisor," even though your overall grade average is closer to C and another former supervisor rated your work performance below average.

Trick questions and answers rely on the listener's ability to decode equivocal language, for example:

Question: When does a boat show affection?

Answer: When it hugs the shore.

Waiter: "How did you find your steak, sir?"

Diner: "Just by accident. I moved the baked potato and there it was."

In both formal and informal communication, equivocal language can create difficulty for listeners in decoding messages.

Complicated Messages

Complicated messages require intense attention, sustained concentration, and persistent effort on the part of the perceptive listener. Ideally one encounters complicated messages as a prospective listener or one who can prepare for a future message, for example, the student who studies an assigned chapter for the next lecture.

Instructions

We listen to countless oral instructions during each day. Yet a common complaint is that many instructions are not followed correctly. Both speaker and listener can be at fault. Two words contain the solution to the problem: *Don't activate.*

When giving instructions, don't activate the listener. When receiving instructions, don't be actively involved in doing any task except listening to the instructions.

- The wrong way to give and listen to instructions: The supervisor approaches Marcia who is absorbed in checking a division audit sheet. He hands her a report while saying, "Sections 3 and 5 relate to your division. Those sections are unclear and redundant. Please review the report and come to my office in twenty minutes with your suggestions."

  It is doubtful that Marcia will follow the instructions completely. The supervisor activated her by placing the report under her eyes; she began reading it without listening to the complete instructions. The supervisor erred in activating Marcia to read and forcing her to stop listening to the instructions.

- The right way to give and listen to instructions: The supervisor approaches Marcia and waits until she raises her eyes from the audit sheet. He holds the report at his side, makes eye contact with Marcia and states the instructions. Then he hands Marcia the report. He returns to his office knowing that Marcia will arrive in twenty minutes with her suggestions.

- The supervisor gave the instructions properly. He waited to get Marcia's attention. He held the report out of sight while giving the instruction. Marcia used her one–process brain to concentrate on his words. Then he handed Marcia the report and walked away as she began to read and revise the report.

For instructions to be transmitted, received, and implemented correctly, as speakers we must retrain *not to activate the listener*. As listeners we need to *deactivate ourselves* and concentrate only on the speaker's words.

Retraining: Guidelines to Listen to Unfamiliar and Difficult Material

1. Determine whether or not you respond effectively when listening to unfamiliar and difficult expository material. If not, make plans to listen regularly to informative messages that require arduous listening efforts.

2. Even though initial improvement appears to be slight, do not become discouraged about retraining yourself to become a competent listener of difficult messages.

3. Seek personal help and guidance from speech communication educators, particularly instructors of listening. Discuss your problems frankly. Plan a specific program for self-improvement in listening to reports, presentations, lectures, and other types of challenging messages.

4. When possible, join with others interested in listening to live and televised speeches and panel discussions on controversial subjects that require great concentration.

5. Generate a feeling of excitement and anticipation about acquiring new

knowledge. Remain determined and confident that you will become competent in listening to complex, challenging expository material and instructions.

6. Practice self-preparation to listen. Be extremely attentive. Concentrate to develop listening power.

9. LISTEN TO SILENCE

Our need as communicators to listen to silence has been noted in two previous chapters: Chapter 5, Five Kinds of Listening We Do, and Chapter 9, Listening to Nonverbal Messages.

We learned that the empathic listener allows the speaker to pause for as short or long a time as needed. This is an act of empathy that prevents the listener from interrupting and causing the reversal of speaker-listener roles. We learned that silence can be positive or negative and always affects another person. Because we tend to feel uncomfortable listening to pauses, speakers often use silence to elicit listener response.

We know that nonverbal or silent speaker cues and listener clues transmit powerful messages. Even in the absence of words, *we cannot not communicate*. Deliberately making no response or avoiding a person is itself a response. Our silence communicates just as intensely as the words we speak, and silence performs specific functions in the communication process.

Functions of Silence

In order to correctly decode and respond to messages, perceptive listeners need to understand the functions of silence. Let's examine six functions of silence noted by Joseph DeVito: to provide thinking time, to inflict hurt and anger, to isolate oneself, to prevent communication, to communicate feelings, and to communicate "nothing."[18]

To Provide Thinking Time
Silence allows the speaker and listener time to think. Both need thinking time to connect and permit previous messages to sink in and to prepare future messages. Following a profound statement, a speaker may pause to emphasize the importance of the words for the listener to interpret and transmit nonverbal feedback to the speaker. In addition to providing short segments of silent time to think, it is beneficial to arrange extended time periods for communicating within — involving self-speaking and self-listening.

To Inflict Hurt and Anger
Silence can be used to inflict hurt and anger. After a conflict, adults refuse to talk to spouses, colleagues, friends. Children, who learn such behavior, give playmates the same treatment. Refusing to acknowledge another is a dramatic, angry act of *disconfirmation*, or refusing to recognize a person as a person. A disconfirmed

person is treated as one would treat an inanimate object. For example, a feuding neighbor silently disconfirms by turning the head to avoid speaking or listening to the other party. Yet the "silent treatment" coupled with hurtful and angry nonverbal behavior *does* communicate as it disconfirms.

To Isolate Oneself

Some persons isolate themselves with a shield of silence in an attempt to handle shyness, anxiety, and fear. The shy person remains in a corner rather than converse at a cocktail party. The anxious person avoids normal and intimate contacts rather than risk rejection. The fearful person retreats physically and psychologically in response to a life–threatening phone message rather than seek proper protection.

To Prevent Communication

Silence can prevent communication. By "clamping" our lips and "plugging" our ears, we withhold information as a speaker or refuse to respond to messages as a listener. A positive aspect of using silence to restrict speech is that we acquire time to monitor and restructure messages. Remember, once spoken, words cannot be unspoken. As a speaker, we use silent time to cool off before uttering inappropriate words. As a listener, we use silent time to perform self-preparation to listen (see Chapter 6, Three Basic Concepts to Enhance Listening Comprehension) and to decode messages.

To Communicate Feelings

Silence can communicate feelings of love, joy, excitement, hate, jealousy, fear — in fact, any emotional response processed by sensory systems. Listeners listen to silence via nonverbal cues of a person's eyes, face, hands, attire, movement, and stance, as discussed in Chapter 9, Listening to Nonverbal Messages. Lovers gaze into each other's eyes, patriots pay silent tribute to the flag, and religious congregations silently bow their heads in prayer. We use silence to express anger, disappointment, and annoyance, reinforced with body language.

To Communicate "Nothing"

Silence is the best policy when there is nothing to say. James Russell Lowell wrote, "Blessed are they who have nothing to say, and who can not be persuaded to say it."[19] Listeners appreciate not being subjected to trite, redundant, incredible messages. Jean Parvin writes:

> In business or personal relations, a word not spoken may be the choicest word of all. Like a composer who knows that the space between the notes is as important as the notes themselves, each of us must realize that our silences can be as expressive as the words we choose. The result is greater harmony and effectiveness.[20]

Retraining: Guidelines to Listen to Silence

1. Be aware of the impact silence has on the listening process by recognizing and responding to the six speaker functions of silence: think, inflict hurt, isolate

oneself, prevent communication, communicate feelings, and communicate "nothing."

2. Accept silence as a powerful nonverbal message and refrain from breaking silence by talking and ignoring pauses.

3. While performing the role of listener, frequently remind yourself of the universal human desire to talk rather than listen. Respect the speaker's complete message, including silence.

4. During silence, observe the speaker closely to determine which function of silence is being used by the speaker. Integrate this information in the listener decoding process.

5. Remember, to retrain as a holistic perceptive listener, one must learn to decode and respond to silence as a meaningful message.

10. LISTEN AND APPLY THE LISTENER BEHAVIOR FORMULA

We discussed segments of the listener behavior formula in Chapter 4, Five Power Tools of Listening, and in Chapter 9, Listening to Nonverbal Messages. We now present the formula as a complete and final power tool of listening to be included in the listening retraining process.

Listener Behavior Formula

LF: Lean Forward.

LSEF: Look into the Speaker's Eyes and Face.

UMF: Use My Face (in response to the speaker's message).

DDOT: Don't Do Other Tasks.

DMP: Don't Make Plans.

DD: Don't Daydream.

DJ: Don't Judge.

Retraining Guidelines: Final Tips

1. Stop talking; we can't listen while talking.

2. Be a holistic listener of telephone messages. Other than the sound of the speaker's voice and use of silence or pauses, telephone listeners are unable to decode nonverbal messages which clarify up to 90 percent of the meaning of messages. Don't "jump in" to fill silence and pauses; respect them as meaningful speaker cues.

3. Use silence as a "turn-taking" regulator to indicate and signal the reversal of roles. After noting the speaker's pause, the listener responds verbally to the message.

4. When excessive speakers ignore listeners' turn-taking signals, take control kindly and ask a question to get the interaction "on track."

5. Be careful not to "jam our receiving sets." We cannot do self-listening while decoding the speaker's message because of our one-process brain.

6. Ask questions to clarify the message.

7. Start listening immediately—to the first word and to the nonverbal message, too. Decoding incomplete messages leads to a breakdown in communication.

8. Plan to use one or two retraining techniques each day to improve listening behavior. Occasionally, you may fail, but persevere in your retraining efforts as you listen perceptively and creatively for depth and growth. Above all, listen to yourself.

WRAPPING IT UP: A SUMMARY

Habits determine the way we listen. It is possible to retrain or change listening habits and upgrade the level of listening competency.

Ten listening retraining techniques and specific guidelines are presented in this chapter, including the complete seven rules of the Listener Behavior Formula, and final tips for retraining to listen.

DISCUSSION AND STUDY GUIDES

1. Define a habit, a technique, and a skill. How do these terms apply to the process of listening? What criteria should be applied to determine which listening habits, techniques, and skills we should retain and which ones we should modify or eliminate?

2. What is meant by "retraining"? Specifically, what are your plans for retraining to improve listening competency? Discuss several ways you can begin immediately to retrain to become a more competent decoder of aural messages.

3. Of the ten listening retraining techniques discussed in this chapter, which ones do you apply inconsistently and incorrectly? Discuss your selection with a friend or colleague. Do they tend to agree with you?

4. After learning about the ten listening retraining techniques, how would you evaluate your overall listening behavior: Excellent, Very Good, Fair, Poor, Very Poor? Justify your assessment by writing a summary report in the Listener Log.

5. Why is to listen with an open mind considered the most important retraining technique? In the Listener Log, list five reasons to support this central idea.

LISTENING EXERCISES THAT WORK

EXERCISE 1. (**Experiencing a Nonjudgmental Day**) Select one day during which you are determined to communicate only by listening and responding without judging or refuting the speaker's message. At the end of the day, reflect on this experience. What are your feelings at the end of the nonjudgmental day in comparison to an ordinary day? Did any friends and acquaintances relate and respond to you differently? Throughout the day, how much restraint did you exercise to listen nonjudgmentally? What have you learned about yourself and others as the result of this experience?

EXERCISE 2. (Listening to Unfamiliar and Difficult Messages) Arrange with a friend to attend a lecture on a difficult topic that is unfamiliar to you, but relates to an area of your friend's expertise. Do planned and on-the-spot self-preparation for this listening event (see Chapter 6, Three Basic Concepts to Enhance Listening Comprehension). During the lecture, concentrate to listen and take minimal notes regardless of the difficulty in understanding the message. After the lecture, discuss with your friend what you have learned. Was the effort and hard work of listening worth the kind and amount of knowledge gained? Would you recommend this type of listening experience to another friend? Explain.

EXERCISE 3. (Assessing Your Retraining Listening Efforts) Complete the chart to assess your listening retraining efforts. As you check one of the five columns for each technique, ask yourself if your friends, family or colleagues would agree with your assessment.

	ALMOST ALWAYS	USUALLY	SOME-TIMES	SELDOM	ALMOST NEVER	SCORE
1. Listen with an open mind	____	____	____	____	____	____
2. Listen to generate interest in and concentrate on the speaker's topic	____	____	____	____	____	____
3. Listen and adapt to the speaker's appearance, personality, and delivery	____	____	____	____	____	____
4. Listen for concepts and central ideas instead of facts	____	____	____	____	____	____
5. Listen to curb and overcome decisions	____	____	____	____	____	____
6. Listen without faking attention and pretending to listen	____	____	____	____	____	____
7. Listen to the entire message without judging and refuting	____	____	____	____	____	____

	ALMOST ALWAYS	USUALLY	SOME-TIMES	SELDOM	ALMOST NEVER	SCORE
8. Listen to unfamiliar and difficult material	_____	_____	_____	_____	_____	_____
9. Listen to silence	_____	_____	_____	_____	_____	_____
10. Listen and apply the listener behavior formula	_____	_____	_____	_____	_____	_____

EXERCISE 4. (Calculating Your Listening Retraining Score) To complete the sixth column, calculate your score for each item as follows:

For every "Almost Always" checked, give yourself a score of	10
For every 'Usually" checked, give yourself a score of	8
For every "Sometimes" checked, give yourself a score of	6
For every "Seldom" checked, give yourself a score of	4
For every "Almost Never" checked, give yourself a score of	2

EXERCISE 5. (Interpreting Your Listening Competency Score) Interpret your listening competency score as follows:

90 and above: You are an extraordinarily competent listener.

70 to 89: You listen well.

69 and below: You need to exert more effort in listening retraining.

What does your total competency score reveal about your overall listening behavior? How does your total assessment level compare with your personal assessment of listening competency in Question 5 of the Discussion and Study Guides? Noting your strengths and weaknesses in this assessment, what is the most significant knowledge you have gained? On which techniques should you concentrate most and least of your retraining effort?

NOTES

1. Guy R. Lefrancois, *Psychology* (Belmont, CA: Wadsworth Publishing Co., 1980), 427.
2. Ronald Lee and Karen King Lee, *Arguing Persuasively* (New York: Longman, 1989), 130.
3. Ibid.
4. Henry W. Johnstone, Jr., "Some Reflections on Argumentation," *Validity and Rhetoric in Philosophical Argument* (University Park, PA: Dialogue Press of Man and World, 1978), 109; cited in Ronald Lee and Karen King Lee, *Arguing Persuasively*, 130.
5. Michael S. Hanna and James W. Gibson, *Public Speaking for Personal Success* (Dubuque, IA: Wm. C. Brown Publishers, 1989), 108.
6. Lawrence B. Rosenfeld and Roy M. Berko, *Communicating with Competency* (Glenview, IL: Scott, Foresman, 1990), 306.
7. Lefrancois, 561.
8. Joan E. Grusec, Robert S. Lockhart and Gary C. Walters, *Foundations of Psychology* (Toronto: Copp Clark Pitman, 1990), 572–75.
9. Gloria Borger, Kenneth T. Walsh, Jeannye Thornton and Ted Gest, "Judging Thomas: A Supreme Court nominee—and the nominating system—on trial," *U.S. News & World Report*, October 21, 1991, 33–36.

10. Donald Baer, "Asking the questions that really matter," *U.S. News & World Report*, Outlook, October 21, 1991, 16.
11. Ella A. Erway, *Listening: A Programmed Approach*, 2nd ed. (New York: McGraw-Hill, 1979), 23.
12. Charles U. Larson, *Persuasion: Reception and Responsibility* 5th ed. (Belmont, CA: Wadsworth Publishing Co., 1989), 209.
13. John C. Condon, Jr., *Semantics and Communication*, 2nd ed, New York: Macmillan, 1975), 18.
14. Richard L. Weaver, II, *Understanding Interpersonal Communication* (Glenview, IL: Scott, Foresman, 1979), 103.
15. R. Tamborini and D. Zillmann, "Effects of Questions, Personalized Communication Style, and Pauses for Reflection in Children's Educational Programs," *Journal of Educational Research*, 79 (1985), 19–26; cited in Robert N. Bostrom, *Listening Assessment: Measurement and Application*, 187.
16. John Rosemond, "Different generations: Teachers say today's students want school to be 'entertaining,'" *Dayton* (OH) *Daily News*, September 9, 1991, 2-C.
17. Ronald B. Adler and Neil Towne, *Looking Out, Looking In*, 6th ed. (Fort Worth, TX: Holt, Rinehart and Winston, 1990), 312.
18. Joseph A. DeVito, *The Interpersonal Communication Book*, 5th ed. (New York: Harper & Row, 1989), 258–59.
19. Ibid., 259–61.
20. Jean Parvin, "When to Keep Your Mouth Shut," *Reader's Digest*, March 1991, 79–82.

CHAPTER 11

THE IMPACT OF CULTURE AND GENDER ON LISTENING

Ignorance of cultural differences is one of the chief causes of misunderstanding in a world that is getting more and more interdependent, on the one hand, and increasingly torn with strife on the other.
— *Falichothia*[1]

THESIS Both culture and gender influence listening behavior. Perceptive listeners must learn how to recognize and use these powerful social dimensions to enhance listening performance.

CHAPTER OBJECTIVES

1. Recognize, accept, and begin adapting to various cultural norms as a perceptive listener.
2. Recognize and understand the impact of gender roles on listening.
3. Sensitively apply the retraining tools presented in this text to improve listening to intercultural and gender-related messages.

CHAPTER PREVIEW

- Listening to a medley of subcultures.
- Listening in organizational culture.
- Communication and gender.

Most large American colleges, universities, and corporations are rapidly acquiring a multicultural character. Students and employees can expect to interact with persons from a variety of different countries and cultures.

LISTENING IN THE GLOBAL VILLAGE

We live in a global village. Never again can the world community return to an isolated existence confined to clearly defined borders. Television enables us to view the shooting of Chinese youths, missile attacks on Israel by Iraq, starving children in Africa. These global events documented in news broadcasts claim the attention of listeners worldwide. The impact of culture on listening needs to be recognized in the classroom, the workplace, the professions.

The Global Village Classroom

We listen perceptively when we are aware of culture insights as we interpret and re-create messages. Being aware of the diversity of cultures can enhance intercultural listening. For example, we need to know that Arabs express their feelings without inhibition in loud voices when speaking to equals, Latin Americans have little regard for time constraints and deadlines, Asians are unlikely to disagree openly with a teacher, Jamaicans believe that looking at a teacher is disrespectful while looking away is respectful, Germans require more space than others during inter-personal encounters to satisfy the ego, and the French are open and sensitive communicators.

Perceptive listeners should be aware of the diversity of cultural backgrounds of students and teachers in the global village classroom as well as in the workplace.

The Global Village Workplace

Each workplace has its own culture or system of values and rules clarifying how you are to act as you perform quality work. Become a network listener in order to learn about company culture; arrange to speak frequently with those who are informed and respected by other employees. Remember, perceptive listening is the key to effective networking.

Unfortunately certain employees are closed-minded. They nonverbally communicate an "unwelcome" attitude toward members of different subcultures. Blacks, Hispanics, Japanese, and Chinese Americans — together with those workers who are aged, handicapped, homosexual, or suffering with the AIDS virus — face serious problems in the workforce. We perceptive listeners can help overcome culture bias by seeking out those not meeting some "expected image." We can listen and learn from those of different subcultures. In doing so, we nurture in them a positive image of self. Also, as listeners, we grow and prosper personally and professionally.

The Global Village Professionals

Professionals, too, are affected by the diversity of different cultures and subcultures. Professionals need to be more cautious and understanding while listening to clients, patients, and customers of different cultures.

Establishing and meeting deadlines are facts of life in America. However, an American businessperson aspiring to negotiate a contract in India should know that Mid–Eastern people consider deadlines a threat, that in an elevator everyone faces front and men exit before women, and that one never gives or takes food with the left hand. An American negotiating a European contract should know that French negotiators are talkative, confrontational, and competitive and British negotiators are polite and tend not to interrupt.

Professionals in the global village—including physicians, nurses, lawyers, engineers, chemists, writers, and others—need to plan for more listening time. All need extra time to assess, adapt, and respond to members of different cultures and subcultures.

In Chapter 1, Listening to Succeed, we described how perceptive listeners can succeed in the classroom, the workplace, and the professions. In this chapter, we show how awareness of the impact of culture and gender on listening will increase the possibility of success in the global village classroom, workplace, and professions of the twenty-first century. Thus we can become more successful perceptive listeners in modern American melting pot culture.

The "Modern" Melting Pot of America

In the twenty-first century non–European racial and ethnic groups in the United States will outnumber Americans of Western European ancestry. Americans will include many individuals of African, Hispanic, Asian, Middle Eastern, and European backgrounds.

In 1990, whites accounted for approximately 78 percent of the nation's population; this figure is expected to drop to 54 percent by 2080. Ethnic minorities, now comprising 30 percent of the public school population, are increasing at a much faster rate than the dominant white culture.[2]

In classrooms and workplaces, we note a persistent inclusion of diverse cultures that will profoundly affect all forms of communication—particularly listening. The concepts and retraining techniques learned in this text need to be adapted to international and cross-cultural communication. To do so, we need to be familiar with the terms noted in the Definition Box 7.

DEFINITION BOX 7:   Terms Related to Culture and Listening[3]

culture: pattern of values, beliefs, symbols, language, norms, and behavior that have been transmitted to and shared by a given group of individuals.

subculture or co-culture: groups influenced by a dominant culture.

intracultural communication: interaction among persons from the same culture or subculture.

intercultural communication: interaction among persons from different cultures or subcultures.

international communication: interaction between two persons from different countries.

cross-cultural communication: study of one particular phenomenon in two or more cultures.

low-context culture: those people using verbal patterns of speech as the explicit part of messages. (Low-context cultures tend to be individualistic.)

high-context culture: people using verbal patterns of ambiguous language so that what *is* *not said* may determine the meaning of the message rather than what *is said*. (High-context cultures tend to be *collectivists* who support group harmony.)

ethnocentrism: a belief that one's native culture is superior. Ethnocentric listeners interpret messages by the norms of their culture.

To listen perceptively, we need to understand the cultural diversity of people. Let's examine three of the largest American subcultures: black Americans, Hispanics, and Japanese. We will also highlight differences in other cultures.

BLACK AMERICANS IN A WHITE AMERICA: AN OVERVIEW

The rich, diverse history of black Americans has its roots in slavery beginning in the seventeenth century.

Researcher and author Richard T. Schaefer states that approximately 29 million blacks reside in the United States, about 12 percent of the population. There are more blacks in New York and Chicago than in any other cities, including those of Africa.[4] While recent antidiscrimination legislation and major court decisions have guaranteed blacks the same rights as American citizens, they continue to struggle for recognition and financial security in a dominant white culture. The average income of blacks is significantly lower than the income of whites, yet the rich heritage of their language permeates American culture.

No displaced people have ever completely lost the language forms of their native culture. The black American language, called Ebonics, reflects the powerful African heritage cherished by the first slaves sold in the American colonies in the early 1600s.

Ebonics

Ebonics is an American *dialect,* a distinctive variation in a language as spoken in subcultures. Blacks tend to use Ebonics or Black English for special occasions or when communicating among members of their culture.

Nonblack listeners can relate to Black English slang. The concept of "soul" has a unifying and mystic significance to blacks. Thus we listen to such slang expressions as: soul food and soul brother or sister; also, chick (girl), vines (clothes), Hog (Cadillac), bread (money) and Oreo (a black who is "white" on the inside).[5] In addition to slang, listeners are exposed to another Black English form called the argot.

Argots in Ebonics

Since *culture is communication*, we gain valuable insight by listening to the way black Americans use *argots*, a code system of special language forms. Argots enable members of subcultures to communicate with each other without being understood by others.[6] Thus they are a means of defense against a dominant culture.

Three argots listeners can recognize are: rapping, shucking, and jiving and a verbal game called the Dozens.

Rapping is a lively manner of speech used to create a favorable impression or receive a favor. It is an interactive, operative procedure. Originally it referred to conversation between a black man and woman through which the man sought to win the admiration of the woman. One does not rap *with* someone but *to* someone.[7]

Descriptive rapping can also be an attempt to create a sense of importance and "belonging" in a narrative form. Additionally, rapping can be cajoling — an attempt to control or exploit others. The expressions "take the rap" and "beat the rap" (meaning to accept and avoid punishment) stem from this argot.

Shucking and jiving are language forms used to manipulate the listener's mind and emotions to control a situation by faking and creating false impressions. Historically this argot stems from a background of mistreatment by the dominant white culture and is generally used when confronted by establishment authority figures. It has become a means of survival, helping blacks stay out of trouble.[8]

The Dozens, another notable aspect of black language, is a verbal battle between speakers interacting with a barrage of cruel and humorous insults, sometimes encouraged by a group of onlooking peers. The origin of the Dozens evolved from the early, degrading practice of selling twelve impaired slaves at a discount price. The group of listeners may select a winner based on the number of original insults tossed around during the impromptu speaking warfare. The verbal battle continues until the loser gives up, walks away, or begins to fight physically. Even if a fight erupts, the winner is not determined by the physical encounter but rather by the intensity and creativity of the verbal confrontation.[9]

Family and Religion

Historically, the family has been the main support as blacks endured the hardships leading to the anti-slavery or Abolitionists Movement and the Civil Rights Movement. Today the majority of black households are single–parent households. Traditionally, the mother assumes the responsibility of raising and providing for her children. Because of the extended single–parent role, the number of blacks finishing high school is increasing.

Continued use of Black English is not reflective of blacks' education. Because blacks experience the world differently from other cultures in America, it is necessary for them to have a language to impart that knowledge. Thus, the black language communicates across surface barriers of education or social position. This language binds and creates community for blacks.

The black community represents Christian and nonChristian believers. At a black church service, the congregation may emotionally express love of God by singing, talking back, shouting, and stomping. Many black Americans reject European–imposed Christianity and follow Black Judaism and Muslim religions, among others.

....

Culture is Communication

Listening to Black Americans: Helpful Tips

1. Remember that Ebonics or Black English is a second language. Its ethnic structure affects our language. It is a rich part of our English language.
2. Respect the cultural heritage of Black English as an informal language. Many black Americans are fluent and articulate speakers of Standard American English.
3. Gaining insight into black American culture helps us understand and listen more perceptively to black Americans. Thus, we can more fully appreciate their rich and diverse heritage.

THE HISPANIC CULTURE: AN OVERVIEW

To understand the largely Spanish-speaking Hispanic population, listeners need to know something about those who share the group label "Hispanic" or "Latino" — where they reside and the symbolic forms of their co-cultures. Definition Box 8 can simplify this task.

DEFINITION BOX 8: Terms Related to the Hispanic Culture[10]

Hispanics: Americans of Mexican, Spanish, or Latin origin with an ancestral home in Central and South America. Cultures of Latin America are sharply divided; 16 million Hispanics reside in the United States (1 out of 20 Americans); most are Chicanos (in the Southwest), Puerto Ricans (in the Northeast — primarily in New York City) and Cuban Americans (in Florida).

Hispanos: descendants of those living in the Southwest in Mexican lands colonized by the United States after the Mexican-American War.

Chicanos: Americans of Mexican origin stretching back to the Aztec civilization; the Spaniards conquered the land and merged with the Indians to centralize the Mexican people; 10 million Chicanos live in the United States (the largest *ethnic group* in the country, representing 60 percent of the Hispanic population).

raza: the Chicano's intense pride of their Spanish, Indian, and Mexican heritage.

barrios: segregated neighborhoods populated by Chicanos, Puerto Ricans, or other poverty-level Hispanic groups.

English immersion: pupils taught by English-speaking teachers who know the native language but use it *only to clarify information*.

fiesta politics: blatant messages to Hispanics by candidates seeking election.

anglo: the term used in this text to refer to non–Hispanics (primarily white).

In Chapter 4, Five Power Tools of Listening, we noted the importance of identifying the listener self, developed through one's total experiences. How has the Hispanic concept of self been affected?

Forces Influencing the Hispanic Subculture

Three powerful forces have had great influence on the Hispanic subculture.[11]

1. Bilingual Problems: Most Hispanics speak both English and Spanish. Because proficiency in English was a standard for achievement, Spanish-speaking pupils, taught by English-speaking teachers, were expected to listen and learn lessons taught in English. This kept many Hispanics from adapting to the dominant culture. Today, bilingual education is helping to eradicate this problem.

2. The False Culture of Poverty: Hispanics, as well as some other subsubcultures, have been stereotyped as being exclusively poor, having an irresponsible lifestyle, and thus creating their own poverty. Bilingual education enables Hispanics to participate productively in the workplace and gradually change their standard of living. Once the Supreme Court mandated bilingual education (teaching subject matter in the native tongue as students learn a second language), Hispanics began to achieve academically. In the growing Hispanic consumer market, economic conditions improved; soon Hispanics could fill positions requiring proficiency in both English and Spanish.

3. Family and Church. Hispanic lifestyle centers around the family unit and the Roman Catholic Church. Headed by two parents, the average family consists of five or more members. Family obligations, including the care of the elderly, are placed above individual needs.

Listening to Hispanic Speakers: Helpful Tips

1. As we listen to Hispanics, we need to discard negative stereotypic images.

2. It is important to remove distorted images as we listen to members of *any* subculture. The PIM (picture in mind) and the STTD (Speech-Thought-Time Differential) Power Tools, explained in Chapter 4, Five Power Tools of Listening, can help us do the job. Replace distorted cultural images with accurate and vivid pictures of the speaker and the message.

   Upon encountering any member of these subcultures and extending a perceptive listening ear, we indicate our desire to reaffirm the speaker's "self."

JAPANESE AND CHINESE CULTURES

In the United States, Asian–American subcultures are the most heavily represented by descendants of Chinese and Japanese immigrants. Any knowledge we acquire about the Japanese and Chinese cultures and the Japanese–American and Chinese–American subcultures enhances our performance as holistic perceptive listeners.

Americans want to know what the Japanese are really like now that Japan is a world power in a global economy. Americans interact with Japanese entrepreneurs in Tokyo and Nagasaki as well as with Japanese–Americans in Houston, Chicago, and other U.S. metropolitan areas.

Japan is a formal country, stressing etiquette more strongly than do European countries and the United States. Japanese respect the customs of foreigners and expect visitors to respect the customs of Japan. Japanese especially admire the combined qualities of sincerity and politeness;[12] silence is considered polite and appropriate behavior while excessive talkativeness is considered rude. Group interaction remains a vital part of the decision–making process, during which one should listen intently to words and silence.

Japan is a very education-conscious society with an adult literacy rate well in excess of 90 percent, a result of the post–World War II education revolution.[13] Communicating to maintain group harmony is a high Japanese priority in business as well as in social settings. Identification with, and support of, the group are highly regarded, and perceptive listening plays an important role. Group homogeneity is achieved by listening and respecting the decision-making thoughts of group members, thus always making the group a stronger entity than the individual.

While Japanese-Americans have not escaped discrimination — indeed, thousands of them were interned during World War II — they have made significant contributions within the social fabric of the United States. Accomplishments of Japanese-Americans over the past three decades have resulted in one of America's great success stories.

As we listen to members of this subculture we are soon aware that assimilation of Japanese–Americans into U.S. culture is occurring at a faster pace than in other Asian–American subcultures. In one generation, Japanese–Americans have attained remarkable upward mobility in education and earning power.

The United States' sizable population of Chinese descent can be traced back for at least five generations.[14] Tending to cluster together from the outset in tight–knit communities, many Chinese-Americans live in numerous "Chinatowns," located throughout the United States, mostly in deteriorating sections of large cities. Chinese–Americans who leave Chinatowns elect to live and work in the mainstream of the dominant white culture.

Only recently have the public and U.S. government agencies become aware that Chinatowns are essentially settlements for the poor working for substandard wages. Why have Chinese immigrants and many Chinese–Americans flocked into Chinatowns and continued to remain in such ghettos? Apart from linguistic barriers on the part of non–English–speaking inhabitants, there have been several reasons for their doing so.

Chinese culture for millennia preserved a rich history of organizational life, which Chinese immigrants carried over from China. Three of those life patterns continued to offer security to Chinatown inhabitants:

1. Clans, or *tsu*, served to unite families with common ancestors and those sharing a last name. Some families still dominate in certain cities: Toms in New York, Moys and Chins in Chicago, Lees in Philadelphia, for example. Clan strength depends on the important role of the extended family (parents, children, and other kin).

2. Benevolent associations, or *hui kuan*, helped to unite members based on the person's district of origin in China. For example, the Chinese Consolidated Benevolent Association makes loans, settles disputes, protects its members.

3. Secret societies, or *tongs*, flourished early and were instrumental in clandestine activities ranging from political issues to exploitation of Chinese workers, illegal drugs, and gambling. Like the *tsu* and *hui kuan*, the *tong* influence has dwindled as acculturation into mainstream America has progressed.

Outside Chinatowns, Chinese–Americans have proved to be high achievers. Like the Japanese–Americans, many have attained high levels of education and earned income. Indeed, as a group, Chinese-Americans have the lowest unemployment rate in the nation, and they are, per capita, more significantly represented in professional fields than is the general population.[15]

LISTENING IN THE ORGANIZATIONAL CULTURE

Every organization has its own culture. Millions of organizations operate within the legal framework of laws enacted and enforced by the government. Thus one might classify a nation as a dominant culture and each organization within the country as a subculture or coculture.

Each organization has its own set of regulations and symbols, forming a subculture. Listening to family, friends, and professionals may have influenced your decision to join and participate in various subcultures or organizations. Among them might be a certain bank or university, a social agency or church, health spa, an accounting club, investment firm, or an Army Reserve unit. Each are unique subcultures in their own right. (Briefly, stop reading long enough to think about the subcultures you have joined and the tasks you perform as a member to support the organization.)

High school and college students prepare themselves for responsible membership in organizational subcultures. Those already in the workforce have been supporting an organizational subculture in accordance with the policies and regulation applicable to all people who work there. Quality performance by each member of an organization is vitally important to the success of the enterprise, and reflects the strength of the subculture itself.

An explicit definition of organizational culture is "a cohesion of values, myths, heroes and symbols that has come to mean a great deal to the people who work there."[16] It is important that all employees, from delivery staff to chief executive officer, understand the formal and informal systems of rules in a corporation, a small business, or military branch of service. Only then can there be a systemized approach for each member of the subculture.

The way we listen in an organization often determines the manner in which others communicate and work with us. We need to listen perceptively to learn about others, and we need to listen in order to learn how to do what is expected of us as productive workers in a subculture.

COMMUNICATION AND GENDER

In Chapter 7, Objectivity Can Be Attained: Maintaining Emotional Control, we learned it is necessary for us to identify the source of an emotional filter before we

As we begin to look at some elements of gender–impacted communication and listening, let us consider some terms we will use.

DEFINITION BOX 9:   Terms Relating to Gender and Listening

sex: biological characteristics present from birth

male: sex condition of having XY chromosomes

female: sex condition of having XX chromosomes

gender: sex-linked differences described in communication, family, school and intimate relationships (One may be female [sex] but act in a masculine [not feminine] style [gender].)

masculine: term for male gender ideal

feminine: term for female gender ideal

sexism: prejudicial attitudes of behavior toward either sex based on cultural stereotypes and myths

androgyny: possessing qualities of male and female

---

can deal with it. Let us attempt now to determine the source for gender–impacted listening barriers by looking at some elements of gender–impacted communication.

Women and men have spent years puzzling over why they misunderstand each other. We find ourselves saying, "the trouble with men," and "just like a woman." Not satisfied with repeating the same old statements, perceptive listeners want to improve listening. They want to know what causes the problems. Nurture or nature? Biology or socialization?

There are some basic differences between female and male brains at birth.

> The female cortex is more fully developed. The sound of the human voice elicits more left-brain activity in infant girls than in infant boys, accounting in part for the earlier development in females of language. Baby girls have larger connectors between the brain's hemispheres and thus integrate information more skillfully. This flexibility bestows greater verbal and intuitive skills. Male infants lack this ready communication between the brain's lobes; therefore, messages are routed and rerouted to the right brain, producing larger right hemispheres. This size advantage accounts for males having greater spatial and physical abilities and explains why they may become more highly lateralized and skilled in specific areas.[17]

This seems to give biological support to the accepted differences between females and males: Girls have greater verbal ability, boys excel in visual and spatial development; also, boys excel in mathematics, and they are more aggressive.

Many people, however, believe female and male differences can also be attributed to socialization.

Socialization or Cultural Differences Between Women and Men

Certainly, some socialization differences between females and males appear almost at birth. If we look into the window of a nursery of newborns, we often see pink blankets on girls, and blue ones on boys. Parents may peer into the nursery holding toys they believe are appropriate. They may buy a son a football even though it will be years before the child can use it or buy a daughter a doll long before she can play with it. Additionally, we may find that we talk to each child differently and accept different ways of talking from them.

Two Communication Cultures

Our talking to each child differently and accepting differing ways of talking from them makes it possible to say that women and men grow up in two distinct communication cultures. Although girls and boys are almost never segregated from each other, most homes, schools, and communities demonstrate gender patterns for behavior.

Boys are urged to be physical and aggressive, girls to be "ladylike" both in action and in "feminine" and "masculine" communication styles. Children spend most of their playtime in same–sex groups.

Boys play outside in hierarchical groups. Their games have leaders and many rules. Players frequently argue about rules and jockey for center stage. They tell stories and jokes, and challenge the stories and jokes of others.

Girls play in small groups or pairs. Within the group everyone gets a turn. Many of their games do not have winners and losers. Girls often center their play around a best friend; they do not grab center stage. They prefer to be liked over being in charge.

Once they have grown up, men talk to present information, knowledge, and skill. As they talk, they take center stage by storytelling, joking, or interrupting. Women talk as a way of establishing connections and negotiating relationships. This creates an intimacy which says, "We are close and the same." Men's talk contributes to an independence that says, "We are separate and different."[18]

Such differences help explain why women and men are often confused by each other's communication. Men may have little use for small talk because they are in the habit of talking to impart information. Women may find telling personal weaknesses and secrets creates closeness and popularity while men believe this very telling would weaken them. Listeners, aware of these differences, have observed two different communication cultures. Just as in any cross-cultural communication, gender–based stereotypes have evolved.

Gender Stereotypes and Listening

Stereotyping means assigning people, groups, events or issues to a particular conventional category. Listeners who assign women and men to stereotypical categories forget the unique characteristics of individuals and develop an expectation of the role each will fill.

Female Communication Stereotypes
Gender expectations tell us that the stereotypical woman speaker is a soft–spoken, self-effacing, compliant female. More emotional than logical, she is prone to be disorganized and subjective. Many have learned to expect women to adhere to these "feminine" stereotypes. They can be shocked by the woman who does not. This shock often leads listeners to discount what the woman says or to criticize her for "unwomanly" actions.

Male Communication Stereotypes
Male communication has been stereotyped throughout history. The "masculine" model is direct, confrontive, forceful, and logical. His few well–chosen words are focused on making a particular point. Uninformed listeners expect male speakers to adhere to this stereotype and may become nervous when they do not. Men who adhere to the accepted stereotype are also ineffective listeners who interrupt often, make categorical assertions, and dominate discussions.

Both female and male communication stereotypes have been with us for centuries. It will take time and effort for listeners to learn to focus on the actual message and to ignore stereotypes. But we must take care to monitor our own expectations of female or male communication styles.

Communication Styles and Listening
Women and men use language differently. Whether this is a result of biology or culture is not important. Learning to identify differences in vocal, verbal, and nonverbal communication is important.

Vocal Behaviors in Women and Men
Women and men use articulation, pitch, and intonation in different ways. Articulation refers to the way we use standard phonetic pronunciation. Women use more precise and more standard articulation. *Pitch* refers to how high or low one's voice sounds. In general, women's voices are higher pitched than men's. Because humans have the ability to change pitch, some experts believe that both men and women tend to adjust their pitch to conform to cultural standards. *Intonation* refers to pitch swings or changes within a phrase or sentence. An upward inflected statement is used mostly by women and a downward inflection by a man.

Verbal constructs for women and men also differ. Tag questions, qualifiers, vocabulary differences, disclaimers, and compound requests are used more often by female speakers.

- Tag questions illustrate hesitancy or doubt. An example would be, "We have an appointment at three o'clock, don't we?" "Don't we?" is the tag.
- Qualifiers such as "maybe," "probably," "rather," "kind of," "I think," or "I guess" can show a speaker's lack of confidence.
- Vocabulary differences refer to which gender uses which word. Adverbs of intensity (terribly, awfully, quite) and certain adjectives (lovely, charming,

divine) are seen as elements of women's rather than men's vocabulary. In our society, women may use typically male expletives like "damn" and "hell," but men are not likely to use typically female terms.

- Disclaimers are used by speakers who see themselves as part of the subordinate group. Women, in our culture, use disclaimers. ("I'm not really sure about this," or "I could be wrong, but. . . .")

- Compound requests are most often used by women who have more difficulty voicing requests than do men. A male speaker in our culture would likely use the imperative, "Type this now," whereas a female speaker might say, "If you're not busy, would you type this now?" which creates more harmonious relationships.

Several researchers have referred to male speaking styles as "power" communication and female speaking styles as "powerless" communication used as a social medium to build rapport. Tag questions, qualifiers, and disclaimers are considered to be more polite and less direct—useful in creating consensus and rapport. Men have learned to communicate in order to exchange information. When women use their rapport–building style in what traditionally have been male arenas—law, medicine, management, for example—these constructs may appear to be powerless when they are meant to be courteous.

Women's and Men's Nonverbal Behavior

Listeners know that nonverbal use of space, posture, movement, touch, eye contact, and facial expression can also communicate power or powerlessness, dominance or submission. As we recall the elements of nonverbal communication discussed in Chapter 9, Listening to Nonverbal Messages, we can consider the ways women and men use each and which are the result of culture.

- Space can indicate power. In our culture women and people of lower status take up less space than men and people of higher status. Women are taught to keep the knees together, cross the legs at the ankle or knee, keep the elbows near the body and hold belongings on the lap. Men, on the other hand, habitually take up space by sprawling and spreading out their belongings.

- Height can also show power. The person who stands over the one who is seated communicates power. Men are generally taller than women, and thus appear to have more power. (Tall women, however, have not learned to use their height in a powerful way.)

- Smiling can show happiness, appeasement, or submission. Dominant members of a hierarchy smile less than submissive members. Perceptive listeners are aware that women smile more frequently and for longer duration than men, but this does not signal happiness—it is a communication style.

- Eye contact is also used more often and for longer duration by women when they listen. They avert their eyes more often when looked at. Listeners must note the context in which eye contact is experienced. While eye contact may signal listening or giving respect, prolonged eye contact can deliver a threat or a sexual invitation.

- Nodding (and sometimes saying "yes" while nodding) is often employed by women listeners to mean, "I am listening." Men often presume this means agreement, because, to them, silence means, "I am listening and agreeing."

As interesting as it is to speculate on what women and men signal by certain nonverbal cues, we must take care in interpreting them. "There is much potential for much misunderstanding in cross–sex communication exchanges. Both women and men listeners need to be able to identify very precisely those behaviors which seem intrusive or inappropriate."[19]

Improving Gender–Impacted Listening

Perceptive listeners must learn to overcome female and male stereotypes and cultural expectations of female-male communication. Perhaps the best way to do this is, first, to confront our own sexist attitudes and, second, to monitor our performance when listening is impacted by gender.

Here are three examples of sexism and stereotypes we encounter in listening to female and male communicators.

1. Males cannot describe feelings. We learned in Chapter 7, Objectivity Can Be Attained: Maintaining Emotional Control, that identifying, describing, and finding the source of emotions and feelings is an important listening and communication skill. Yet many men are still unable to describe or voice their feelings and have great difficulty developing this skill.

   We can confront this difficulty by considering in what way we have helped to create it. How often have we told little boys that "big boys don't cry" or to "take it like a man" when things go wrong? Do we provide children with male role models who do not express feelings? When we allow children to presume that men should not communicate feelings, we prepare men to grow up not able to express nor listen for feelings and women not to expect men to express feelings nor listen to gender–impacted issues.

2. Women seldom act assertively. Just as men have been conditioned to "keep a stiff upper lip" when dealing with feeling, many women have been conditioned to be passive. If we have suggested to little girls, "Nice girls don't talk back," and "Be a little lady," we should not be surprised if grown women do not know how to stand up for themselves. Often women think they can't express an opinion because men do not wait for them to give one.

   A woman who was passed over for promotion because her male bosses said she didn't seem to assert herself and enter into conversations said, "I never can get in. You never quit talking." "Well," they answered, "Sure you can! You start talking whenever you're ready." Interrupting is part of the male game. That's how they change the topics.[20]

   If we have urged little girls not to interrupt and to wait their turn, they become women who don't know that they can break in and simply enter a mixed–gender discussion in order to contribute knowledge and expertise.

3. Society values masculine over feminine behavior. Most of us — female and male — have learned to admire and defer to what is thought of as traditional masculine behavior. This has been called the white male system (WMS). Its beliefs are: The WMS is innately superior, the WMS knows everything, it is possible to be totally logical, rational, and objective.[21] Of course, not all communicators believe this, but it can create problems in cross–gender communication. These circumstances make it difficult to establish a climate of equality between women and men.

Our culture has contributed to this inequality and preference for male behavior. Urging young men to participate in sports and young women to cheer them on as cheerleaders is one example. Identifying medicine, law, and engineering as prestige fields of study and urging young men to enroll in them once again contributes to signaling this preference.

Monitoring Gender-Impacted Listening

In the various roles humans play, each of us may contribute to stereotypes and sexist attitudes which affect our listening. We can attempt to repair this situation by learning ways to monitor and improve our listening behavior.

As listeners, we can remind ourselves to concentrate on the content of the message. If a nonverbal signal — eye contact, facial expression, paralanguage, for example — does not conform to the content of the message, we can apply a perception check. We can do the following:

- Observe sender cues.
- Describe sender cues to yourself as listener clues.
- Ask: "What do these clues mean to me?"
- Put your understanding into words.

In putting the understanding into words, the speaker should use "I" statements rather than "you" accusations. This gives the listener a way to concur.

Male listeners need to recognize women communicators' use of metamessages. Most of us have learned that the meaning of a message is conveyed in words. But a male listener who considers only words for meaning may be puzzled by why he and a female listener apparently hear different messages. Women listen for metamessages — the unspoken meaning behind the words we speak.[22]

Your authors suggest that men listening for messages in words and women listening for metamessages also should practice perception checking. Experts suggest that males begin their discussions of perception by using "we" or "us" (pronouns of inclusion) rather than "I" or "me" (pronouns of exclusion). "Let's look at why we're not understanding each other," might be an excellent way to begin a perception check when exploring female and male understanding of messages and metamessages.

We must learn to value and accept differing communication styles. What we sometimes see as weak or passive female communication is seen that way only if it is compared to a masculine style. Men and women can learn to accept an androgynous model in which traditional masculine and feminine traits are blended.

As listeners, let us recognize traditionally female and male communication styles as just that, styles. Recognize that there is room in communication for many styles—female, male, and the androgynous combination of both. We can adopt those elements of each style which would enhance, add to, and improve our own.

> If sensitivity, emotionality and warmth are desirable human characteristics, then they are desirable for men as well as women. . . . If independence, assertiveness and serious intellectual commitment are desirable human characteristics, they are desirable for women as well as for men.[23]

As listeners, women and men must look at communication with *people*. It is our attending, interpreting, and re–creating that determine how we will respond to the messages we hear. We can open the lines of communication by learning to take each other on our own terms rather than applying the standards of one group to the behavior of the other.

We can recognize that Anita Hill and Clarence Thomas may both have told the truth as they perceived it and remembered it. Many hearers who could not listen responded out of their "feminine" or "masculine" culture. They applied the standards of one group to the behavior of the other and could not listen.

It is possible to accept, and even admire, the way others communicate. Perceptive listeners can recognize that while women and men each communicate in different ways, both ways are worthwhile. Just as we recognize that different artists present the same scene in different styles, different automobile manufacturers provide the same options in different styles, and different musicians express the same emotion in different styles, women and men can present the same message in different styles. If we learn as many elements as possible of each style, we can learn to recognize the message in each.

When we listeners have learned there are communication styles that are different from ours and accept and value them, we are ready to begin to change. We can achieve behavioral flexibility where we can listen with empathic understanding when it is appropriate (feminine communication) and be assertive when these communication behaviors are called for (masculine communication). While it is difficult to learn, this is what leads to androgynous communication style.[24]

To begin work on listening flexibility, we must:

- Monitor our reactions to nonverbal messages.
- Recognize female communicators' awareness of and use of metamessages.
- Recognize male communicators' adherence to content and message sending.
- Learn to value and accept communication styles different from our own.
- Aim for the ability to change in order to listen holistically to gender–impacted messages.

Retraining: Guidelines for Female and Male Communication

1. Take care to objectively confront our own sexist attitudes and the ways in which they affect our listening performance.

2. Monitor our own reaction to male and female stereotypes. When we recognize a stereotype, we can make use of STTD listening time to remind ourselves that stereotypes limit understanding. Concentrate on the message sent—devoid of gender ramifications.

3. Recognize our own female— or male—dominant communication style. Ask ourselves which elements will limit the way listeners receive our message. Be ready to recognize and retrain to change those possible limitations.

4. Consider ways in which perception checking could improve our performances as listeners to gender—impacted messages.

WRAPPING IT UP: A SUMMARY

We examine five American subcultures: Black American, Hispanic, Japanese, Chinese, and organizational settings.

We discuss the impact of gender on listening, especially considering those "feminine" and "masculine" behaviors that impact the way we listen and communicate, cultures, stereotypes, and biases toward female and male communication styles.

DISCUSSION AND STUDY GUIDES

1. What are the five most positive and the five most negative qualities of your own culture? Why do you consider each to be positive or negative?

2. What stereotypes about another culture have you believed? ("French are great cooks," "New Englanders are cold," "Women are emotional," "Orientals are smart," "Blacks are good dancers.") Have you come to know any members of one of the groups and learned that they are pretty much like you? How did you arrive at that conclusion?

3. Have you observed professors or supervisors treating female and male students or co—workers differently? If so, how? If not, how do they avoid doing so?

4. What stereotypes about female and male behavior and communication styles have been apparent in your world? (Examples are: "Men don't cry," or "Ladies don't smoke in public.")

5. In what ways must we use Retraining Technique 4, Listen to the Entire Message without Judging or Refuting (from Chapter 10, Ten Productive Listening Techniques) in listening to members of the opposite sex or to members of another culture?

LISTENING EXERCISES THAT WORK

EXERCISE 1. (Intercultural Sensitivity) Choose and attend any intercultural event available in your geographic area, such as an international club meeting, a foreign–language film, a talk or seminar presentation by members of another culture. After the event answer the following questions:

a. What elements of nonverbal communication were different from yours?
b. What evidence did you observe showing different values?
c. What listening retraining techniques did you use in adjusting to these differences?

EXERCISE 2. (Intercultural Listening) Choose a listening situation in which you regularly communicate with a person from another cultural background: large city vs. small town, Native American vs. African–American, Northerner vs. Southerner, etc.

A. Over a period of three weeks, observe and record:
   1. What nonverbal signals did you observe that were different from your own?
   2. What verbal signals did you observe that were different from your own?
   3. What methods of perception checking did you use to clarify misunderstandings?

B. In small groups, discuss:
   1. What you learned about intercultural communication differences.
   2. What you learned about listening across cultures.

EXERCISE 3. (Identifying and Profiting from Organizational Networking) We know the importance of understanding organizational culture in addition to having qualifications for a position. Considering the position you now hold or hope to hold, answer the statements below by putting "yes" or "no" in the blank.

_____   1. When I first go to work in an organization, I ask questions and listen to the responses.

_____   2. If I am in a position of power, I am careful not to make abrupt changes in the way the organization operates.

_____   3. I look for the communication networks within the organization.

_____   4. I try to learn the history of the organization (the "myths" and "legends" about the beginning of the company) as a clue to the culture.

_____   5. I try to recognize the organization's major symbols (logos and letterheads) to learn how the organization views itself.

_____   6. I observe the way the organization celebrates (potluck dinners, picnics, black–tie dinners) as a clue to its culture.

_____ 7. I observe what the organization rewards (complaining, creative solutions to problems, carrying gossip to supervisors) as a clue to its culture.

_____ 8. I observe how the organization rewards productive work (promotions, bonuses, titles).

_____ 9. I observe the way space is used within the organization (closed doors, individual offices, large offices) to determine the general culture.

_____ 10. I base my organizational behavior on what I have learned through careful listening (to verbal and nonverbal messages) within the organization.

After totaling the number of "yes" and "no" answers, calculate your use of networking to understand organizational culture. The more "yes" answers, the better your understanding of the concept.

10–9: High level of understanding of organizational cultures

8–6: Moderate level of understanding of organizational cultures

5–3: Low level of understanding of organizational cultures

2–0: Study this chapter to learn more about adjusting to the organization in which you work.

EXERCISE 4. (Gender–impacted Listening) Choose a listening situation in which you regularly experience difficulty with a member of the opposite sex.

A. During two weeks follow the same steps outlined in Exercise 2.

1. Observe differing nonverbal signals.

2. Observe differing verbal signals.

3. Make use of perception checking to clarify misunderstandings.

B. Discuss the following:

1. What you learned about female and male communication differences.

2. What you learned about your own gender–impacted listening.

EXERCISE 5. (Female-Male Communication Styles) Select a career you are now pursuing or intend to pursue. Identify:

a. Model female-male verbal communication behavior for this career.

b. Model female-male nonverbal communication behavior for this career.

In a group of five to seven members (mixed gender) discuss the model behaviors considering:

a. How many identified traditionally masculine behavior for traditionally male careers, and traditionally feminine behavior for traditionally female careers?

b. Discuss evidences of gender stereotypes.

c. Did any choose traditionally male behavior as ideal for most careers? If so, discuss this evidence of preference for male communication styles.

Designate one member of each group to report to large group.

NOTES

1. Larry A. Samovar and Richard E. Porter, *Communication Between Cultures* (Belmont, CA: Wadsworth Publishing Co., 1991), 230.
2. Ben J. Wattenberg, "Tomorrow," *U.S. News & World Report*, February 13, 1989, 31; cited in Larry A. Samovar and Richard E. Porter, *Communication Between Cultures* (Belmont, CA: Wadsworth Publishing Company, 1991), 12–13
3. John K. Brilhart and Gloria J. Galanes, Effective Group Discussion (Dubuque, IA: William C. Brown Publishers, 1992), 135–137.
4. Richard T. Schaefer, Racial and Ethnic Groups, 3rd ed. (Glenview, IL: Scott, Foresman, 1988), 214 (See especially Chapter 8, "The Making of Black Americans in a White America," 213–50).
5. J. L. Dillard. Black English: Its History and Usage in the United States (New York: Random House, 1972), 240.
6. Andrea L. Rich, Interracial Communication (New York: Harper & Row, 1974), 142.
7. Larry A. Samovar and Richard E. Porter, Intercultural Communication: A Reader, 6th ed. (Belmont, CA: Wadsworth Publishing Co. 1991), 279.
8. Samovar and Porter, Communication Between Cultures, 161.
9. Samovar and Porter, Intercultural Communication, 280.
10. Schaefer, 285–320 (See especially Chapter 10 "Chicanos: The Nation's Largest Ethnic Group".)
11. Ibid., 288–90, 313, 316.
12. W. Scott Morton, The Japanese: How They Live and Work (New York: Praeger Publishers, 1973), 138.
13. Frederick M. Bunge, ed., Japan: A Country Study (Washington, D.C.: United States Government, 1983), 94–95.
14. Schaefer, (See especially Chapter 13, "Chinese Americans: Continued Exclusion," 365–81).
15. Ibid., 367.
16. Terrance E. Deal and Allan A. Kennedy, Corporate Cultures: the Rites and Rituals of Corporate Life (Reading, MA: Addison-Wesley, 1982), 4.
17. Jacquelyn Wonder and Priscilla Donovan, *Whole-Brain Thinking*: *Working From Both Sides of the Brain to Achieve Job Performance* (New York: William Morrow, 1984), 24.
18. Deborah Tannen, *You Just Don't Understand*: *Women and Men in Conversation* (New York: William Morrow, 1990), 43–44.
19. Deborah Borisoff and Lisa Merrill, *The Power to Communicate*: *Gender Differences as Barriers* (Prospect Heights, IL: Waveland Press, 1985), 40.
20. Peg Meier and Ellen Foley, "War of Words: Women Talk About How Men and Women Talk," *Minneapolis* (MN) *Star Tribune* (January 6, 1991), 6.
21. Anne Wilson Schaef, *Women's Reality* (St. Paul: Winston Press, 1981), 7.
22. Deborah Tannen, *That's Not What I Meant*: *How Conversational Style Makes or Breaks Relationships* (New York: William Morrow, 1986), 127.
23. Borisoff and Merrill, 97–98.
24. Judy Cornelia Pearson, *Gender and Communication* (Dubuque, IA: Wm. C. Brown Publishers 1985), 29.

COPYRIGHTS AND ACKNOWLEDGMENTS

INDEX

(Glossary words in italics are defined on the pages noted.)